Digital Culture, Play, and Identity

Digital Culture, Play, and Identity

A WORLD OF WARCRAFT® READER

edited by Hilde G. Corneliussen and Jill Walker Rettberg

The MIT Press
Cambridge, Massachusetts
London, England

For information about special quantity discounts, please email special_sales@mitpress .mit.edu

This book was set in Minion and Syntax on 3B2 by Asco Typesetters, Hong Kong. Printed and bound in the United States of America.

Library of Congress Cataloging-in-Publication Data

Digital Culture, Play, and Identity: A World of Warcraft Reader / Hilde G. Corneliussen and Jill Walker Rettberg, eds.
    p.   cm.
Includes bibliographical references and index.
ISBN-13: 978-0-262-03370-1 (hardcover : alk. paper)
1. Computer games—Social aspects. 2. World of Warcraft. I. Corneliussen, Hilde G. II. Rettberg, Jill Walker.
GV1469.27.D55   2008
794.8—dc22   2007020839

10   9   8   7   6   5   4   3   2   1

Contents

Acknowledgments

This anthology has two origins. The first is an international online research network for research on *World of Warcraft*. The Truants, a guild for scholars researching the game, was formally established in January 2006 at a meeting in the gameworld. In addition to our weekly in-game meetings and ongoing informal discussions within the guild online, we have used a blog, a wiki, and a mailing list to discuss and share ideas, research, and experiences related to the game. The guild has grown from a handful of people who knew each other from their research to a larger and highly inspiring group of researchers united by their interest in the game. All the contributors to this anthology are members of The Truants, not because it started as an exclusive Truants project, but because the network has grown steadily since its start. Thus, we want to thank all the members of The Truants, and in particular our guild master Nuuna, a.k.a. Torill Elvira Mortensen, for creating such a warm and vibrant academic community. For the Horde!

The book's second origin was a workshop held in Bergen in November 2006, made possible by funding from the Faculty of Humanities at the University of Bergen. Being able to discuss drafts of the chapters with other researchers was invaluable, and of course it was both inspiring and fun to finally meet many of the other researchers with whom we had talked online but not previously met; before the workshop, some of us had only known each other as green orcs or pale undead mages.

We are grateful to Blizzard Entertainment, who have kindly granted us permission to print screenshots from the game. Thanks are also due to Atle C. Gandrudbakken, who arranged for workshop participants to have a more physical experience of one of the most common activities in computer games: firing a weapon. Although we would resent the claim that online activities are not real, it is still a difference to have your flesh, rather than your mind, feel the recoil of a shotgun.

Hilde G. Corneliussen and Jill Walker Rettberg

Introduction: "Orc Professor LFG," or Researching in Azeroth

Hilde G. Corneliussen and Jill Walker Rettberg

In 2007, *World of Warcraft* is the world's most popular massively multiplayer online game (MMOG), with as many players as Sweden or Bolivia has inhabitants. Subscribers to the game spend an average of twenty hours a week playing (Yee 2006), and like Sweden or Bolivia, *World of Warcraft* has a culture and a language all its own. To players of the game the customs and cultural rules of the game rapidly become familiar, but to outsiders, they can be quite baffling.

"I can't write the assignment about *World of Warcraft*. I don't understand the game. Last time I logged on, someone spat at me." These words came from a despairing student in one of our classes on digital culture. After analyzing the situation, she found a way around her problem: being new to the culture of *World of Warcraft* could be compared to being an immigrant in a foreign culture. The spitting episode was the result of the student's lack of knowledge of the game's unwritten rules (Sniderman 1999). Playing a healer, she had fought instead of healing fellow players, a mistake that a more established resident of Azeroth, the universe of *World of Warcraft*, would recognize as a deadly sin. As she began to understand more of this local knowledge and language, the student could finally laugh at how she had thought that the text "LFG WC" in the in-game chat channel meant that the player had to go to the toilet. Now she knew that it meant someone was Looking For a Group of fellow players to kill monsters in a place called Wailing Caverns.

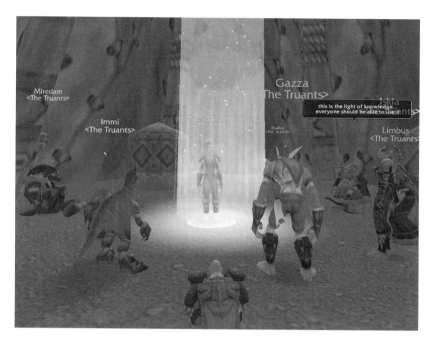

Figure I.1
Guild meeting in the Truants.

The articles in this anthology are written by researchers who have immersed themselves in the culture and customs of *World of Warcraft*, and have gone from being newbies confused by cryptic chat messages like LFG WC to leading guilds and raids, exploring the possibilities for making big money on the in-game auction house, and engaging in large role-playing events. We have spent months and years within the *World of Warcraft* universe, playing different factions, races, and classes to learn about this particular culture. The game universe has been explored through in-game observations, interviews with players, and online surveys. We have studied the game design as provided by Blizzard Entertainment, the game developer, as well as the player-created user interfaces, mods, and add-ons, which are small pieces of code that alter the presentation of the game to the player. The articles collected in this book are all based on this first-hand experience of being a resident of Azeroth as well as on data gathered and interpreted by the authors themselves.

We have not only played the orc professor LFG, but have also performed research in Azeroth. This group of contributors was brought together by a shared scholarly fascination with *World of Warcraft*, and we have various research backgrounds from a wide variety of humanities- and media-related disciplines. Espen Aarseth is one of the founders of the field of game studies, and those familiar with the field will recognize the names of several other games scholars contributing here. Other contributors have solid groundings in the study of digital culture, both as researchers and educators, while others have backgrounds in disciplines that have only recently become relevant to the study of games.

In many ways, our diverse backgrounds are typical of games researchers today. The academic study of computer games is still a very young field. Although the first computer games were developed in the 1950s and became readily available in arcade halls in the 1970s, the academic study of computer games has developed into a field of its own largely in the last seven or eight years, as evidenced by new journals, conferences, research networks, dedicated university courses and degrees, and a steady increase in research literature and textbooks.

This book is a contribution to the new research literature of game studies, presenting thirteen in-depth analyses of *World of Warcraft* from different perspectives and employing analytical tools and theoretical traditions from various academic disciplines. This collection includes analyses of *World of Warcraft* using theories and methodologies from, among others, textual analysis, gender studies, history, narratology, postcolonialism, and ethnography. Each contribution tells a different story about *World of Warcraft*, and each offers a different perspective. This is one of the first books to provide multiple perspectives on a single game. Such casebooks, or readers, of critical approaches to canonical works have been common in media studies and literary studies for decades, and as games studies matures, we are also beginning to see anthologies devoted to single games. *World of Warcraft* is an enormous game, both in terms of hours spent playing it and in terms of the number of players and the ways in which it can be played. Multiple approaches to the game may be required to grasp its multiplicity.

The book's primary audience is academic scholars and students of game studies and other disciplines dealing with digital culture. A digital culture is, like every culture, constructed according to norms, rules, and traditions. This book proposes a number of different perspectives on the study of digital cultures, be it in a MMOG like *World of Warcraft*, an online world like *Second Life*, or a Web-based community such as Wikipedia. We also believe that the articles in this book will interest gamers and residents of Azeroth or other synthetic worlds. And we hope that anxious parents or worried journalists also will find, if not redemption, then at least a source of knowledge that can help them understand the MMOG phenomenon which is an increasingly important form of digital culture.

How to Find a Group in Azeroth

World of Warcraft was launched in November 2004, and by March 2007 it had 8.5 million active subscribers spread across four continents: Europe, North America, Asia, and Australia. The game is played online on servers run by Blizzard Entertainment. Hundreds of servers run independent copies of the game, each server allowing several hundred players to be online at the same time. Servers are designated for different geographical regions and run different languages. Players buy a copy of the game on CD and pay an additional monthly fee for access.

The first MMOG was *Ultima Online* (made by Origin Systems, Inc.), which was released in 1997. MMOGs also have roots in the tabletop role-playing game *Dungeons and Dragons* (1974) and in text-based online games known as MUDs, or multiuser dungeons (Mortensen 2006). These roots in earlier forms of role-playing games are evident in the alternative acronym used to describe MMOGs: MMORPG, where the last three letters stand for role-playing game. The first MUDs appeared in the early 1980s, and enjoyed a certain popularity throughout the 1980s and 1990s. However, while MUDs were influential, they did not enjoy the mass appeal of the graphical MMOGs. In the decade following the release of *Ultima Online*, many MMOGs have been released, with *EverQuest* as the most popular up until the release of *World of Warcraft* in 2004. *EverQuest* has received a great deal of interest from academics, such as Castronova's study of the economy of Norrath (Castronova 2001) and T. L. Taylor's book *Play Between Worlds* (Taylor 2006b). MMOGs have likewise received much attention from mainstream media. While most nongamers may not know exactly what a MMOG is, *World of Warcraft* has received interest from the press to such an extent that almost everybody today has heard of it. Thus, one of the interesting aspects of this game is not only the large number of players it has attracted, but also the way it has entered the offline culture's everyday speech to a greater extent than have most other computer games.

As Torill Elvira Mortensen has argued, *World of Warcraft* is not faithful to any one game genre, but is "eclectic and opens up for a very diverse set of uses" (2006). Thus, many different kinds of player types (see Bartle 1996) can find activities that interest them in *World of Warcraft*. Like MUDs, *World of Warcraft* draws on the traditions of adventure and role-playing games such as *Dungeons and Dragons*. An important feature of these genres is the construction of a coherent background story for the players. The story of *World of Warcraft* has been developed through earlier games (Blizzard Entertainment's *Warcraft I–III*, 1994–2002) and in novels and comics produced under license to Blizzard. Additionally, the gameworld history is outlined in detail both in the manual included in the game box and on the official Web site.

Azeroth, the planet on which *World of Warcraft* takes place, has a long history of wars and conflicts between different races in earlier times. The conflict lines were eventually consolidated in the formation of two opposing factions: the Alliance and the Horde. The playable races in the game (such as humans, orcs, trolls, or night elves) are all assigned to one of these two factions. Although the background story claims that there is a truce between the Alliance and the Horde, the game itself encourages players to actively fight players from the opposing faction, as Esther MacCallum-Stewart discusses in chapter 2. In January 2007 the expansion pack *The Burning Crusade* was launched by Blizzard, and introduced new playable races, new quests and dungeons, and even a new planet—the Outland, where the Alliance and the Horde join forces to fight the ultimate enemy, the Burning Legion.

Players from the two factions cannot communicate with each other (except from a limited set of predefined emotes), and each faction has designated areas where opponents cannot enter without being attacked by the local guards. The level of hostility between the two factions—that is, the possibility of killing other players (see "corpse run" and "ganking" in the glossary at the back of the book)—is, however, also determined by the type of server the player selects. Normal servers guarantee that players will not be attacked by opponents unless consenting to fight, while players on Player vs. Player (PvP) servers will be flagged as legal targets for the opposing faction when moving into contested or hostile territory. A third type of server is also available, the Role-Playing (RP) server (which can be either normal or PvP), where players are encouraged to engage in their characters through role-playing.

The player's choice of faction will affect his or her experience of the game not only in terms of geographically available areas, but also in terms of character representation through the choice of available races and classes. Classes are defined in rather traditional ways for MUDs and MMOGs as specialized in melee or ranged combat, in healing, or in magic. Player characters can learn professions that give them the ability to make objects or perform services, which can then be sold to other players, vendors, or at the in-game auction house. Gaining experience points by killing *mobs* (mobile objects, see glossary) and solving quests are the most important activities for leveling up, thus making your character more and more powerful. However, players can engage in many different activities, from peaceful role-playing sessions to battlegrounds and in-game PvP competitions between the Alliance and the Horde. Even though the world can be explored alone, many quests and areas of the gameworld require that groups of players cooperate. Thus the social aspect of this world is vital, and the guild system is the most important tool for holding social groups together.

This short description of the game by no means does justice to its complexity, which will be the topic of the chapters to follow, but it may serve as a first guide for those "Earthlings" (Castronova 2001) who have not yet moved into synthetic worlds. The glossary at the end of this book will also help newcomers who are confused by the jargon and language of the game.

Players and Cultures

World of Warcraft has received a lot of attention from the press, making it an important topic in the everyday life of a far broader group than its 8.5 million players (as of March 2007). Although the game is often met with skepticism, it has also been described as giving important training that is useful in business life, as Scott Rettberg discusses in chapter 1.

According to Nick Yee, a scholar who has explored MMOGs for a number of years and presents his findings through the Daedalus project, it is "easy to dismiss video games as pointless activities that only teenagers indulge in. The truth is that the average age of MMORPG players is around 26. In fact, only 25 percent of MMORPG players are teenagers. About 50 percent of MMORPG players work full time. About 36 percent of players are married, and 22 percent have children" (Yee 2004). Thus digital or synthetic worlds (see Castronova 2005) such as *World of Warcraft* are inhabited by people of various ages, cultural contexts, and social backgrounds, from many different parts of the world. MMOGs represent an important element of a networked society and of digital culture, and as the contributors to this book argue, the gameworld created in *World of Warcraft* challenges many of our traditional notions of game, play, and society.

Even though *World of Warcraft* hit the player market with unprecedented force and broke records for number of copies sold shortly after its release, it has yet to hit the academic world with the same force. Although the scholarly journal *Games and Culture* dedicated a special issue to essays about the game (April 2006), other work on *World of Warcraft* has until now been scattered and difficult to find. Thus our book represents one of the first deep dives into *World of Warcraft*, seen from a number of different academic perspectives and disciplines by authors from several European countries, as well as from the U.S., Canada, and Australia. We hope this anthology will be a first step toward larger cross-cultural analyses of this gameworld, which at present exists in a number of very diverse cultural contexts.

Blurred Definitions

Several games and new media researchers have emphasized the importance of studying computer games as *games*, with their own logic and rules that are different from film, literature, or hypertext (Aarseth 2001, Eskelinen 2001, Buckingham 2006). This interest in studying games as games has led researchers to build on and examine earlier definitions to hone their understanding of games (Huizinga 1955 (1938), Caillois 1958, Juul 2003, Salen and Zimmerman 2004). Several aspects of common definitions are particularly interesting when considering what kind of a game *World of Warcraft* is.

Johan Huizinga's frequently referenced definition of "play" (1938) states that play is an activity that happens outside "ordinary" life. In their influential book *Rules of Play*, Katie Salen and Eric Zimmerman (2004) use Huizinga's concept of the magic circle to emphasize that the rules, space, and time of a game are separate from real-life rules, space, and time. Importantly, players are aware of the boundary of the magic circle, and know when they enter it (Buckingham 2006). Huizinga also claims that play provides no real-life material interest or profit for the player (1938). Jesper Juul, on the other hand, argues that games can be played "with or without real-life consequences" (2003), thus allowing for the possibility that games affect players' lives outside of the game.

In a game like *World of Warcraft*, the magic circle is less clear than in a game of hopscotch or a single player computer game. The economist Edward Castronova (2001) showed this very literally in his analysis of the economy of the MMOG *EverQuest*, finding that Norrath, the world of *EverQuest*, had an economy just as viable and valid as that of many real-world countries: "The nominal hourly wage is about USD 3.42 per hour, and the labors of the people produce a GNP per capita somewhere between that of Russia and Bulgaria. A unit of Norrath's currency is traded on exchange markets at USD 0.0107, higher than the Yen and the Lira." Today, there are people who earn their livings as MMOG players (Dibbel 2006). Farming for *World of Warcraft* gold is against Blizzard's terms of service but is still a sizeable industry (Taylor 2006a, chapter 10 in this book). This touches on another aspect of game definitions: what Juul calls the player's attachment to the outcomes of the game, where a player will be happy if she wins and unhappy if she loses (Juul 2003). However, in a multilayered game like *World of Warcraft*, one that resists being confined within traditional genres and provides different goals and activities, definitions of winning and losing conditions may differ from player to player, as Torill Elvira Mortensen discusses in her chapter on deviant strategies.

Another frequent element in definitions of "game" that is blurred in a game like *World of Warcraft* is the expectation that a game should have a clearly defined ending. According to Salen and Zimmerman, games have a "quantifiable goal or outcome," which means that the player in the end has "either won or lost or received some kind of numerical score." This is what distinguishes games from "less formal play activities" (Salen and Zimmerman 2004, 80). *World of Warcraft* has no clear ending. There are many attainable goals with quantifiable outcomes, such as reaching level 70, or acquiring the highest level in a profession, or killing the dragon Onyxia, but when each of these goals is reached, many still remain. In addition, the game is constantly being expanded. This is made explicit in the FAQ on Blizzard's official Web site, which states that the game offers "thousands of hours of game play . . . and nearly infinite goals for players. Because we'll have a live team regularly adding new quests, creatures, and items, the game will never truly end."

These are only glimpses of various elements that game researchers have argued are important in games. But definitions like these do raise some questions in relation to a MMOG like *World of Warcraft* where, as Blizzard states in the FAQ, "thousands of players will have the opportunity to adventure together in an enormous, persistent gameworld, forming friendships, slaying monsters, and engaging in epic quests that can span days or weeks." *World of Warcraft* is a game with a time, place, and space of its own, with rules defined through the game design (kill monsters and earn experience points to level up), as well as unwritten rules (heal, don't fight, if you are a healer), and as mentioned, a number of varying goals for players to strive for. Additionally, *World of Warcraft* is a social framework for communication. And with communication, we get culture. We get players who define their own rules or challenge the rules as given by Blizzard (Taylor 2006a and, in this anthology, chapter 11) and players who define their own goals (see chapter 10 in this volume). Some of the defined goals, like role-playing, do not lead to the quantifiable goals, like leveling up. And for some following the goal of role-play, the rewards for other goals (such as acquiring good battle gear) might even be unwanted (see chapter 11).

According to David Buckingham, "the fundamental difference between games and other kinds of cultural texts [is that] games are *played*" (Buckingham 2006, 6; his emphasis). While this, like many of the game definitions, points to the difference between real life and gameworld, *World of Warcraft* seems to challenge the concept of the magic circle in several ways, both in relation to what is going on in the game—for example, when the research guild meets to discuss the chapters of this book—and what goes on outside it—for instance, gold farmers who play the game to acquire real-life profit. Thus, in order to understand *World of Warcraft* we must study it both as a game and as a cultural site requiring the application of multiple disciplines' analytical tools, concepts, and methods so that we may fully comprehend this phenomenon.

Researching in Azeroth: A Reader's Guide to the Book

The anthology consists of thirteen chapters that we have organized into four sections. The first, Culture, examines the various ways in which gameworlds reflect, represent, or reconstruct stories that are relevant to or originate in our world. The second, World, discusses ways in which the gameworld is established and made to feel "real"—or not. Play, the third section, explores role-playing and the options for and limitations of play. The final section, Identity, looks at ways characters are established and developed.

Culture

The first section of the anthology opens with an essay by Scott Rettberg in which he questions the enormous amount of time that Blizzard intends a player to spend playing *World of Warcraft*. If you have never immersed yourself in a game like *World of Warcraft* you probably think that all game playing is fun. But, as Rettberg demonstrates, reaching the most advanced goals in *World of Warcraft* requires hours of repetitive work. Rettberg continues this discussion by interpreting *World of Warcraft* as a simulation of Western market-driven economies, a "capitalist fairytale," offering everyone equal access to training in basic economics and promising wealth and status to the hard-working laborer, thus acting as a form of "corporate training." The narrative aspects of the game, Rettberg argues, simply serve as "window-dressing," glossing over the repetitive work required to advance in the game.

Esther MacCallum-Stewart also discusses the links between our real-world culture and the in-game scene, but from a different perspective, as she discusses the representation of the warfare and conflict in *World of Warcraft* in light of the military history of the last century. Azeroth is a world with an uneasy truce between the Alliance and the Horde, according to the game lore, and yet players on the two opposing factions are encouraged to fight and kill each other. MacCallum-Stewart discusses how this tension is constructed in the game as an ambiguity by providing both factions with stories that can justify their conflict as a fight for what is a historical "right." Signifiers across the landscape also contribute to historicize and produce idealized versions of war, and place the warfare of Azeroth within traditional discourses of chivalry and honor. Chapter 2 thus challenges the understanding of what it means to be at war, in a struggle between heroic stories and the popular dislike of war.

Chapter 3, by Hilde G. Corneliussen, explores the construction of gender in *World of Warcraft*. By using three different feminist positions exemplifying different possibilities of organizing gender in society, Corneliussen illustrates how a complex mixture of possible and available gendered positions opens up the gendered space in *World of Warcraft*, making multitude and variety important keywords for gender constructions in the game. However, she also points to the limits of the gender constructions, like the unused opportunity to use fantasy genders within this fantasy world, and she demonstrates the game's built-in limits for masculinity and femininity: the first along lines of power, and the second along lines of aesthetic.

Jessica Langer explores yet another aspect of the relationships between the in-game world and our real world, by focusing on the construction of race in *World of Warcraft*. Taking a postcolonial perspective, Langer discusses how the races of the Alliance are presented as familiar, while Horde races are depicted as the Other, modeled on races seen as different from a white Western perspective. Langer shows how the representation of Horde races draws on colonial images of African, Jamaican, Native American, and other peoples. Like MacCallum-Stewart, Langer finds that the difference between the Alliance and the Horde is not a simple dichotomy of good versus evil. Instead, through careful readings of each race and the use of aspects of postcolonial theory, Langer argues that the division is between the familiar and the foreign, and that this division has consequences not only within the game but in the real world as well.

The important contribution of the chapters in this section is their definitive rejection of the idea of an innocent game, and their examination of the ways in which game references are constructed by and construct meaning in offline culture. As John Dovey and Helen Kennedy point out, this is a much-needed task: "We need to consider the ways in which these stereotypes reflect and reintroduce offline power imbalances within the play environment. In this regard, the visual imagery in many mainstream games seems to be entirely ignorant of the critiques that have been made of these stereotypes in other visual media and appear to import some of the worst examples in an entirely unreflexive and uncritical way" (Dovey and Kennedy 2006, 93).

World

The second section, World, contains four chapters discussing how *World of Warcraft* sets up a cohesive gameworld from four perspectives: geography, mythology, death, and narrative. Espen Aarseth's chapter examines the geography of Azeroth, calculating what the size of this world would be if it were a physical space, and discussing the way in which the world is represented. Aarseth argues that *World of Warcraft* is a very small world, comparing it to a theme park in a Fordist paradigm of assembly-line mass entertainment. As judged from its popularity, *World of Warcraft* is an utterly successful computer game. However, it is not among the most visually advanced, and the surface of the game is static, leaving the game a hollow world. This hollowness is in fact one reason for the game's multicultural success, according to Aarseth.

In chapter 6, Tanya Krzywinska discusses this hollowness from a different perspective, pointing to the ways in which the mythology and historical background that Blizzard has created for *World of Warcraft* play upon established mythological constructs from other stories and traditions, and thus create a "rich text" that is "richly populated with various allusions, correspondences, and references." Although many players never read up on the backstory, Krzywinska argues that the use of mythology in the game provides "a symbolic language" and "constitutes a sense for the player of being in a world." This chapter also furthers the discussions of cultural meanings that were raised in the previous section by its analysis of how references to myths and popular culture provide shortcuts to meaning, making the gameworld a meaningful world filled with references to stories familiar to players.

Lisbeth Klastrup, in chapter 7, uses the representation of death in *World of Warcraft* as a means to understand players' experience of playing the game. Death in *World of Warcraft* is a temporary state that is frequently experienced in regular play. Klastrup explores the way in which dying is used to structure the game experience, comparing the design of death in *World of Warcraft* to other games, considering sociological theories of death and its rituals in the real world, and using players' own stories of dying in the game to examine ways in which players use and understand death as an element of play.

Jill Walker Rettberg analyzes the structure and rhetoric of quests as they are used in *World of Warcraft* in chapter 8, comparing this to previous work on quests in games. She proposes that the quests of *World of Warcraft* are primarily characterized by the theme of exploration and by the rhetorical figures of deferral and repetition, and discusses how the narrative networks established in quests contribute to creating a cohesive gameworld.

The chapters in this section thus all explore ways in which aspects of the gameworld and the gameplay contribute to what Lisbeth Klastrup calls the "worldness" of the game. While the previous section examined the connections between the gameworld and the offline world, this section explores the internal mechanisms of the game. Yet it is clear from these analyses that the game draws upon many other genres and experiences: myths, narrative structures, theme parks, and notions of death among them.

Play

The third section of the anthology, Play, explores the ways players play the game, looking at role-playing and at the ways in which players choose to play that differ from what the developers planned.

In chapter 9, T. L. Taylor discusses the use of player-created mods and add-ons to the game that assist players in group play. Many scholars have lauded these player-initiated developments as evidence of emergence, but Taylor warns us that "emergence should not be equated with the free, utopic, non-hierarchical, or unfettered." The tools she looks at in fact allow raid leaders to track group members' performance in intricate detail, a form of surveillance that has not only become compulsory in many high-end guilds, but that also has significant effects on the relationships between players and the style of play.

Torill Elvira Mortensen explores the ways in which many players set their own goals when they play, engaging in what she calls "deviant strategies," playing in ways that do not seem to be in line with the game designers' intentions. In chapter 10, she explores the motivations of players who prioritize socializing, leading guilds, role-playing, or catching gold farmers rather than killing monsters and leveling up.

Esther MacCallum-Stewart and Justin Parsler in chapter 11 use their extensive background as role-players and as organizers and designers of live action role-playing games to present the ways that players who wish to role-play in *World of Warcraft* do so. Although *World of Warcraft* is presented by Blizzard as an MMORPG, or massively multiplayer online role-playing game, the game design presents many challenges for players who genuinely wish to roleplay their characters. MacCallum-Stewart and Parsler discuss what role-playing is, and explore strategies used by players who wish to engage in role play despite the limitations of the game's interface and design.

Identity

The last section of the book, Identity, focuses on how players (can) identify with the characters and how the characters are given identity through naming, thus discussing players' identification with and investment in the characters from two different perspectives. Ragnhild Tronstad's chapter 12 discusses the possibilities for players to identify with their characters as either an experience of "being" the character or by feeling empathy toward the character. Earlier computer game research has argued that players' experience of being their character relies on the character's capacities in the game rather than on its appearance, implying a split between character appearance and capacity. Tronstad, however, argues that in MMOGs such as *World of Warcraft* this is an artificial split, and that appearance and capacity here rather inform and affect each other, thus contributing equally to the player's processes of identification.

The last chapter is by Charlotte Hagström, an ethnologist and name researcher who has studied the norms of naming a player character in *World of Warcraft*. The name is the only aspect of the character that a player can create freely rather than simply select from available options. Once chosen, a name cannot be changed, and it is one of a character's main distinguishing features. Hagström has surveyed names in use in the game and collected players' own stories of how they chose their character names. She compares her findings about *World of Warcraft* naming conventions to our naming customs outside the gameworld.

World of Warcraft is an expansive game in every sense of the word. As the chapters in this collection demonstrate, there are many different ways to understand the shape of this world and the activities that take place within it. These contributions offer a wealth of approaches to the game, as well as a sampler of the breadth of research currently being conducted on *World of Warcraft* and other MMOGs. However, even the thirteen researchers' perspectives presented in this book cannot cover everything. Our experiences in the gameworld also differ from one another, and so topics like race, gender, or character identification are treated in different ways by different authors of this book. This is one indication of the complex world that is constructed in the gamespace of *World of Warcraft*—a complexity not unlike the complexity found in the rest of our society.

References

Aarseth, Espen. 2001. "Computer Game Studies, Year One." *Game Studies* 1, no. 1 (July). Available at ⟨http://gamestudies.org⟩.

Bartle, Richard. 1996. "Hearts, Clubs, Diamonds, Spades: Players Who Suit MUDs." *Journal of MUD Research* 1, no. 1. Available at ⟨http://www.mud.co.uk/richard/hcds.htm⟩.

Buckingham, David. 2006. "Studying Computer Games." In *Computer Games: Text, Narrative and Play*, ed. Diane Carr, David Buckingham, Andrew Burn, and Gareth Schott, 1–13. Cambridge: Polity Press.

Caillois, Roger. 1958. *Man, Play, and Games*. New edition, Chicago: University of Illinois Press, 2001.

Castronova, Edward. 2001. *Virtual Worlds: A First-Hand Account of Market and Society on the Cyberian Frontier*. CESifo Working Paper No. 618, December. Reprinted in 2006 in *The Game Design Reader: A Rules of Play Anthology*, ed. Katie Salen and Eric Zimmerman, 814–863. Cambridge, MA: MIT Press.

Dibbell, Julian. 2006. *Play Money, or, How I Quit My Day Job and Made Millions Trading Virtual Loot.* New York: Basic Books.

Dovey, John and Helen W. Kennedy. 2006. *Game Cultures. Computer Games As New Media.* Maidenhead: Open University Press.

Eskelinen, Markku. 2001. "The Gaming Situation." *Game Studies* 1, no. 1 (July). Available at ⟨http://gamestudies.org⟩.

Huizinga, Johan. 1955 (1938). *Homo Ludens. A Study of the Play Element in Culture.* Boston: Bacon Press.

Juul, Jesper. 2003. "The Game, the Player, the World: Looking for a Heart of Gameness." In *Digital Games Research Conference*, ed. M. Copier and J. Raessens, 30–45. Utrecht: Utrecht University.

Mortensen, Torill Elvira. 2006. "WoW is the New MUD: Social Gaming from Text to Video." *Games and Culture* 1, no. 4: 397–413.

Salen, Katie and Eric Zimmerman. 2004. *Rules of Play. Game Design Fundamentals.* Cambridge, MA: MIT Press.

Sniderman, Stephen. 1999. "Unwritten Rules," *The Life of Games* 1 (October). Available at ⟨http://www.gamepuzzles.com/tlog/tlog2.htm⟩.

Taylor, T. L. 2006a. "Does WoW Change Everything? How a PvP Server, Multinational Player Base, and Surveillance Mod Scene Caused Me Pause." *Games and Culture* 1, no. 4: 318–337.

Taylor, T. L. 2006b. *Play Between Worlds: Exploring Online Game Culture.* Cambridge, MA: MIT Press.

Yee, Nick. 2004. "Player Demographics." *The Daedalus Gateway: The Psychology of MMORGs.* Available at ⟨http://www.nickyee.com/daedalus/gateway_demographics .html⟩.

Yee, Nick. 2006. "The Demographics, Motivations and Derived Experiences of Users of Massively-Multiuser Online Graphical Environments." *PRESENCE: Teleoperators and Virtual Environments* 15: 309–329.

Culture

Corporate Ideology in *World of Warcraft*

1

Scott Rettberg

Hours have gone to blade: days, weeks of my life. To be precise, in the past year I have spent eighteen days, two hours, and seventeen minutes in Azeroth.[1] And my level 57 hunter, Ulcharmin, is one of lesser lights in our guild, the Truants—an active group of academics, a full contingent of PhDs and advanced graduate students who dedicate a significant portion of their lives to the study of MMORPGs. By my estimation, about 5 percent of my total life during the past year has gone into the *World of Warcraft*, perhaps 7.5 percent of my waking life. While I'm no more addicted to *Warcraft* than I am to scotch, chocolate, or sex, I've spent more time killing trolls over the past year than I have drinking alcohol, eating candy, or making love (combined). During this same year, I watched the first two seasons of the narrative-rich, multi-sequential TV series *Lost* on DVD, forty-eight episodes, all in a row. That took about thirty-five hours total, about 8 percent of the amount of time I spent playing *World of Warcraft*. During the course of my life, I've read James Joyce's *Ulysses* three times, twice carefully. I estimate that took about six days of twenty-four-hour time, about eighteen full eight-hour working days, about 33 percent of the time I've spent playing *World of Warcraft*. Is the world that the team of developers at Blizzard have created twelve times more compelling than the island of *Lost*? Am I three times more engaged, illuminated, and challenged by the topography and multifarious virtual life-forms of Kalimdor and the Eastern Kingdom than I was by the topology and folk of Joyce's Dublin? I don't think so. What then, could compel me, a grown man of thirty-six years with a fully developed personality and real-world responsibilities, to spend so much time engaged in this alternate universe, riding a timber wolf, with my faithful pet Houndcat padding along beside me? Why would hardcore gamers spend considerably more time than I do, perhaps eighty days of real time per year, shunning the world of the flesh for a virtual fantasy world?

Playing *World of Warcraft*, sometimes referred to by its 8.5 million (and likely more by the time you read this) players as "World of Warcrack," is indeed a compelling experience. I will argue here that though the world Blizzard has created offers an engaging gameplay experience, and is not without some visual beauty, wit, and narrative subtlety,[2] the principle reason why Blizzard has been able to build such a large and devoted audience for their flagship product is in fact because it offers a convincing and detailed simulacrum of the process of becoming successful in capitalist societies. *World of Warcraft* is both a game and a simulation that reinforces the values of Western market-driven economies. The game offers its players a capitalist fairytale in which anyone who works hard and strives enough can rise through society's ranks and acquire great wealth. Moreover, beyond simply representing capitalism as good, *World of Warcraft* serves as a tool to educate its players in a range of behaviors and skills specific to the situation of conducting business in an economy controlled by corporations. While it's certainly true that some students are failing out of college, some marriages are falling apart, and some bodies are slipping into flabby obesity as a direct result of *World of Warcraft* addiction,[3] in a larger sense the game is training a generation of good corporate citizens not only to consume well and to pay their dues, but also to climb the corporate ladder, to lead projects, to achieve sales goals, to earn and save, to work hard for better possessions, to play the markets, to win respect from their peers and their customers, to direct and encourage and cajole their underlings to outperform, and to become better employees and perhaps, eventually, effective future CEOs. Playing *World of Warcraft* serves as a form of corporate training.

The form and structure of players' engagement with video games have always been to a large part determined by the economic goals of game developers, and for completely logical reasons. Video games are primarily entertainment products, not forms of art. Each type of video game and computer game is developed with an idea in mind of how to most effectively extract money from its players and provide a reliable income stream for its producers.

From an economic perspective, the purpose of classic arcade games such as *Pac-Man*, *Centipede*, *Asteroids*, and *Galaga* was to extract as many quarters from as many players as possible as quickly as possible, while still providing an experience compelling enough that the player[4] would rather *wait in line* to play the game of his choice than play something else instead. The value proposition of those early arcade games had much in common with that of horror movies. The idea was to deliver the player a quick dose of adrenaline, as each level became quickly and progressively more difficult, with more aliens, more spaceships, more missiles coming at the player faster, faster, *faster*, until he died and was prompted to feed the machine another quarter.

In contrast, the developers of console-based and computer games faced a different challenge. Console game developers wanted to first convince the player, with his or her limited budget, that their particular cartridge, and not one produced by the competition, was among the few that the player absolutely *needed* to own. The producers were charging a nontrivial per-unit price for the cartridges,[5] so the notion of replay value became more important. The idea was to hook the player, both on a particular console system and on a particular brand of game. Games then were structured to offer compelling experiences that could either be replayed until the new version of the game came out (for example, the *Madden NFL* football games) or to offer game experiences that could be played through and mastered just in time for the release of the next game in the series (as with Tom Clancy's fill-in-the-blank military escapades). The amount of playing time the player was expected to spend with each title increased dramatically, though the developers would never want to produce a game so compelling that the player would not want to buy another game from them. That would be a stupid business practice.

The business model of the massively multiplayer online game is significantly different from those that preceded it. Though there is a significant upfront cost for the client software,[6] the real money is made in the monthly churn. Depending upon the plan they choose, *World of Warcraft* players pay between $12.99–14.99 per month (as of March 2007). While players are likely to spend money on other types of games and other entertainments,[7] a low percentage of these players are likely to pay for more than one MMORPG at a time. The logical goal of MMORPG producers, then, is to immerse players in one single game for as long as possible, without diversion to other virtual world environments, and without end. The fewer new games that a particular company has to develop, the lower their development costs will be, and thus the higher their profits. From an economic perspective, it is in the interests of an MMORPG's producers that their game be as addictive as cigarettes.[8] Game developers don't want you to go and find another dealer. They want you to develop a taste for their brand and keep buying the same product, from the same company, over and over again. The subscription model has made video games into a kind of utility, a fixed cost that becomes for the gamer just another fact of life.

As the economic models of games have changed, so too has the nature of the reward systems used to motivate players to continue playing. In his essay "Narrative, Interactivity, Play, and Games" Eric Zimmerman defines "game" as "a voluntary interactive activity, in which one or more players follow rules that constrain their behavior, enacting an artificial conflict that ends in a quantifiable outcome" (2004, 160). The quantifiable outcome was certainly less complex in early video games than it is in contemporary massively multiplayer online games. In *Pong*, the first of two players to reach a predetermined score won. In games such as *Centipede* or *Galaga*, arcade players struggled to achieve seemingly absurd high scores (for example, 567,841). Each monster, insect, spaceship, ghost, and so on shot had its own point value. Arcade players were motivated both by progressing through levels and by achieving a localized, ephemeral kind of preteen immortality by having their initials enshrined on a game's "All Time High Score" screen. While these scores were tied to specific events in the course of play, in a larger sense they were mere abstractions, with little to no metaphoric relationship to reality. To be a high-scoring player simply meant that you had achieved a level of mastery over a particular entertainment device.

In *World of Warcraft*, the quantifiable aspect of a player's achievement is not marked with a single number, but by many different types of metrics. The avatar has an overall level between one and seventy. Attributes such as strength, intelligence, agility, spirit, and stamina define the player's avatar quantitatively. The basis of these metrics is determined to some extent by the character's race and class (for example, Orc hunter) and to a greater extent by the level the player has achieved. The particular weapons, armor, and other items the player has looted from slain enemies, been awarded for accomplishing quests, been given as gifts from other players, and purchased in the auction house also affect those basic attributes, which in turn affect the player's armor, melee attack, and ranged attack abilities. Additionally, the player has a quantifiable reputation with different factions and militaristic ranks of honor. To further complicate matters, a player's performance is also measured informally by his or her fellow players, particularly fellow guild members. In addition to the "hard" metrics calculated by the system, there are numerous "soft" outcomes in terms of the effects a player's given actions will have on his or her relationships with other players. The types of ways players evaluate others might range from their ability to effectively perform a given task during a raid to their generosity, their dedication, their conversational abilities, or their adherence to complex systems of social mores and etiquette—including those of the *World of Warcraft* as a whole, those of a particular server,[9] and those specific to a given guild. While to players of *World of Warcraft* this likely does not seem complex, as players have internalized the majority of this system during the course of many hours spent playing the game, to people unfamiliar with MMORPGS I suspect this sounds like a very tangled web indeed. The player's actions have multiple and complex effects, not on a single score, but on multiple quantifiable and nonquantifiable attributes. In fact, it is probably safe to say that the state and performance of an avatar in *World of Warcraft* is measured and analyzed[10] in more ways, more often and more closely, than most of us are in real-life situations such as our working lives.

Part of the appeal of *World of Warcraft* is that while all players are accessing a shared universe of possible activities and choosing from the same pool of available quests, all of these metrics and choices allow for a very high degree of personalization. From the first moment the player "rolls" a character and gives it a name, she is defining an avatar, a character that will be distinct from all of the other characters in the game. The player defines a second self, with traits and physical qualities far different from his or her own real embodied personality. For many players this represents an opportunity to escape from the confines of their own situation (their Heideggerian "thrownness") in the world. While we all find ourselves living lives that we have in part determined by our choices and in part been thrown into by virtue of being born into them, in *World of Warcraft* and in other MMORPGs we have the opportunity to wipe the slate clean, to start again and choose new lives in a new world. As Castranova notes in *Synthetic Worlds*, "We are no longer stuck with the Game of Life as we receive it from our ancestors. We can make a new one, almost however we like" (2005, 70). While the nature of this virtual existence is constrained by the limits and affordances of a strictly defined virtual world within a particular software platform,[11] it is still a world in which, for instance, an orphan orc can rise through the ranks from killing pigs for a camp chef to being the CEO of a guild—leading, conducting, and directing massive expeditions of forty other players to slay dragons.

Just as in the *Sims Online* and other contemporary MMOGs, the metrics of achievement in *World of Warcraft* have shifted from the abstraction of a numerical score to more complex social and economic metrics that are familiar from everyday life. Rather than asking how high a score you have achieved, today's games might ask questions like "How much money did you earn? Have you achieved the highest possible position within your profession? Are you well-liked and respected by your peers?" The game has become a simulacrum of the world, an imaginary real.

We can imagine nearly as many possible metrics of achievement within virtual worlds as we can within the real world.[12] Perhaps because *World of Warcraft* is a truly *massive* massively multiplayer online game, with more players than the populations of Norway and Rhode Island combined, in creating their imaginary reality, the developers at Blizzard have defaulted to the values, ethos, and methodologies of the contemporary world's most popular ideology, market capitalism. While the acquisition of (virtual) material goods is only one of several metrics of achievement in *World of Warcraft*, and while the market is less explicitly the point of this game than it is in other popular MMORPGs and virtual worlds,[13] this world is nevertheless very clearly one in which gold rules. The spirit of capital in *World of Warcraft* is not simply reducible to more gold = greater achievement. Money is not a meaningless abstraction; gold is more often a means to an end. It can be used to buy special weapons and armor, for instance, or to motivate or reward guild members. Once players have achieved the highest possible level, achievement is no longer marked by leveling up but by getting better stuff. Even honor, earned through battle, is ultimately rewarded in a materialist way—certain "epic" items are only available for purchase by players who achieve a particular rank.

Louis Althusser, in his "Ideology and Ideological State Apparatuses," asserts that ideological state apparatuses contribute to the formation of our values and desires, our positions as subjects. As opposed to repressive state apparatuses, such as the military, prisons, and the police, which enforce ideology by controlling and disciplining the body through violence, ideological state apparatuses such as religion, educational institutions, mass media, and literature shape subject positions through ideology. They interpellate subjects, establishing and reifying certain rules of behavior to which the members of a given society should adhere. According to Althusser, ideology is not something a subject consciously chooses. While I think Althusser is mistaken both in his portrayal of ideological state apparatuses as monolithic entities and in the antihumanism of conceiving individuals as pure subjects with little or no free will, I think there is value to the idea that ideology suffuses all cultural institutions. Althusser argues that when children are in school, they learn not only practical "know-how," but in a larger sense, "how to be":

> besides these techniques and knowledges, and in learning them, children at school also learn the "rules" of good behavior, i.e., the attitude that should be observed by every agent in the division of labour, according to the job he is "destined" for: rules of morality, civic and professional conscience, which actually means rules of respect for the socio-technical division of labour and ultimately the rules of the order established by class domination. They also learn to "speak proper French," to "handle" the workers correctly, i.e., actually (for the future capitalists and their servants) to "order them about" properly, i.e., (ideally) to "speak to them" in the right way, etc. (1994, 103)

In Althusser's formulation, even those aspects of culture we might think of as mere entertainments carry a great deal of ideological freight. There is more at stake than simply winning or losing the game. In *World of Warcraft* and other contemporary MMOGs that are not narrowly defined contests but complex social systems, we need to consider the nature of both the "know-how" and the "how to be" that the game teaches us. The process of advancing in *World of Warcraft* is itself to some extent modeled on the process of getting an education.[14] You begin at level one, with very few skills and only the unrefined abilities that you were "born" with by virtue of your race and class. During the course of the game, by working hard and completing quests (tasks assigned by higher-level NPCs, or non-player characters), players progress to higher levels. While these quests comprise the main mode of play during the earlier parts of the game, they are also clearly a kind of work. There are several different types of quests in the game, but most of those designed for solo players involve a repetitive task of some kind, such as slaughtering twenty giant spiders or thirty owlbeasts. Keeping in mind Althusser's suggestion that one of education's ideological functions is to teach future managers how to "speak proper French" so that they can order workers about more effectively, consider one of the first quests low-level orcs are asked to complete in the beginner's area of Durotar, the "Valley of Trials." The quest is titled "Lazy Peons." The low-level orc encounters an NPC, Foreman Thazz'ril, who says: "Cursed peons! They work hard gathering lumber from the trees of the valley, but they're always taking naps! I need someone to help keep the peons in line. You look like the right orc for my task. Here, you take this blackjack and use it on any lazy peons you find sleeping on the job. A good smack will get them right back to work! Return the blackjack when you're done. Lousy slacking peons...." While the peons in question are cartoonish figures akin to Shrek, found emitting green ZZZZZs rather than engaged in work of any kind, it is nonetheless the case that one of the first acts of play during *World of Warcraft* training is performing an act of violence on behalf of management, clubbing a worker over the skull with a blackjack to set him back to work. On the player's completion of the task, Foreman Thazz'ril expresses his gratitude: "Good, good. Maybe they'll think twice before slacking next time! Thanks for the help!"

Though this is only one of many quests, most of which have little to do with labor relations, the implicit message to the *World of Warcraft* player is quite clear. The *World of Warcraft* is a world in which work is valued as an end in its own right. It is also a world in which slacking will bear little fruit. Though playing the game is itself a form of escapism from the demands of life in the real world, it is somewhat paradoxically a kind of escapism into a second professional life, a world of work.[15]

There is a complex in-game economy in *World of Warcraft*. The work the player does in *World of Warcraft* quests, instances, and PvP battlegrounds has its rewards. Most enemies that a player kills will drop items and often in-game currency as well: copper, silver, and gold pieces. The player can use this currency to purchase necessities, such as food, drink, weapons, ammunition, potions, and armor from vendors. Money is also necessary for players to continue their educations. After completing every second level, players can learn new skills or spells from their class trainers.[16] Education is not subsidized in *World of Warcraft*. To learn these skills, players must both have leveled up and have the gold to pay for the training. Typically, players will have earned enough by grinding up to the level that they can afford their training. In addition to killing enemies and animals that drop gold, players can sell other items that these creatures drop to vendors, or on the open market via the auction house. In addition, each player can choose two primary professions and three secondary skills, including fishing, cooking, and first aid. The practice of each of these professions and skills can result in the production of marketable commodities. Thus, in addition to their primary duties of slaughtering enemies for the glory of the Alliance or the Horde, *World of Warcraft* avatars earn their keep picking herbs, skinning dead animals, mining thorium, crafting weapons, sewing clothes, and so on. Some players are known to log in to spend hours doing nothing but fishing.[17]

The phrase "time is money" takes on a new meaning in *World of Warcraft*. While players pay real money to subscribe to *World of Warcraft* for a set period of time measured in days or hours, within the game they acquire virtual objects, gold, and reputation by expending their time, whether by repeatedly grinding the same mobs over and over again, picking herbs, mining precious metals, or tailoring garments. Indeed, as Torill Elvira Mortensen notes in chapter 10, there is a small industry of actual *World of Warcraft* sweatshops, where "Chinese gold farmers" toil away at these repetitive activities in exchange for the real-world currency of some Western players who can't be bothered to earn the virtual gold for themselves. There are some odd versions of real-world economic behaviors in the game. While no one I know[18] would be motivated to work for more than a day or two by the prospect of purchasing a new pair of trousers, *World of Warcraft* players will happily put in dozens of hours of labor in order to acquire a particular pair of magic pants.

Currency becomes particularly important to players as they attain level 40. In their survey of *World of Warcraft* player behaviors, Ducheneaut, Yee, Nickell, and Moore note that the amount of time players spend playing the game spikes in the few levels around level 40, when players are allowed to purchase a mount and need to acquire the necessary currency to do so (2006, 3). Players who have simply soloed and grouped their way through quests up to this point will likely find themselves short of the hundred or so gold pieces required to train in riding and to purchase their mount.

It is worth considering how the mount functions within the game, and why the purchase of a mount (and at higher levels, an *epic* mount) is so important to players. Mounts are riding animals that function as a form of ground transportation within the game. The most important reason for a player to acquire a mount is the pragmatic one that most directly affects gameplay: mounts increase the player's movement speed. As the player proceeds through the game, quests increasingly require the player to travel greater and greater distances. While the developers of *World of Warcraft* put a great deal of effort into creating beautifully rendered landscapes that can be wondrous to behold, most *World of Warcraft* players will attest that the "travel time" feature of the game, which perhaps serves to enhance the player's perception of the game world's realism,[19] is also one of the most pain-inducing aspects of the game.

There is a great deal of traveling to and fro in this world, and once the player is past the initial landscape-appreciation stage, most of this travel is about as exciting as traveling from Des Moines, Iowa, to Lincoln, Nebraska, in the back seat of your parents' station wagon. While getting a mount does not eliminate the need to travel within the game, it does cut some of this dead time. Owning a mount is also a mark of achievement. *World of Warcraft*'s site attests that "Owning a mount is an impressive accomplishment in the game (not to mention the fact that it makes you look cool)." Just as is the case with other objects in the game, the possession of a mount is a status symbol. All the other players within the game know that a player who has achieved level 40 is allowed to purchase a mount. One can assume that those players who ascend levels after 40 without purchasing a mount lack one because they have failed to marshal their resources effectively. Thus, while the mount is not essential to gameplay, higher-level players seen strolling around the plains of Kalimdor without a mount are in a sense marked as failures, as unskilled players of the game. With the release of *The Burning Crusade* expansion pack, *World of Warcraft* players who achieve the new highest level of 70 can get flying mounts. Blizzard is raising the bar of the cool factor. What teenager would want to tool around in a parent's Oldsmobile when he or she could drive a *flying car* instead? Just as in the contemporary American marketplace that *World of Warcraft* to a great extent mimics, these vehicles serve both the pragmatic function of getting the players around the fictional world more quickly and conveniently than their feet, and as status symbols to differentiate the haves from the have-nots.

I hesitantly admit that because I had not managed to squirrel away enough gold to purchase a mount, Ulcharmin progressed through levels 41, 42, and 43 without ever feeling the thrill of riding wolfback. I began to question my own virtual fiscal management skills. As my peers vaulted past me on their vaunted steeds while I trudged through the mud of the Swamp of Sorrows, the importance of the in-game economy became radically clear to me. I was mortified, and I needed to make some fast cash.

Around this time during my experience of the game, I became much more interested in the market dynamics involved in the game's auction system. While NPC vendors will buy many items from players, in most cases the value of those items to vendors is far lower than their value to other players on the open market. There are separate auction systems for the Horde, the Alliance, and in neutral cities. The auction system, like the mail system, involves a convenient anachronism. While much of the *World of Warcraft* seems modeled on a very analog, medieval/feudal-style culture, both the game's mail system and auction system are based on more contemporary electronic mail systems and markets.[20] The market system functions much like eBay: players can choose the length of the auction, set an opening bid price, and can optionally choose a buyout price at which the item will immediately be sold to the first buyer to hit that price. Very rare items are worth the most gold in the auction house. The developers of the game have a certain amount of control of the in-game economy, in that they control the "drop rate" of rare "blue" items and very rare "epic" or "purple" items. Around level 40, however, most players will have gathered only a few blue or purple items. At this point in the game, most of their activity in the auction house will likely have to do with what I would call trading in commodities.

Because of their professional skills (such as herbalism, alchemy, or skinning), players are able to earn salable goods not only by looting them from the corpses of the beasts, monsters, and other enemies they kill, but also in the more peaceful manner of the gentle gatherer and skillful tradesman. After I managed to obtain a short-term loan from Nuuna, the CEO of my guild, to pay for the mount, Ulcharmin quickly skilled up in herbalism, spent much time picking flowers, and went to work playing the commodities market in the auction house.[21]

While I earned the bulk of the capital necessary to repay my loan slaughtering pirates and miners in Stranglethorn Vale and looting their lifeless bodies of silver and copper coins, I earned a good deal of supplementary income by selling my wares in the auction house. Just as in real-world commodities markets, the prices for individual herbs fluctuate a great deal depending on the supply of and the demand for various commodities.[22] Market timing also plays an important role in the pricing of *World of Warcraft* commodities. As I used the auction houses, I realized that there were arbitrage opportunities, and other players were taking advantage of those opportunities as commodities traders. At this time, I was playing *World of Warcraft* on a European server while living in and playing from the USA, typically during my evenings, which were the wee hours of the morning in Europe. As a result, the servers were typically less populated while I was playing. While the market remains open during these off-peak hours, most players time their auctions to take place during peak play hours—and this allowed me a greater deal of control over the market price of certain herbs during Europe's off hours. While fewer buyers were online, lesser quantities of the herbs were listed. Furthermore, while some players use add-ons such as "Auctioneer" to scan the auction houses and determine the likely price at which a given item or commodity will sell, less-informed players will often list their herbs at lower prices. Some players or groups of players have this down to a science, and are able to more or less control the market price, stockpiling huge quantities of herbs, skins, metals, and such, and selling them in large batches. By buying up batches of herbs listed with inappropriately low buyout prices, however, and by taking advantage of my time differential (listing items while any sensible European was asleep), I was both able to build up large stores of herbs and often to underprice my European competitors, so that my lots would often be sold in the late night (USA)/ early morning (Europe), while the competition slept. I was able to turn a tidy profit and pay back my loan much more quickly than I would have been able to by simply grinding mobs.

In modeling a moderately complex economy, *World of Warcraft* offers its players training in the basics of supply-and-demand economics, markets, and arbitrage. While players are encouraged to perform repetitive labors throughout the game on behalf of their higher-ranking superiors, during the mid-level (middle management) portion of the game, the game structure encourages a degree of entrepreneurship by motivating the player to participate in the auction house economy. Young players of *World of Warcraft* learn economic lessons far more sophisticated than saving pennies and nickels in their piggy banks for a desired toy. They learn how to engage with and play the fluctuations of an electronic marketplace that operates twenty-four hours a day. It is not a far leap to move from the auction houses of *World of Warcraft* to electronic trading of stocks, bonds, and commodities with an online broker. *World of Warcraft* certainly offers a more realistic model of the operations of financial markets than more traditional games used as tools to indoctrinate young capitalists, such as Parker Brothers' *Monopoly*.

While playing the commodities markets in the auction house is clearly a form of training in capitalism with an entrepreneurial bent, the majority of the play involved in advancing a *World of Warcraft* character is mindless and repetitive to the extent that it verges on Taylorism. There is an assembly-line mentality to many of the quests, many of which involve killing a staggering number of a certain type of beast or enemy (grinding), over and over again. There is little more novelty involved in grinding than there would be in welding two sections of a fender together, over and over again, all day long. Combat is a form of production, through which the avatar generates experience, currency, and reputation.[23]

A case in point is the cluster of nonrepeatable and repeatable quests involved in enhancing one's reputation with the furbolgs of Timbermaw Hold. Furbolgs are a race of creatures that appear to be something between Wookies and a demented nightmare version of teddy bears. While the majority of furbolgs are somehow "corrupted" and therefore make for good hunting, the furbolgs of Timbermaw Hold are a powerful faction. Players who can ally with the Timbermaw can garner a number of benefits from the relationship. Just like levels and character attributes, in *World of Warcraft* reputation is a quantifiable metric. The player can gain or lose reputation with various factions depending on the quests performed and the number of members and enemies of the factions killed. All players start out with a hostile reputation with Timbermaw Hold. This might not be important were it not for the fact that one of the upper-level regions in the game, Winterspring, is nearly impossible to get to without going through Timbermaw Hold.[24] To get through Timbermaw Hold and secure safe passage to Winterspring, a player needs to earn a decent reputation with the Timbermaw. In order to do so, the player must kill hundreds of other furbolgs, the Timbermaw's enemies. The act of killing furbolgs lost its novelty within about fifteen minutes of play, yet I carried on for hours upon hours, motivated by the unseen wonders of Winterspring, this mysterious area of the game I would not know until I had proven myself to the Timbermaw. When I finally did get through the tunnel to visit that wintry land on the other side, you can imagine my shock and disappointment at my first Winterspring quest. My charge there was to kill more furbolgs, this time those of the Winterspring clan. Needless to say, I am not among that elite group of players who have achieved "exalted" status and won the Defender of the Timbermaw trinket, which allows the player to summon a pet druid. To reach that goal, I would have needed to slaughter not hundreds, but thousands of furbolgs over perhaps one hundred hours of playing time.

The reputation metric is similar to the honor system, military ranks that players can achieve by waging war in PvP battlegrounds. Esther MacCallum-Stewart's essay in this volume (chapter 2) details the military ranking system, which includes fifteen different steps for both the Horde and Alliance factions. From the standpoint of understanding *World of Warcraft* as a form of training in corporate ideology, the importance of honor and reputation are not trivial.

Players climb a kind of corporate ladder through their efforts in battle, and along the way it is important for them to remain focused on building positive reputations with various factions. In addition, as previously discussed, the player's reputation with other players is important. Just as in corporate life, without a good reputation as an industrious worker, it will be difficult for a player to succeed.

Nevertheless, that grinding is required to level up and achieve reputation cannot alone explain why so many *World of Warcraft* players tolerate, or even welcome, its repetitiveness and tedium. I contend that the appeal of this type of activity is threaded deeper into the subconscious of the capitalist mind, which has been trained to appreciate work itself as a moral good. In writing of the "Protestant Work Ethic," Max Weber asserts that "Waste of time is...the first and in principle the deadliest of sins. The span of human life is infinitely short and precious to make sure of one's own election. Loss of time through sociability, idle talk, luxury, even more sleep than is necessary for health...is worthy of absolute moral condemnation" (1904, 157). Through the lens of the protestant work ethic, the amount of time one spends in a MMORPG would undoubtedly seem a loss of time devoted to play and sociability, a luxury worthy of absolute moral condemnation. Play itself is a kind of sin. A form of play that consumes hundreds and hundreds of hours would almost surely condemn a good soul to hellfire and damnation. But Blizzard and other game developers have found a way to integrate the protestant work ethic into the design of their games: they have created an alternative universe in which play is a form of work. Players are willing to spend hundreds of hours in *World of Warcraft* not in spite of the fact that it often seems like tedious work, but precisely because of it. When play feels like labor, and one toils to achieve objectives, play does not feel like a waste of time. Play that feels like frivolous entertainment would be intolerable for the good capitalist. Play that feels like *work*, on the other hand, must be *good*.

While I believe that the equation between work and play in *World of Warcraft* is a sustained delusion that enables the player to waste time without seeming to—a form of suspension of disbelief—some outcomes of players' engagement with the game are in fact skills applicable in real-world business environments. In the April 2006 issue of *Wired*, John Seely Brown, a person well accustomed to the demands of corporate leadership from his years as the director of Xerox Parc, praised experience as a *World of Warcraft* guild leader as a "total immersion course in leadership. A guild is a collection of players who come together to share knowledge, resources, and manpower. To run a large one, a guild master must be adept at many skills: attracting, evaluating, and recruiting new members; creating apprenticeship programs; orchestrating group strategy; and adjudicating disputes.... Never mind the virtual surroundings; these conditions provide real-world training a manager can apply directly in the workplace."

One could consider grouping, advanced raid groups, and guilds as forms of managerial training. In large raid groups, players must manage their own activities in the context of up to forty other players working toward a common goal. Raid leaders must manage raid members effectively. Each class of player has different ways of inflicting damage on enemies and/or of caring for the well-being of group members. A successful raid is a complex project. It is common for raid leaders to use voice-over-IP software to direct players under their command during a raid. In chapter 9 T. L. Taylor details how some mods (add-on software) allow raid leaders to monitor the performance of individual group members while a raid is unfolding, and to apportion loot as a reward on the basis of each player's individual performance. In short, players who participate in raid groups are often subject to an ongoing performance review, and those who lead raids function as their managers. Guilds, the core social unit in *World of Warcraft*, are also often structured like companies. Most guilds hold regular meetings and have guild leaders (the in-game equivalent of a CEO) and other officers, such as a treasurer, who maintains a guild bank. Guild leaders or an executive committee of officers arbitrate disputes, plan organized campaigns, and distribute loans, armor, and weaponry.

It is also the case that many people who join guilds together are simply moving a real-world social or professional network into *World of Warcraft*. The Truants are far from the only guild that has some professional association outside of the gameworld: it's not even the only guild composed primarily of new media researchers. The virtual world scholars who blog at Terra Nova also have a researchers' guild running on a USA-based server.[25] Venture capitalist and technology guru Joi Ito is the leader of the We Know guild, which also includes many other technology luminaries.[26] Though this form of collegiality is clearly different from gabbing about how to hit the fourth quarter quotas while standing on the fairway waiting for the vice president of sales to take his shot, it is not at all unusual for guild members to talk shop on the same chat channel that they are using to talk about whether or not to sheep the summoner before or after the tank takes out the dragonkin.

On the level of the real-world economy, the millions of players of *World of Warcraft* are, through their subscription fees, supporting a multinational corporation. Blizzard, the developer of *World of Warcraft*, is a subsidiary of Vivendi Games, a subsidiary of the conglomerate Vivendi, which owns a range of telecommunications, television, and entertainment companies. Within the confines of the gameworld, players are also active in a simulation of a society driven by allegiance to one of two multinational conglomerates, the Alliance or the Horde. Players have further allegiance to particular localities and racial groups, guilds, and raiding parties. While each business unit functions with a great deal of autonomy, and certain goal-oriented quests might cross established lines in pursuit of targets of opportunity, the social structures of *World of Warcraft* are in fact very similar to the interlocking and shifting hierarchies of multinational corporations like Vivendi. I have demonstrated just a few of the ways that the game itself trains players how to function within the market economy, of which *World of Warcraft* is a product, and for which it serves as a heuristic device. *World of Warcraft* players are both participating in the globalized economy as consumers and learning how to efficiently operate within it as "players" and good corporate citizens.

Notes

1. I was disappointed to learn that the average player reaches level 60 after 15.5 days of play (Ducheneaut, Yee, Nickell, and Moore 2006). Perhaps, as an herbalist, I have spent too much time stopping to smell the flowers.

2. The majority of quest narratives are simply window-dressing around tasks that could be simply restated as "go kill twenty crocodiles." I do however appreciate the wit of the many intertextual allusions in the game to works of literature, movies, and other videogames. The bankers in Undercity, for instance, are Montagues, while the white-bearded great hunter searching for the lost pages of his book in Stranglethorn is named Hemet Nesingwary. The apes in Un'Goro sometimes drop empty barrels that, while virtually worthless, are an amusing reference to the classic arcade game Donkey Kong.

3. I am nearly certain that the term "addiction" will be unpopular with my fellow players, because the popular media have used the term while terrifying us with stories of teenage *World of Warcraft* players (these stories are typically set in China, and like horror movies, the victims are always teens) literally *dying* because they *forgot to eat* while playing a MMORPG. While I'm sure that at least one of these stories is true, I doubt it's a widespread phenomenon. Your child can and likely will survive *World of Warcraft*. Intelligent adults can spend hours a day play MMORPGs without becoming

pale-faced, sunken-eyed, self-destructive shadows of their former selves. While playing *World of Warcraft* has the hallmarks of a psychological addiction, it may in fact also be a kind of cure. Like MOOs, MUDs, and many other types of online activities, *World of Warcraft* is a social activity, a cure for the deadly human disease of loneliness. None-theless, we can crave human contact in a particular type of structured way just as much as we can crave a cigarette.

4. Say, in my case circa 1982, a sweaty, parched twelve-year-old kid who has just rid-den his ten-speed two miles through traffic to Tin Pan Alley, and decides to forego a cold Coca-Cola so that he'll have two more quarters to feed to Galaga.

5. For example, $10–15 per Atari cartridge in 1987 (atariage.com), $30–50 for Nin-tendo 64 cartridges in the 1990s, and about $30–60 for contemporary PS2 games.

6. $39.99 for *World of Warcraft*, and another $39.99 for the *Burning Crusade* expansion.

7. Even the most dedicated gamers tend to leave the cave a couple times a year to catch the latest Hollywood blockbuster.

8. This is neither to say that MMORPGs are as destructive to your health as cigarettes, nor that Blizzard or other game developers want the players to play the games to the point of neglecting other aspects of their lives (job, family, and so on). In fact, both from public relations and business model points of view, it makes sense for developers to want their players to be healthy, productive members of society who can continue to pay their subscription fees until a ripe old age. *World of Warcraft* even has built-in incentives for players to stay away from the game. Players need to rest their characters in order to gain full experience points for the monsters they kill. It's also more efficient from a business point of view (server maintenance and bandwidth costs) if players only utilize the servers for a limited period of time, and not during every moment of their waking lives. MMORPG developers are seeking a happy medium—one in which players would prefer the game to other entertainment diversions, and would happily pay for the privilege of playing for years on end, whilst simultaneously exemplifying a healthy, mainstream lifestyle.

9. Esther MacCallum-Stewart and Justin Parsler's essay in this volume (chapter 11) discusses the conventions of role-playing servers versus non-role-playing servers.

10. T. L. Taylor's chapter in this volume (chapter 9) discusses ways that players mea-sure and analyze each other's performance in greater detail.

11. For instance, while I can perform a preprogrammed dance in *World of Warcraft*, I can't develop a thriving career as a world-class ballerina.

12. One could imagine achieving the highest score for best dispute arbitration abilities, or best in-game storytelling abilities.

13. In *Second Life*, for instance, players buy and sell property and can develop in-game objects and retain the intellectual property rights to those objects. Players buy both property and in-game currency from Linden Labs, the game's developer.

14. This is perhaps one reason why the academics of the Truants feel so at home in the game. Although the nature of the work one does along the way is quite different, the grind of progressing to level sixty is not all that far removed from the academic grind of achieving bachelor's degree, master's degree, PhD, tenure-track assistant professor, associate professor, and full professor. While master's students are sometimes awarded a tie or a scarf from their home institution upon completing their degree, *World of Warcraft* players are awarded with the ability to ride a mount, such as a timber wolf, at level 40. Though virtual, let me assure you that in purely materialistic terms the mount is a more satisfying token reward for the accomplishment.

15. In his essay, "The Labor of Fun: How Video Games Blur the Boundaries of Work and Play," Nick Yee notes that "It is ironic that computers were made to work for us, but video games have come to demand that we work for them" (2006, 70).

16. Each skill learned adds another layer of complexity to gameplay, as it gives the player another action to choose during a combat situation. At level 57, there are about forty different actions I can initiate. In addition, my hunter carries about forty different objects (potions, food and drink, herbs, bandages, etc.), each of which has a purpose. While the actual manual dexterity of the player is of little importance in comparison to arcade-style joystick-and-button games, the array of choices available to the player at any given time is several orders of magnitude greater in current MMORPGs. My hunter, for instance, can fire a weapon in twelve different ways, each with particular effects. Gameplay in MMORPGs is less about how deftly the player moves, and more about how quickly and how well he or she makes strategic choices from available options.

17. Though it is interesting to note that the player in our guild known to spend the most time fishing says that she does so not for monetary reward in the game, but because she finds it meditative and relaxing after a hard day of work, much like recreational fishing in the real world.

18. That is, no one in an economically advanced "first-world" nation.

19. A great deal of time spent playing *World of Warcraft* is time spent waiting, either to get to a destination, or for some form of transport, or for group members to show up. Rather than giving its players non-stop action, *World of Warcraft* encourages us to "hurry up and wait." There's an argument to be made that this ongoing deferral of gratification makes actual battles and encounters in the game more exciting, by forcing the player to anticipate them in advance of the experience. Jill Walker Rettberg's essay in this volume discusses deferral as a narrative strategy in the game.

20. The postal system would stretch the credulity of the fictional world if one were to think about it too hard. It is difficult to imagine a real-world mail system in which one

could attach a chain mail vest to a memo, which could be picked up by the recipient in whatever town he or she happened to be visiting at the time.

21. As is evidenced by use of "I" and "Ulcharmin," throughout this essay, the interface of *World of Warcraft* invites a good deal of avatarial confusion. While my avatar, Ulcharmin, benefited materially from Nuuna's loan, I was actually responsible for its repayment, and would have encountered social consequences if the debt were not repaid.

22. Though herbs have other uses, alchemists primarily use them as the raw material for potions. Interestingly, on the open marketplace the constituent herbs used to make a potion will often cost more than the potion itself. This seeming contradiction might be explained by the fact that players training as alchemists need these raw materials in order to skill up their professional ability. While potions (such as a healing potion or an elixir of invisibility) can improve a player's performance, only rarely are they essential to gameplay. This is also evidence that in some ways, the drive towards the avatar's personal improvement (leveling up, advancing professional skills) has a stronger pull than any other metric of achievement within the game.

23. Although production takes the form of killing, there is a vast difference between the nature of death in *World of Warcraft* and death in the real world in that NPC enemies killed in *World of Warcraft* regenerate a few minutes after their death. The player kills the NPC, harvests loot from the corpse, and a few minutes later the NPC is back. In many respects, battle in *World of Warcraft* works more like agriculture than war.

24. I say "nearly" because some members of my guild explained a way through that involves ghosts and resurrection without getting through Timbermaw Hold. This alternate route, however, involves subterfuge and a "deviant strategy," not one that is necessarily encouraged by the structure of the game itself.

25. http://terranova.blogs.com/.

26. See CNET article "Power Lunching with Wizards and Warriors" at http://news .com.com/2100–1043_3–6039669.html for discussion of the We Know guild.

References

Althusser, Louis. 1994. "Ideology and State Apparatuses." In *Mapping Ideology*, ed. Slavoj Žižek, 100–140. New York: Verso.

Blizzard Entertainment, Inc., http://www.blizzard.co.uk/wow/townhall/mounts.shtml.

Brown, J., and Douglas Thomas. 2006. "You Play *World of Warcraft*? You're Hired!: Why Multiplayer Games May Be the Best Kind of Job Training. *Wired* 14, no. 4. Available online at ⟨http://www.wired.com/wired/archive/14.04/learn.html⟩.

Castranova, Edward. 2005. *Synthetic Worlds: The Business and Culture of Online Games.* Chicago: University of Chicago Press.

Ducheneaut, Nicholas, Nick Yee, Erick Nickell, and Robert J. Moore. 2006. "Alone Together? Exploring the Social Dynamics of Massively Multiplayer Games." In *Conference Proceedings on Human Factors in Computing Systems: CHI 2006*, 407–416. New York: ACM. Available online at ⟨http://www.nickyee.com/cv.html⟩.

Weber, Max. 1904. *The Protestant Ethic and the Spirit of Capitalism.* Translated by Talcott Parson. New York: Charles Scribner's Sons. Reprinted 1930.

Yee, Nick. 2006. "The Labor of Fun: How Video Games Blur the Boundaries of Work and Play." *Games and Culture* 1, no. 1 (January 2006): 68–71.

Zimmerman, Eric. 2004. "Narrative, Interactivity, Play, and Games: Four Naughty Concepts in Need of Discipline." In *First Person*, ed. Noah Wardrip-Fruin and Pat Harrigan, 154–164. Cambridge, MA: MIT Press.

2

"Never Such Innocence Again": War and Histories in *World of Warcraft*

Esther MacCallum-Stewart

Hello, I'm glad that you've decided to hear me out. The Horde needs all of the help that it can get to prepare for the Ahn'Qiraj War, and that means that we need you! Even now as we speak, official collectors are gathering the necessary material needed for the upcoming war, but we won't be able to meet our goals without your assistance, Chlorr!

You should go speak with the guy in charge, Warlord Gorchuk. What do you say, mage? Will you help out with the vital preparations? (Blizzard Entertainment 2004–present, "The Horde Needs your Help!")[1]

A vast percentage of computer games use some kind of war or conflict as their central underlying narrative. Nowhere is this more apparent than in *World of Warcraft*, where the very name conjures the idea of warfare as an artform, a "craft." Indeed, the Warcraft games have a long history of oppositional combat, stemming from their original incarnation as tactical games between two sides. This is reflected in the name of the first Warcraft game, *Warcraft: Orcs and Humans* (1994), where the two sides fought against each other as deadly enemies.

World of Warcraft sets itself up as a war game between two groups, yet with a vital difference from the customary binary of good versus evil, or orcs versus humans. In *World of Warcraft*, the two sides share an uneasy truce, supposedly united against common enemies that have appeared throughout the Warcraft mythology. This allows a player to choose which side they play on, but it also introduces crucial tensions that question the nature of a world at war. This paper investigates these tensions and asks how they are enforced within the text.

Azeroth (the "world" of Warcraft), is a world shaped by the artifacts of war. Within this world are a series of visual, narratological, and player-engendered signifiers that represent war in various ways. Yet the war that is fought inside this world is curiously stylized—battles for territory become games of "catch the flag." Each side fights the other, yet no consequences for these incursions are ever enacted. A historical vision of war taken from real signifiers makes warfare a central part of the game, yet then diffuses its impact. Like the First World War of 1914–1919, the battles that take place in *World of Warcraft* become attritional, with no side ever winning in the long term. By setting up these factors in an ongoing and historicized conflict, *World of Warcraft* paradoxically challenges its own right to be a world at war.

Going to War

The first decision a player makes when entering *World of Warcraft* is directly related to conflict. Before choosing a side, character, class, or avatar, they must choose what type of server they wish to enter. "Normal" realms are described as follows: "On Normal realms, other enemy players can't attack you unless you allow them to. These realms are labelled Normal in the realm selection screen when you enter the game.... players in those realms ... fight against the monsters in the game rather than against other players. That is why you can think of the Normal realms as 'truce' realms" (Blizzard 2004–present, "Realm Types"). However, a quick breakdown of the English-speaking realms on *WoW* Europe show that the term "Normal" is misleading, since those defined as such are not in the majority: there are only twenty-three Normal realms as compared to 57 PvP (Blizzard 2004–present, "*WoW* Realm Status Europe").

Realms in which players can fight each other on sight—the PvP or "At War" realms—predominate. Despite the narrator's claim in the game's digitized movie introduction that "an uneasy truce" remains between the two sides, it seems from the outset that this truce is in name only. In most cases, combat between Alliance and Horde players is the norm, and in PvP realms, the possibility that a player may be attacked by the opposite side in contested or enemy territory is high.

The second choice that the *World of Warcraft* player makes is which side to be on. The Alliance is formed of elves, humans, dwarves, draenei (a peculiar blue race with hooves), and gnomes; the Horde is composed of orcs, trolls, the undead, blood elves, and taurens—the latter a fantasy race of bovine people. Readers of fantasy texts might recognize these races as representing traditional good and evil factions. The Alliance races derive from the heroes of Tolkien's *Lord of the Rings* (1954) and the playable races in *Dungeons and Dragons* (Gygax and Arneson 1974), while the Horde races comprise enemies in the same texts. In *Dungeons and Dragons*, orcs are a nonplayable race, described in the *Monster Manual* as "aggressive humanoids that raid, pillage and battle other creatures" (Cook, Tweet, and Williams 2000, 146).

The Alliance and the Horde cannot communicate linguistically with each other. Speech is scrambled, and to the opposing side, original emotes are translated as "[the player's name] makes some strange gestures." Players are unable to enter certain areas, including encampments and cities, without being attacked by the guards surrounding them. A designated chat channel, "Local Defense," broadcasts a warning message to every nearby friendly player if opposing players move into these areas: "[Location] is Under Attack!" Cleverly, this simple message carries no further information or advice, leaving oppositional action to the players themselves. All servers permit players to duel each other formally when they meet and opposing sides can fight directly, resulting in the death of the losing avatar.

All realms have battlegrounds. These range from simple games of "catch the flag" to huge outdoor skirmishes across entire regions. Prior to *The Burning Crusade* expansion, good performance in battlegrounds earned players military rankings. Rank works on a sliding scale, taking into account factors such as number of kills, the player's level, the comparative performance of other players in the same realm, killing blows dealt, and the most obvious element, winning or losing a battleground (see the "Honor System Guide" on the official game Web site). Persistent kills of one person, or killing a weakened or significantly lower-level character, generate very little or no honor. These titles represent the only formal nomenclature available in-game (players cannot take surnames) and operate on a quasimilitary structure. There are strong leanings towards medieval titles for the Alliance and Roman names for the Horde, as shown in table 2.1.

Once a rank is gained, it must be consistently maintained; thus it is possible to find that a player has been cashiered from one week to the next as their

Table 2.1
The Rank and File of *World of Warcraft*.

Rank	Alliance	Horde
14	Grand Marshal	High Warlord
13	Field Marshal	Warlord
12	Marshal	General
11	Commander	Lieutenant General
10	Lieutenant Commander	Champion
9	Knight-Champion	Centurion
8	Knight-Captain	Legionnaire
7	Knight-Lieutenant	Blood Guard
6	Knight	Stone Guard
5	Sergeant Major	First Sergeant
4	Master Sergeant	Senior Sergeant
3	Sergeant	Sergeant
2	Corporal	Grunt
1	Private	Scout

Adapted from the documentation of the "PvP Ranking System" at the official game Web site.

ranking slips downward. After *The Burning Crusade* expansion, players who had previously taken part in battlegrounds gained a default military rank based on their best average performance, which they could choose to display as part of their character's name.

These fundamental elements of *World of Warcraft* mean military tension within the game is clearly established from the outset. It is strongly suggested that the two factions would be at war with each other, and indeed, this is encouraged in the gameplay. Overall, fighting between Horde and Alliance players is a central part of the game dynamic.

The Landscape of War

In *World of Warcraft*, the classic aspects of historical and mythological warfare blend and change. The simplistic notion of a fantasy landscape where rural equates with good and technological with bad is deliberately problematized. Simon Schama argues that "landscapes can be self-consciously designed to express the virtues of a particular political or social community" (1995, 15), and

Azeroth capitalizes on this action to represent various landscapes through rich text (see chapter 6).

The use of traditional fantasy races would seem to suggest that the Alliance are good, and the Horde are evil. However, this is specifically not the case. Within the game, the Alliance races are ecologically destructive, aggressive colonizers, whereas the Horde races live harmoniously with the land around them. Humans, dwarves, and gnomes are presented as technologically progressive, supported by their love of gnomish engineering, dwarven mining, and archaeology, and the farming communities of Redridge, Elywnn, and Westfall. Conversely, tauren, trolls, and orcs have backgrounds implying harmony with the land, collectivism, and ecology.

The Alliance races may be progressive, but they live amongst a rural idyll of forests, lakes, farmland, and the elven World Tree, Teldrassil. In contrast, the Horde live in darkened forests, barren plains, deserts, and refugee cities. The tauren Mulgore perhaps comes closest to pastoralism, but unlike the arable lands of the Alliance, Mulgore is bland; the eye travels over vast expanses of open field punctuated by a few trees. The Horde, it seems, worship nature in all its forms—the Alliance are only happy with a conventional, fertile landscape that they have quickly industrialized.

The Horde's representation as five races of survivors seems to have given them a more adaptive attitude toward their habitats. Their cities reflect an ability to creatively remodel terrain. Orgrimmar, the main Horde settlement, has been abruptly hollowed into a mountainside; background noises are war drums beating, dogs barking, and hammers ringing on anvils. Its haphazard construction reflects all at once a military base camp, a bustling souk, and a refugee station. Half of the city lies inside a natural series of tunnels, whereas the rest is clustered outside. A short fortified wall encloses the entire structure, but has been adapted so that an entrant must travel through its length in order to enter, increasing defense capability. Undercity appears at first a deserted ruin, but the undead have what amounts to a hidden base lurking beneath the ruined architecture. Thunder Bluff, the most militarily relaxed of the settlements, is on a peninsula, well-protected from invasion.

The Horde have a sense of dynamism, but in contrast, Alliance cities are long established. They include the medieval castle of Stormwind, a mountainside fortress; Ironforge; and Darnassus, which is so far away from anything that it scarcely needs protection and is a barely defended lakeside complex of art deco beauty redolent of Tolkien's Rivendel. Yet the Alliance appear to be suffering from classic elements of social collapse. Humans are led by a corrupt government and a juvenile king, the gnomes have lost their city as a result of their own experimentation, and the dwarves live in a city without windows, reflecting their introspection.

Quests reflect this differing cultural makeup. It becomes quickly clear that some have specific geographical undertones. The humans, gnomes, and dwarves carry out many quests focused on intrusion: finding mechanical objects, protecting farmland, and discovering places or new ways to make things.[2] The tauren, orcs, and trolls are more concerned with reparation—protecting the land in the form that it is, chasing off invaders, and gathering materials.[3] The Alliance are clear aggressors upon both the land and its people, with the Horde working to keep the ecology in balance. This capitalizes not only on the pastoral, but expands it in military terms. Paul Fussell argues that the literature of the First World War relies heavily on descriptions of landscape, and in particular those that portray the land as whole (often through remembrance of a green and pleasant land), or broken, as it was when trench warfare and continual bombardment destroyed the landscape (1975, 36–74). He also argues that soldiers used the memory of a whole landscape as key to their conceptualization of "home": "The language of literary pastoral . . . can fuse to assist memory of imagination" (ibid, 235). Thus in war, the depiction of landscape as either broken or whole is intrinsically linked, often ironically, to the perception of warfare and warlike attitudes.

Case Study: Warsong Gulch

"The armchair general faced with a computer did not have to concern himself or herself with questions of right or wrong, or separate the good guys from the bad guys. It all depended, quite literally, on your 'point of view'" (Atkins 2003, 4).

Azeroth is, theoretically, a world sharing a fragile truce. This should suggest cohesive and common backstories providing a threat from outside, alongside monsters and NPCs to support this. Although this is a significant part of the game, both sides also fight each other. This is partly an act of player agency, but at the same time it is carefully engineered within the game to provide narrative friction. This is very clearly demonstrated by the battleground Instance of Warsong Gulch.

The battle in Warsong Gulch against the Silverwing Sentinels is of great importance. Under the guise of protecting a forest that doesn't belong to them, the Alliance seeks to deny the Horde one of our largest sources for lumber.

Do not let this happen, Chlorr! Come back to me with proof of serving the Horde in a worthy manner! (Blizzard 2004–present, Horde Quest, "Battle of the Gulch")

The Silverwing Sentinels are at war with the Warsong Outriders due to the destruction the Orcs are causing to the forest. There are, however, more reasons to defend this particular forest than the preservationist philosophy the Silverwings espouse. The forest forms a strategic barrier that makes Ashenvale defendable against a large-scale attack. Without it, Astranaar would last a day or two before being annexed to the Barrens. Do your part in fighting the Warsong Outriders! For the Alliance! (Blizzard 2004–present, Alliance Quest, "Natural Defenses")

Blizzard has spent considerable time ensuring that the battlegrounds have valid backstories, encouraging enmity between the Horde and the Alliance, but carefully ensuring both sides are equally justified.

The argument over deforestation in Warsong Gulch appears initially to heavily favor the elves, in particular given modern concerns over ecology and the destruction of rainforests. The elves wish to preserve the land that the orcs are rapidly cutting down for military supplies. Astranaar, the zone in which Warsong Gulch is set, is dotted with small pockets of orcish lumber mills and elven defenders. The area is one of the first sections of contested territory a player may encounter—areas of the game where in PvP realms, players can attack each other on sight. Even a player who never enters a battleground can see that the territory is disputed. To the north of Astranaar lie the elven lands: Darkshore, Teldrassil, and Darnassus. These are all forested areas. To the south lie the Horde lands: the Barrens, Stonetalon Peak, and Mulgore. Without exception, all of the Horde lands are more geographically hostile. In Stonetalon Peak, mercenaries are actively cutting down trees and polluting the land—a large stretch of this area, Cragpool Lake and Windsheer Crag, contains nothing but hacked-off tree stumps and dirty pools of water full of oil and debris. In short, the Horde simply does not have the access to lumber that their Alliance counterparts possess in plentiful quantities. Thus, the orcs have no lumber and need to defend themselves in their new city. The elves have plentiful supplies but wish to preserve their forests.

The narratives of Warsong Gulch deliberately suggest that there is no correct answer. This taps into a fundamental debate about modern war, which asks whether it is ever necessary. In Azeroth, there are shared enemies, so why do players choose to fight each other as well? In *Synthetic Worlds*, Edward Castronova points out that the natural state of any MMORPG is anarchy: "Players, given the opportunity to use weapons and spells against one another, used those abilities to complete[ly] destroy what nascent social order the world had. Given the opportunity to get away with murder, players took it. It would seem that allowing violence among the players would produce fun gameplay and also add to the social cohesion of the world...but the effect was...more death. Lots more" (2005, 209).

The contradictions of this statement are perhaps more visible in chapter 7 in this anthology; namely that "death" is a word used in the game for a temporary removal from it rather than death itself, and thus has less meaning than it might. Additionally, the impetus for players to act in a destructive manner toward each other is also something inscribed into games since their inception, since they usually encourage players to break or otherwise eradicate the opposition. However, Warsong Gulch enables these aspects to work successfully together and diffuses the tension of players "killing" other players. Players have the opportunity to destroy each other as much as they want, yet taking part in a battleground engenders social cohesion. The satisfaction of doing this can be seen in the congratulations that players issue after a battleground is won.[4] It may not be right, since a battleground involves destroying one's fellow human/orc/gnome/tauren, but winning *is* both gratifying and rewarding. There is nothing but gain from taking part—players are showered with reputation, titles, and access to better armor and items.

Finally, there remains the intensely stylized nature of this combat. In Astranaar, orcs chop down lumber, and elves sneak around them or guard areas from deforestation. This is the natural response to such an incursion. Arathi Basin involves capturing and holding a set level of resources, and Alterac Valley is a tactical battle in which players must ultimately kill the opposition's general. Both of these battlegrounds symbolize familiar and logical actions in a battle or conflict. In Warsong Gulch, the battle over territory is resolved by playing a game of "catch the flag." This reverts the battle to a game rather than anything to do with warfare itself. Quite simply, "catch the flag" does not equal "solve the territorial dispute."

Warsong Gulch questions the rightness of war by giving each side a justified reason for a territorial dispute. Castronova's argument supports the idea that battlegrounds diffuse the temptation to destroy, yet in a world supposedly sharing a truce, players meet and actively kill each other. This conflict will never be resolved, and is played out in such a stylized way that the reasons for the conflict are occluded. While Warsong Gulch is a self-aware reflection by Blizzard on players' desire for conflict and antagonistic play toward each side, it jars with the representation of a world fighting to preserve a fragile truce, reducing Warsong Gulch to a "game" rather than a "battle."

Fictional History

"We still live in a world where the encounter of 'fiction' with 'history' is often read as a traumatic moment when written history is in danger of falling into 'falsehood' or 'deception'" (Atkins 2003, 88).

The Warcraft games have a long narrative history, beginning with the events of *Warcraft: Orcs and Humans* (1994). This typical fantasy narrative of conquest and war is available on the *World of Warcraft* Web sites and is frequently alluded to by NPCs (see figure 2.1). However, while the earlier games specifically encouraged the playable races to fight each other, specific changes have been made in *World of Warcraft* to incorporate the idea of a truce.

World of Warcraft shifts emphasis away from the idea of the Alliance and the Horde fighting each other (as they did in the earlier *Warcraft* games), stressing instead their joint struggles. In effect this avoids the focus of earlier

Figure 2.1
An NPC in the human city of Stormwind explains the backstory of *World of Warcraft*.

Warcraft games, where the objective was to play one side and destroy the other. Now the complicated backstory available on the *World of Warcraft* Web site deliberately emphasizes acts of unity. Thus Jaina Proudmoore's unquestioning trust of the orcs is lauded, and displeasure is directed at such people as "King Llane, who believed the bestial orcs to be incapable of conquering Azeroth, [and] contemptuously held his position at his capital of Stormwind" (Blizzard 2004–present, "Warcraft Historical Library"). This rewriting of *Warcraft*'s own history brings into play the old cliché that there is little to separate the fighting man on either side. This modified backstory reconfigures the Horde as a group who have largely realized the faults of their ancestors and changed their actions accordingly. Despite being victims of persecution and warfare, they have actively recognized and fought against exterior threats (such as the opening of the Dark Portal), losing their original homelands in the process:

The war had wounded each race deeply, but they had selflessly banded together to attempt a new beginning, starting with the uneasy truce between the Alliance and Horde.

Thrall led the orcs to the continent of Kalimdor, where they founded a new homeland with the help of their tauren brethren. Naming their new land Durotar after Thrall's murdered father, the orcs settled down to rebuild their once-glorious society. Now that the demon curse was ended, the Horde changed from a warlike juggernaut into more of a loose coalition, dedicated to survival and prosperity rather than conquest. Aided by the noble tauren and the cunning trolls of the Darkspear tribe, Thrall and his orcs looked forward to a new era of peace in their own land (Blizzard 2004–present, "Warcraft Historical Library").

In contrast, the Alliance appear responsible for most of the incursive activities of the game, including allowing the Burning Legion (the centrally shared enemy) into Azeroth. The humans and the elves are also directly accused of genocide in their attempts to wipe out the trolls and the orcs. It is, in fact, difficult to find positive Alliance figures in the *Warcraft* backstory unless they are sympathetic to Horde persona.

Azeroth's leaders epitomize this reconstruction. The Horde leader, Thrall, is a noble warrior who has dragged himself from obscurity to rightful leadership. The Alliance leaders are a juvenile human king, a bad-tempered elf who utters derisive comments such as "Tyrande has no idea how to lead our people!," and a stereotypical beer-loving dwarf. Whereas Thrall is depicted as a leader struggling to hold together forces with contradictory aims, pictures of the human King Anduin Wrynn found in various dungeons suggest that

Wrynn is unaware of corruption in the Alliance; his image is still being used by those who wish to harm all. The King is guarded by Lady Katrana Prestor, who is also the traitorous dragon Onyxia. Other symbols, such as the torture chambers in the Stockades beneath the city of Stormwind or the internment camps at Lordaeron, suggest unpleasant undertones to Alliance rulership.

Real History: Biplanes and Zeppelins

Historicized responses to warfare exist all around Azeroth. Flight is the first stage at which it is possible to determine a specific reference to historical warfare—namely the First World War.

It takes time to travel across Azeroth, and this makes transport important. On flight routes players use individual transports, which include bats, hippogryffs, and gryffons, and large-scale transport such as a tram, galleons, and zeppelins. Zeppelins are the major large-scale transport for the Horde. "Of course there's no danger in everything catching flames and exploding like a huge helium bomb," says the smiling goblin on the Orgrimmar flight platform, warning players that "smoking is not allowed while on board the zeppelin, and fire spells are banned from being cast during the trip."[5]

Since the First World War and the Hindenburg air disaster in 1937, the image of the zeppelin has been used to signify progress run amok, often along explicitly totalitarian lines. Raids carried out over British cities during the war were condemned and feared for their devastating physical and mental effect on civilians. This fear was exacerbated by H. G. Wells's prophetic *The War in the Air* (1908), which identified the airship as a key factor in warfare and helped to sustain panic toward zeppelin attacks during World War I.[6] When the war ended, zeppelins became more commercially successful, and were indeed regarded as the future of flight. Their monetary potential, plus the romanticism of dining beneath the great balloons, became an aspirational motif across Europe and America. In 1936 the *Hindenburg* airship made the first transatlantic flight between Frankfurt am Main, Germany and Lakehurst, New Jersey. However, on her maiden flight in the next new season in 1937, the airship exploded and crashed. Several prominent politicians traveling on the flight were killed. The incident was filmed, recorded, and broadcast across the United States in the first live coast-to-coast radio broadcast. Obviously this made radio history, but it also permanently destroyed the zeppelin's positive reputation. From this point on, the zeppelin became a signifier of technology run on too fast—a dangerous instrument of warfare that could not be tamed for peacetime uses.

In science fiction, the zeppelin is repeatedly used as a dystopian icon in visions of the future. *Equilibrium* (Wimmer 2002), *Sky Captain and the World of Tomorrow* (Conran 2004), *The Forever War* (Haldeman 1975) and a recent series of *Doctor Who* (Davies 2006) have used the zeppelin in this context. It is at once seen as profoundly historical, yet at the same time too progressive for the society in which it is placed. A zeppelin in a fantasy or science-fiction setting is a signifier of dystopian fear.

In *World of Warcraft*, these cultural assumptions provide a strong undertone to the Horde's use of zeppelins. Their appearance brings with it suggestions of aggressive colonization, technology outstripping need, and a potentially fascist militarism insinuating itself into normal life.[7] Indeed, there are several zeppelin crash sites around Azeroth and the Outlands, two of which are the source of multiple quests to retrieve lost supplies. The *Hindenburg* is referred to by the flight goblin's comment that the zeppelin might explode in flight (in fact, helium is inert and no one really knows what caused the crash). All of these signifiers suggest the Horde is preparing for war quickly, perhaps too quickly. However, lest things get too dark (in particular to avoid the fascist undertones of the use of zeppelins in fantasy texts), the appearance of Horde zeppelins has been offset. Instead of the sinister, sleek machines of the past, the Horde zeppelins are tubby-looking boats, seen in figure 2.2, which distinctly resemble the Montgolfier Brothers' balloon.

Above the city of Ironforge lies an airfield. This area is inaccessible;[8] however, it can be clearly seen by players flying through a gully on the way to various terminals (see figure 2.3).

Within the "instance" dungeon (see the glossary for a definition) of Gnomeregan, more biplanes can be found (figure 2.4). Gnomeregan, once home to the gnomes, is abandoned. The biplanes are surrounded by groups of unfriendly, poisoned goblins and gnomes who attack players on sight. The planes cannot be interacted with—they do not move if touched, nor do any quests involve their restoration.

The biplane functions rather like an antithesis to the zeppelin. During the First World War, flight took massive technological leaps forward. At first aeroplanes were only flown by the upper classes (who often brought their own machines to the front with them), and the singular nature of the lone pilot dueling in the sky on a one-to-one basis with skill and nerve quickly cap-

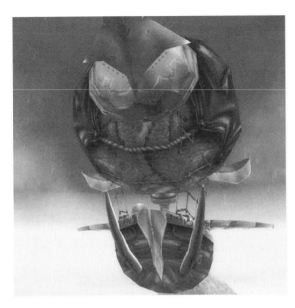

Figure 2.2
A zeppelin transport in Stranglethorn Vale.

Figure 2.3
Ironforge Airport from the air.

Figure 2.4
A biplane inside Gnomeregan.

tured the public imagination. The media were quick to draw upon the excitement and danger of flight, and a popular romanticism quickly grew around
these "knights of the sky." After the war, the stories of W. E. Johns' fictional
hero James Bigglesworth, "Biggles," cemented the vision of the aeroplane as
on the side of the just and good.

In Gnomeregan, the biplanes are locked dormant underground: technology
unused is technology wasted. Gnomeregan is filled with irradiated monsters,
an accidental by-product of gnomish experimentation and building. This
reconfigures the age-old science fiction concept of technology run amok without thought beforehand. While there is a crashed biplane on a hillside of Dun
Morogh, and the airport lies serenely above the city of Ironforge, the Alliance
use the more retrograde gryphons and hippogriffs as their transport, eschew-
ing the progressive biplane. Once again the suggestion that technology leads to
dangerous, dystopic progress is apparent: the Alliance used to use biplanes,
but they advanced too quickly, and their biplanes either lie wrecked on the
landscape or are underground and unusable. For the Alliance, galleons, along
with a tram strongly identifiable with a deserted New York subway station,
carry players long distances. Neither of these connote the aggressive forces of
dystopic progress that the zeppelins suggest, although the tram is reminiscent
of previous RPG computer games such as *Shadowrun* (1993). Good guys, it

seems, do not ride zeppelins, but since the Horde are not the bad guys either, their zeppelins have been contained with bright linings and comical goblin aeronaught guides.

The First World War as a Site of Conflict

"A generation that had gone to school on a horse-drawn streetcar now stood under the open sky in a countryside in which nothing remained unchanged but the clouds, and beneath these clouds, in a field of force of destructive torrents and explosions, was the tiny, fragile human body" (Benjamin 1936, quoted by Lodge and Wood 2000, 12).

It might seem odd to single out one war as more culturally significant in the *World of Warcraft* narrative than another. However, the crucial point at which World War I stands in our understanding of how wars are fought makes it a vital point at which the tension inherent in *World of Warcraft* can be understood.

The First World War is often seen as engendering a fundamental change in the way people conceptualized warfare. After 1918, the world's eyes opened to war's potential to ruin lives, land, and societies. Of course, this is a very modern understanding of the war—often known as the "mythology" of war—but it is a useful one because it provides a point of closure. Before 1914, goes this mythology, war was fought on more noble, possibly even fantastical terms. Afterward, the advent of technology meant that no one could regard war as glorious again.

World of Warcraft makes heavy use of these ideas. The end of innocence through war is counterposed by the growth of mechanized society. The game counterposes "old" war—chivalric, medieval, fought with sword and bow and arrows, and united against an evil enemy, with "new" war—devious and fought with modern weapons against a justified, empathic enemy. *World of Warcraft* uses these themes to deepen the tension inherent in the conflict between the Horde and the Alliance. Attritional warfare, such as that against the Scourge or the Burning Legion, is also portrayed in a negative context. This is not a new theme to *World of Warcraft*, and builds on many fantasy texts using the same idea. However, it is the persistence with which *World of Warcraft* uses tropes of First World War warfare that makes it extraordinary.

Dotted around Azeroth are constant reminders that it is a world at war. These include monuments or shrines to the dead, quests that specifically work toward wartime activities (these are most notable in the central plot arcs that govern the instances and higher-end quests), individual markers in the text such as the zeppelins, or the annual festival to honor dead heroes that comes just before Armistice Day on November 11. These signifiers may seem insignificant when seen separately, but taken collectively they produce a picture comparing Azeroth's Great Wars to that of 1914–1919. Along with the history of this war comes the emotional baggage inherent in its depiction by writers, poets, and artists: that of mud, blood, and futility.

Direct references to the First World War are also used. Azeroth's previous conflicts are named "The First Great War" and "The Second Great War," echoing the common name for World War I as "The Great War." In Stormwind, several NPCs mention this in their default conversations; Aedis Brom, a human veteran who walks the city exchanging war stories with his dwarven companion, says "I tell ye, I don't miss the Great War at all. I remember when we fought at Darrowmere. All night in the fog, lying in a muddy trench." The comparison with the dreadful weather experienced on the Western Front and the association with trench warfare is clearly made.

For a modern reader, the act of warfare is always going to be problematic. Only a small fraction of the population currently serves in the armed forces. War is simply not a daily part of most people's lives any more, and their attitudes toward the experience of being at war are often constructed from secondary sources such as literature. A succession of wars throughout the twentieth century has worked to create a dominant cultural belief that war is a bad thing. This cultural construction, known as the parable of war, is a literary, often highly ideological model of the war based on a series of emotive ideals and key themes. This parable is best represented in A. J. P. Taylor's infamous statement about the Battle of the Somme:

Idealism perished on the Somme. The enthusiastic volunteers were enthusiastic no longer. They had lost faith in their cause, in their leaders, in everything except loyalty to their fighting comrades. The war ceased to have a purpose. It went on for its own sake as a contest in endurance. Rupert Brooke had symbolised the British soldier at the beginning of the war. Now his place was taken by Old Bill, a veteran of 1915, who crouched in a shell crater for want of "a better 'ole to go to." The Somme set the picture by which further generations saw the First World War: brave helpless soldiers; blundering obstinate generals; nothing achieved. After the Somme men decided that the war would go on forever. (1963, 140)

What is so notable about Taylor's writing is his emphasis on emotion, loss, and futility rather than actual historical detail. Yet his book *An Illustrated His-*

tory of the First World War remains one of the most frequently read history books about the war.

The 1960s, and specifically the Vietnam War, changed the way war was represented in popular culture. Ben Shephard has called this development "the birth of trauma" (2005). From this point on, to survive a war without emotional degradation was seen as almost unthinkable. The men who served were to be pitied after the horrors they had experienced, and it was also strongly suggested that not to react with shock and active protest to these conditions was wrong. None of these ideals really represent the attitudes of soldiers or civilians at the time, but they have come to be seen as historically insoluble.

All of these ideals heavily affect the construction of a MMORPG where the backdrop is a land actively engaging in combat, in particular combat between two equal sides. While many games construct a nebulous other who never becomes "us," the sheer fact that in *World of Warcraft* the Horde and the Alliance can meet, fight, and "see" each other as people, as well as actively encouraging antagonistic relationships, throws the ideas of the war parable sharply into focus. War is awful and terrible; it takes lives and destroys land, races, and friendships. It is dehumanizing and barbaric. Azeroth has its heroes, but the players within it are very much seen as cogs in a huge, attritional machine.

This is one view of the war. It is certainly one that the players themselves often rely on. *World of Warcraft* uses the ethos of World War I to make its players self-aware. In considering why they might be fighting, players are also forced to consider their fellows, what part they might be playing in this conflict, and whether the enemy that they fight is a sympathetic one. The backstory of war against shared enemies provides a common theme—and at the same time players are able to return from the dead an infinite number of times with little ill effect, meaning that often they are fated to meet and to kill each other repeatedly (see chapter 7).

Player-Led Activity

T. L. Taylor's *Play Between Worlds* (2006) argues that within a game, agency is often removed from the designer and given to the player. While designers can create the world, they have little control over what may happen within it. The narratives provided engender characterization and role play, which may then move in unexpected directions. In MMORPGs very little of this agency exists, as the paths which a player may tread to succeed are very narrowly defined. In

World of Warcraft, fundamental precepts such as fighting must take place. The use of conflicting ideas about warfare in *World of Warcraft* is an attempt to drive play beyond the confines of the quest and experience point-gaining objectives of the game. *World of Warcraft* encourages the player to think about what they are doing, even though there is little more that they can do to engender active role playing.

However, the cultural parable of World War I states very specifically that to fight in a war is wrong, and that if one does so, it must be respectfully handled. War, says the parable, is a terrible thing, and contact with the horrors of war drives a person to madness. In *World of Warcraft*, players must fight and kill to survive, not only destroying the targeted enemy, but also killing each other. Obviously there is a paradox here. One technique to overcome this paradox is to rewrite the agenda, thus subverting narrative for personal ends. The construction of narrative videos (machinima), which take painstakingly filmed moments from the game and reconstruct them as stories, is one example of how this is done.

In a video posted on YouTube.com, the guild The Collective Order (of the Destromath server) dramatizes a series of incidents involving PvP combat and raiding enemy territories ("Beer for My Horses" 2006). These are counterposed with staged shots of the guild riding or walking through Azeroth on their mounts, meeting in a tavern, and tending to their horses. The figures in the video are self-consciously equipped with cowboy-style equipment—most notably in their headgear and horses, and the locations chosen for the filming of the video match this style. The emphasis in the video is that the guild members are meting out justice through their actions, and that their killings are justified. The situation within the video is displaced even farther, away from the combat-oriented location of Azeroth and toward a Western-style scenario. The guild, it seems, are fictionalizing their warlike actions within a secondary genre (the Western) in order to displace them.

This act is reversed in the video "My Life For the Horde" (Bannerman 2006) and the events that took place at the role-playing event "The Steamwheedle Faire" (Darrow 2006) on the Moonglade EU server.[9] "My Life for the Horde" is a lengthy video telling the story of Seemos, an aged orc warrior. Having retired in order to train more warriors, Seemos learns of an insurrection in Alliance lands by an evil mage. He arms himself for battle and destroys the mage in single combat, but is killed as a result. Many people visit his body as it lies in state before burial.

The video is an unself-conscious celebration of being a warrior, but it draws on feudal ideas rather than recent ones of individual heroism and glory, and also specifically names the enemy as "other."[10] Seemos is not fighting the Alliance, he is fighting a dangerous splinter group. The fact that Seemos does not survive, and that considerable time is spent at the end dwelling on his funeral, is testimony to conceptions of warfare in which he who has killed (and is therefore morally in the wrong) cannot be allowed to re-enter society, especially if it is an act he has enjoyed or performed excessively.

At the Steamwheedle Faire, over 200 Horde and Alliance players met peacefully to tell stories, drink on the beach, participate in boxing matches, and dance in front of campfires. One guild (The Mithril Guard) performed a military parade. While some acts, like the dancing, were spontaneous, the parade was planned. A demonstration of the military pride that the guild felt, the parade also showed a curious tension. In the middle of this peaceful gathering was a staged act of military force.

Figure 2.5
The Mithril Guard practice for their parade.

The Steamwheedle Faire subversively reconstructed mythologized events of warfare. Shared activities showed a willingness to act communally in the same way that soldiers did—by sitting together and sharing drink, stories, and campfires.[11] The event is comparable to the infamous Christmas Truce of 1914, when soldiers fraternized, played games, and shared food in No Man's Land on Christmas Day.

All of these activities blend representations of war with a shared understanding of how conflict should be approached in order to diffuse its central tenet—that of killing one's fellow men. The participants at the Steamwheedle Faire chose to contain this through their joint role play as equals in the same lands. The makers of the machinima "Beer for My Horses" and "My Life for the Horde" did it by alternatively displacing or glorifying the act of fighting. Both however, moved the participants away from normal activities in *World of Warcraft*, one by linking warfare with a different genre in a comedic style, and the other by killing its perpetrator.

Conclusion: Being at War

I know all about landmines. I'm the one that lays all the mines on the front lines here, after all.

If you want to defuse the Stormpike mine fields, all you have to do is kill their explosives expert. That dwarven coward is no doubt hiding in the first tower on the Field of Strife. Take him out and those landmines won't come back after they've been disarmed.

If you do happen to kill him, come back here and let me know. No good deed should go unrewarded (Blizzard 2004–present, "Defusing the Threat").

The narrative of *World of Warcraft* presents a society where the state of warfare is naturalized. This is at odds with real society, where war in the Western world is an isolated and minor aspect of public life and where the difficult connection between games and war is long established: "...the interdependence of game-playing and warfare develops in two stages: first, an abstracted model of individual combat is transposed onto the sphere of game-playing; in a second step, the model of artificial warfare represented here becomes a measure for real combat" (Richard 1999, 339–340).

In order to placate ideas of militarism and warmongering, as well as lay to rest the perennial bugbear that violence in computer games engenders real-life violence, *World of Warcraft* questions the discrepancy between good and evil, suggesting not only that both sides are equal, but that they are equal in being wrong. If anything, Blizzard have rather overcompensated in their construction of the Horde as beleaguered, persecuted good guys and the Alliance as grasping sybarites. These constructions tie directly into the modern unease with warfare and the question of who, if anyone, is on the right side.

Of course, a great deal of warfare is part of the game dynamic: going on quests, building reputation, fighting other people in the designated battlegrounds, or simply fighting the enemies of the world itself. Many players are unaware of the tensions that the backstory creates, and indeed, these issues do not figure in their experience of the game. However, many of these also connote specific ideas about war itself, specifically by engaging the ideology of the First World War as a moment of change: sometimes unconsciously, sometimes overtly. The war as a cultural parable permeates the game, from shared NPC conversations to the physical appearance of items and artifacts. It is strongly suggested that signifiers of later wars—the internment camps in the Hillsbrad Foothills, the nuclear explosion appearance of Loreadan—are emphatically wrong. World War I acts as a point of closure in the game's representations of war in the same way that it does in modern cultural perception.

A cautionary note to conclude: *World of Warcraft* was produced during a period when warfare *was* an important part of society, during the Iraq–America conflict of 2003–present. Perhaps this accounts for its apparent encouragement of warfare throughout the game in the form of battlegrounds and the Alliance versus Horde dichotomy. Alongside *World of Warcraft* are computer games such as *America's Army* (2002–present), which actively encourage recruitment into the American army and aim to present the U.S. forces in a positive light. The tension within *World of Warcraft*—presenting the war as a naturalized part of society, but at the same time questioning its underlying concepts—may be an attempt to address some of these issues. Guy Westwell argues that this pattern is endemic to American war films, especially during times of active conflict: "for all their protestations to the contrary, Hollywood movies tend to show the war as necessary, if not essential, and present the armed forces as efficient, egalitarian and heroic institutions" (2006, 3). It seems logical that this ideological bias should also apply to games.

As a conclusion this is sobering—if the game is influenced by representations and assumptions about more recent events, this also politicizes it, an argument confirmed by Jessica Langer's discussion of in-game races as depictions of real life races in chapter 4. In putting forward a vision of a world in which war is a fundamental part of the economy, history, and landscape, Blizzard is also sending out less overt messages about the rightness of warfare as an everyday activity.

Notes

1. As well as being accessible through gameplay, all quests listed in this paper can be found at "The Goblin Workshop" at http://www.goblinworkshop.com by searching under title.

2. See, for example, "Filthy Paws," "Supplying the Front," and "Powder to Ironband" (Blizzard Entertainment 2004–present).

3. See, for example, "Zehvra Dependence," "The Disruption Ends," and "The Defense of Grom'Gol" (ibid.).

4. The ability to do this was removed after the application of Patch 1.1.12 (8/24/06), which allows cross-realm battlegrounds but instantly degroups players once the battleground ends.

5. Smoking is not possible in the game—although there is a quest that refers to it, "The Great Fras Siabi"—and it is not possible to cast fire spells on the zeppelins anyway, unless one is duelling. There is in fact no adverse penalty for doing so.

6. See, for example, the first-person accounts detailing this in Richard Van Emden and Steve Humphries, *All Quiet on the Home Front: An Oral History of Life in Britain During the First World War* (Headline, London, 2003).

7. Although zeppelins were not used extensively in World War II, they were used by the Germans before the war, and are often associated with Nazism. See for example the proto-Nazi symbols used on flags in the same scene that introduces the zeppelins in *Equilibrium,* or the extended fight (and flight) scene in *Indiana Jones and the Last Crusade* (1989).

8. The airfield can be accessed, but only by using "cheats," which include a fast mount, potions, or clothing that allows the player to float through the air, as well as knowing the way across a steep range of mountains.

9. A commemorative video of the event can be seen at http://video.google.com/videoplay?docid=1257027171107285010.

10. Jill Walker Rettberg has also pointed out that the guild structure itself is feudal, drawing on ideas of military togetherness that also help to answer the question of whether or not Alliance and Horde are at war—many role-playing stories created by players often revolve around interguild rivalry rather than the direct opposition of the Alliance versus the Horde.

11. Ironically these acts are some of the only things opposing players can do to show community, since clicking on an opposing character makes the player automatically attack her target, and languages are scrambled.

References

Atkins, Barry. 2003. *More Than a Game*. Manchester: Manchester University Press.

Bannerman, Corey. 2006. "My Life for the Horde." WarcraftMovies video. Available at ⟨http://www.warcraftmovies.com/movieview.php?id=9508⟩.

Blizzard Entertainment. 2004–present. "World of Warcraft Europe: Official Web site." Available at ⟨http://www.wow-europe.com⟩.

Castronova, Edward. 2005. *Synthetic Worlds: The Business and Culture of Online Games*. Chicago: The University of Chicago Press.

Cook, Monte, Jonathan Tweet, and Skip Williams. 2000. *Monster Manual: Core Rulebook III*. Renton, WA: Wizards of the Coast.

Cranius. 2006. "Beer for My Horses," You Tube Video. Available at ⟨http://www.youtube.com/watch?V=XWU_gZgUkZQ⟩.

Darrow, Ed (Stormina Teacup). 2006. "The Steamwheedle Faire," Google video. Available at ⟨http://video.google.com/videoplay?docid=1257027171107285010⟩.

Doctor Who: Rise of the Cybermen, directed by Russell T. Davies. First broadcast May 13, 2006. London: British Broadcasting Corporation.

Doctor Who: The Age of Steel, directed by Russell T. Davies. First broadcast May 20, 2006. London: British Broadcasting Corporation.

Equilibrium, directed by Kurt Wimmer (2002, New York: Dimension Films).

Fussell, Paul. 1975. *The Great War and Modern Memory*. Oxford: Oxford University Press.

Gygax, Gary, and Dave Arneson. 1974. *Dungeons and Dragons*. Lake Geneva, WI: TSR Inc.

Haldeman, Joe. 1975. *The Forever War*. London: Weidenfeld and Nicolson.

Indiana Jones and the Last Crusade, directed by Steven Spielberg. (1989, Marin County, CA: Lucasfilm).

Lodge, David, and Nigel Wood. 2000. *Modern Criticism and Theory*. 2nd ed. London: Pearson Education Limited.

Richard, Brigit. 1999. "Norn Attacks and Marine Doom," in *Ars Electronica: Facing the Future: A Survey of Two Decades*, ed. Timothy Druckery. Cambridge, MA: MIT Press.

Schama, Simon. 1995. *Landscape and Memory*. London: Harper Collins.

Shephard, Ben. "Writing about Modern War." Paper given at Queen Mary's University, London, November 23, 2005.

Sky Captain and the World of Tomorrow, directed by Kerry Conran. (2004, Brooklyn: Brooklyn Films II).

Taylor, A. J. P. 1963. *An Illustrated History of the First World War*. London: Hamish Hamilton.

Taylor, T. L. 2006. *Play Between Worlds*. Cambridge, MA: MIT Press.

Tolkien, J. R. R. 1954. *The Lord of the Rings*. London: Allen and Unwin.

Wells, H. G. 1908. *The War in the Air*. Reprinted in 2005, London: Penguin Books.

Westwell, Guy. 2006. *War Cinema: Hollywood on the Front Line*. London: Wallflower Press.

World of Warcraft as a Playground for Feminism

3

Hilde G. Corneliussen

In 1789, during the French revolution, women fought to be included in the category of citizens—the brotherhood—for which the revolutionaries were claiming equal rights. Although it took 155 years before French women got the right to vote, feminists have fought and won many battles since the French revolution, and they have been a major driving force in changing the position of women throughout the Western world. However, one of the recurring challenges of feminist projects in their various facets is the dilemma of "equality vs. difference" (Scott 1996). Should women's equal rights be based on their similarity to men, a standpoint posing a threat to the category of women by dissolving it, or should women claim their rights based on their difference from men, thus running the risk of reinforcing inequality by constructing women as a special group?

The feminists of the French revolution are often mentioned as pioneers in a first-wave feminism that fought for women's equality. Today, in the modern Western world, it is however not primarily *rights*, but rather *representation*, or access to traditionally male-dominated subject positions, that is at stake. A more recent feminist movement in France, the Parité movement, worked for equal representation of men and women in elective political positions in the 1990s and deserves some attention, as it suggests a new solution to the dilemma of equality versus difference, as Joan Wallach Scott explains:

Instead of saying either that women were the same as men (and therefore entitled to equal participation in politics), or that they were different (and therefore would provide something that was lacking in the political sphere), the paritaristes refused to deal in gender stereotypes at all. At the same time, they insisted that sex had to be included in any conception of abstract individualism for genuine equality to prevail. The abstract individual, that neutral figure upon which universalism depended—without religion, occupation, social position, race, or ethnicity—had to be reconceived of as sexed. Here was the innovation: unlike previous feminisms, women were no longer being made to fit a neutral figure (historically imagined as male), nor were they reaching for a separate incarnation of femininity; instead, the abstract individual itself was being refigured to accommodate women (2005, 4).

Thus, the claim from the Parité movement was that individuals were never neutral, but always either male or female, and men and women needed to be recognized as categories in society, but as meaningless categories. According to this view, gender equality is not motivated by the genders' qualities, and the paradox of equality versus difference is irrelevant. Instead, equality is based on a notion of justice and balance within important institutions in society (Skjeie and Teigen 2003, 28). The law popularly referred to as the Parité law was passed in 2000, although with clear limitations compared to the original demand from the paritaristes (Scott 2005, 127), which I will return to later.

Although gender can have different meanings in different contexts, there is a recurring tendency for gender to be perceived as a dualism of men-women, male-female, masculine-feminine. Thus an important aspect of our understanding of gender is the relationship between the genders, and gender as a relational category is a premise in all three feminist positions. The premise for difference feminism is that women are special and complementary to men. The premise for equality feminism is that women are identical to men, which often implies a masculine norm. In her book *Only Paradoxes to Offer*, Scott describes how one of the feminists even broke the law of early twentieth-century Paris and wore trousers, finding pleasure in sometimes being mistaken for being a man (1996, 140–141). The paritaristes rejected the masculine norm, and claimed equality based on the always present, but "essential meaninglessness, of sexed bodies" (Scott 2005, 56). These three feminist positions are not the only ones, but they serve the purpose here by presenting three different suggestions for how to organize gender in a society, and they will help us explore the gender constructions of the game universe of *World of Warcraft*.

Even though gender inequalities still prevail, women in the Western world have gained a lot of ground in terms of equal rights—politically and financially, in education and the workforce, and the uterus is no longer an argument against women's ability to enter higher education, as it was in the nineteenth century (Moi 1999, 15–20). Salen and Zimmerman claim that games can be seen as "ideological systems" that reflect the offline culture in which they are designed and played. They refer to this as "cultural rhetoric," which points to the persuasiveness of the meaning produced by a game and how players are invited to accept the discourse of the game as a meaningful framework to play with (Salen and Zimmerman 2004, 516–517). Computer games have received a large amount of feminist critique for being made by and for boys (Cassell and Jenkins 1998; Gansmo, Nordli, and Sørensen 2004; Haines 2004). However, during the last decade, computer games have developed from being dominated by male protagonists to include more female protagonists. This might be a response to the feminist criticism, but if we accept Salen and Zimmerman's claim, it can also be seen as reflecting the increasing gender equality in Western society in general. A synthetic world that can be "anything we want it to be" (Castronova 2005, 7), can also be a perfect cultural playground for perceptions of gender in our modern world. Although *World of Warcraft* represents a fantasy world, a world inhabited by orcs, night elves, and dragons, it is also a place where gender is being constructed, represented, and negotiated in ways not totally different from hegemonic Western discourses of gender. Meaning is however not created solely by designers in a MMOG like *World of Warcraft*, where millions of users constantly bring in their own cultural baggage. Still, it is important to explore the gendered universe of the game design, to consider how the game, by opening for some, ignoring some, and excluding other meanings of gender, creates a framework for perceptions of gender. Thus the object of study in this chapter is the construction of gender in the design of *World of Warcraft*, analyzed through a gender-sensitive lens tuned by the three feminist perspectives of gender as difference, similarity, and the Parité movement's version, which will help us explore how discourses of gender are woven into the game design.

Reviewing Computer Games and Gender

"Girls do not really like computer games." This has become a truism that is hard to refute, even with plain numbers showing otherwise.[1] There are many research projects and surveys documenting that girls and women—in particular women over 40—enjoy playing computer games. Female gamers over 40 spend more time playing online games (mostly puzzle and card games) than men or teens of both genders, according to research by AOL in 2004 (Carr 2006, 172). According to the Entertainment Software Association (ESA) Web site, "[w]omen age 18 or older represent a significantly greater portion of the game-playing population (30%) than boys age 17 or younger (23%)." Nick Yee, who has done extensive surveys of MMORPG players, claims that women are still outnumbered by men in these games, but interestingly, female MMORPG players are in general older (age 23–40) than corresponding male players (age 12–28) (2003). According to the BBC survey *Gamers in the UK*, 59 percent of the UK population between 6 and 65 years of age played digital games in 2005 (Pratchett 2005). Thus the heterogeneous group of game players is not small and exclusive, and it is not quite as dominated by either youth or men as the hegemonic discourse tries to convince us. The perception of girls' and women's disinterest in computer games has also raised the question of how to expand the market for computer games to "the other half of the population," as one game producer puts it (WomenGamers.Com 2000). Gansmo, Nordli, and Sørensen (2004) list three strategies that have been used to get girls and women to play computer games. The first strategy, most widespread in the 1980s and early 1990s, was to claim that there was nothing wrong with the games; it was girls and women that should change—echoing arguments in other IT fields (Corneliussen 2003). Critics, however, have pointed to how early computer games were dominated by male heroes and passive female victims or "damsels in distress," as well as displays of violence against women (Cassell and Jenkins 1998; Salen and Zimmerman 2004, 524) and storylines creating a space that attracted boys and excluded girls (Jenkins 1998).

This criticism also informs the second strategy, which is to make games for a female audience in particular, based on the assumption that girls have different preferences than boys. In contrast to games involving competition, speed, sports, and violence, which are activities associated with boys' preferences, traditional girls' games have focused on things like "character-centered plots, issues of friendship, and social relationships" (Cassell and Jenkins 1998, 10), romance, role play, or strategy games (Gansmo, Nordli, and Sørensen 2004). This has fostered successful initiatives like *Barbie Fashion* (Cassell and Jenkins 1998), as well as other less successful games for girls. One of the challenges of this strategy has been that (male) game designers have considered girls and women not only a rather mysterious and incomprehensible group

(Gansmo, Nordli, and Sørensen 2004, 189), but also a risky group to target in a business where failure has a high price. "Pink games" (Carr 2006, 172) have also primarily targeted young girls, and thus have not really affected a more mature female audience. Another weakness of this strategy is that conceptualizing male and female preferences implies a static image of gender, ignoring variations and diversity among real men and women. And as Carr has pointed out, a focus on gendered preferences can be used to argue that RPGs are interesting to female players and uninteresting to male players, which is obviously an erroneous inference (2006, 171).

There is another line of games that can be seen—or at least can claim to be seen—in light of this strategy, and that is action games that target an older audience than the "pink games" did, introducing female protagonists as initiated with Lara Croft in *Tomb Raider* (Core/Eidos 1996). Much has been written about Lara Croft and her hypersexualized exterior, questioning whether she was meant to empower female players, as the designer claimed, or was made for the male gaze (Schleiner 2001; Kennedy 2002; Salen and Zimmerman 2004, 524). Lara Croft was followed by a number of other female protagonists with more or less extreme degrees of hypersexualization (Graner Ray 2004). Research has found that female protagonists are presented as sex objects more often than male protagonists; they are more hypersexualized, with exaggerated female bodies; and they are more often presented partially or fully nude than are male characters (Downs and Smith 2005). Male characters have certainly also been stereotyped, primarily through exaggerated muscles and a steroidal kind of masculinity. Whatever intention motivates hypersexualized female protagonists, the fact remains that stereotyped masculinity showing big muscles also can signal power, while big breasts primarily signify sexual availability (Taylor 2003; Haines 2004; Corneliussen and Mortensen 2005). According to Trine Annfelt, sexualized female bodies are used also in our offline culture, "as signs of heterosexuality [that can be] understood as compensatory and dethreatening strategies at a time when the boundaries to masculine behaviours and rooms for action are being put under pressure by women" (2002, 135). Thus, the hypersexualized female characters at best send out ambiguous signals: they are females in untraditional positions, but at the same time the player is invited to play with a (masculine and heteronormative) cultural rhetoric of women as (sex) objects (Graner Ray 2004).

The third strategy for attracting female gamers is to acknowledge that both males and females are important for the computer games market, and consequently to make cross-gender games. "Cross-gender" should not be confused with "gender-neutral," but rather implies an awareness of both genders, including "a bundling of masculine and feminine tastes" (Gansmo, Nordli, and Sørensen 2004, 188) in one computer game. One potential problem with this strategy, however, is the different values ascribed to activities associated with men and women. Boys, men, and masculinity have often been perceived as, or associated with, the (nongendered) norm, and girls and women have been encouraged to act or choose like boys and men do.[2] However, as Cassell and Jenkins have pointed out, it is not equally accepted for boys and men to perform activities associated with girls and women (1998, 35). Thus the challenge for cross-gender games is to introduce activities and values associated with women or femininity without losing male players. Women are no more homogenous as a group than men are, and the following analysis will not focus on activities related to gendered preferences. However, it can be argued that *World of Warcraft* is an interesting case because it does in fact introduce activities with feminine associations, which together with other features, like equal availability of player characters of both genders, clearly points in a direction of a cross-gender game.

Gender Constructions in *World of Warcraft*

Feminists have argued for decades that gender should be seen as a social construction, as negotiable and shifting structures, but simultaneously as discourses specific to cultural and historical contexts (Scott 1988). Gender in a computer game is also constructed, and in most cases it is reminiscent of our nonfictional ways of perceiving gender. Even though the fantasy universe constructed in *World of Warcraft* offers creatures that we do not expect to meet in our offline reality, it does not offer genders outside the most common way of structuring the world, into a dichotomy of males and females. The question we will pursue here is *how* gender is being constructed in the game. The analysis will focus on four areas of the game design. First we will examine how gender is inscribed in the background story, and second, how gender is visually represented through the player characters. Then we will explore the gender distribution among nonplayer characters, which are an often ignored—though important—group, contributing to a general gendering of a game world, before we look at in-game activities that bring with them associations to women or femininity.

His- or Her-story?

The history of Azeroth is a story of endless battles between races and factions, staging the gameplay of *World of Warcraft* during an uneasy truce between the Alliance and the Horde.[3] The history is mainly a "his-story" dominated by male leaders, driven forward by the deeds of males in the shapes of princes, kings, warlords, chieftains, and comrades, and with very few female participants. However, the females who are present take on prominent roles as rulers and war heroines. The following section is not a representative retelling of the story, but a brief summary of female heroines' roles in Azeroth's history, illustrating how they introduce a set of female positions that result in a complex web of traditional and untraditional gender positions.

The night elves' history includes more females than any other of Azeroth's races, with Queen Azshara and the "beautiful young priestess, Tyrande," as well as two female-only groups who help protect the night elves' land. Queen Azshara, who was corrupted by spellcraft, became a victim of the evil Sargeras and helped him to enter the world of Azeroth, which resulted in an implosion of the night elves' sacred well and the splitting of the continent of Kalimdor into a number of scattered islands. In this struggle for power, Tyrande became entangled in a drama between two brothers, Malfurion and Illidan, who both had fallen in love with her. She preferred Malfurion, which caused Illidan to betray the night elves, increasing the damage done during the fight over the sacred well.

There are also prominent females outside the group of night elves, such as Modgud, wife of army leader Thaurissan and queen of Dark Irons, a hostile clan of dwarfs. She led her own army in a battle, but was eventually defeated and killed. Alexstrasza, an ancient dragonqueen, was forced to help the Horde, who threatened to destroy her eggs (future children) if she did not send her children to fight for them—which she did. Aegwynn was "a fiery human girl" who was elected as the Guardian of Tirisfal, as she had "distinguished herself as a mighty warrior against the shadow." Her story could almost be called feminist, as "she often questioned the authority of the male-dominated Council of Tirisfal," and found the "ancient elves and the elderly men" in the council to be "too rigid in their thinking." Aegwynn fought and killed Sargeras, but unfortunately she only killed his shell, which had been his cunning plan, and his spirit entered Aegwynn's body. When Aegwynn was asked to leave her position for a successor, she refused. She wanted to appoint a successor of her own, and she seduced a suitable man, got pregnant, and gave birth to a son. However, Sargeras' spirit had entered the unborn child's body, and evil was reborn with him.

Despite these stories of strong women, most of Azeroth's history is a story of war and conflict played out by men, which leaves most of the population of Azeroth, including most of the female characters, invisible. The concept of her-story has been used occasionally to emphasize the importance of making women visible in history, as they often have remained invisible or unimportant in the "his-story" of "mankind." Although the proportion of females is low in this history, those who are present do in fact take on positions as war heroines, and they are celebrated for their special abilities as warriors, which is still an untraditional position for women in the Western world. If we look more closely at the female characters, most of them seem to fulfill some kind of special female roles: as a replication of Eve meeting the fallen angel Lucifer (Sargeras), thus introducing evil into the world; as a romantic partner constructing the storyline for a harmful betrayal; as a mother acting like a puppet for evil forces to save her children; and through reproduction, including the reproduction of evil. Most of the female characters need to be female in order to enter various relationships with males or the evil forces and drive the story forward. Clearly this history is based on a notion of gender as difference, with special roles to be filled by males and females. Only Modgud does not seem to enter a special female role (except for being the wife of another war leader) and her deeds could just as well have been performed by a male. Aegwynn is also a special case. She obviously needs to be female in order to fulfill her role in the story, but she also replicates traditional masculine positions: she is a brave warrior, an elected leader, and when her power is threatened, she seduces a partner with the sole purpose of producing an heir, and neither love nor marriage is involved. Another untraditional gender role is the father of Aegwynn's heir, who fills the traditionally female role of the one being seduced and used, then left alone to raise the child from birth until adolescence. Thus the history of Azeroth is interesting because it mixes different perceptions of gender, from the traditional "his-story" to breaking away from gender stereotypes by including females in positions with masculine connotations, as well as by opening up alternative feminized roles for males. The history includes examples of all the three feminist positions: we find females contributing with special female abilities, thus acting as complementary to males (romance and childbirth). We also find males and females as equals, with females entering traditional male positions (leaders and seducers), and we find a parité version of ignoring gender, making males and females interchangeable (Modgud).

Visual Gender Representations

A hotly debated topic in the field of gender and computer games is the lack of female heroines and the extreme sexualization of the few heroines available. Despite the fantasy aspect in the story of Azeroth, gender is not subject to fantasy. In the process of creating a player character, there is no option to choose fantasy genders, like neuter, either, Spivak, or other variants found in, for instance, MUDs (Sundén 2003, 28). All playable races do however have the option of being male or female, a choice that makes no technical difference to the playable character's attributes. Not just gender, but also race and bodily features, like face and hairstyle, contribute to the visual representation of player characters. Player characters are simplified simulations—models created through a careful choice of features to be included and excluded (Carr 2006, 166), not unlike the "menu-driven" identities that Jessica Langer discusses in relation to race in chapter 4: in both cases, the available choices are accentuated on behalf of the excluded possibilities. The gendering of characters in *World of Warcraft* is achieved through a limited number of features: primarily a combination of breasts and a feminine waistline for females, and for males most notably through muscles and size, as they are always bigger than females of the same race. Males from one race can, however, be smaller than females from another race, which also makes the in-race relationship between males and females important for the construction of gender. Thus breasts, waistline, muscles, and size are the main features constructing the generic genders, and these generic gender features contribute to demarcating a clear line between males and females.

The limited set of generic gender features, clearly based on ideas of humanness, underlines gender as a *difference* between males and females. However, there is not one gender model for males and another for females, but rather a number of different models, primarily created through the various racial features. Gender models vary from the tall athletic male night elf and the fashion-model look of his night elf sister to the working class male dwarf and the generously proportioned female dwarf, or the more monstrous and steroidal masculinity of male tauren and the almost-plump female tauren with hooves and a big cow-like nose. Thus *World of Warcraft* offers characters of both genders with a high possibility for variation in looks, and does not lock the player into a scheme of playing with young steroidal males and model-like females.

The kind of hypersexualization of female characters that some computer games have been criticized for (Graner Ray 2004; Corneliussen and Mortensen 2005; Downs and Smith 2005) is toned down, or at least made a choice, in *World of Warcraft*. Prominent breasts and a slim waistline clearly feminizes a character, but these features are not as overdimensioned as can be found on characters like Lara Croft in *Tomb Raider*. Clothes with more or less low-cut necks for females are available and clearly put *World of Warcraft* in the category of games featuring heroines with "inappropriate attire" (Downs and Smith 2005), and as Esther MacCallum-Stewart and Justin Parsler discuss in chapter 11, this sexualization can be seen as problematic by players. However, making a character appear hypersexualised because of their clothing is to a large degree a choice in *World of Warcraft*, as it is possible to wear supplemental garments, like a shirt or a guild tabard, to cover up the cleavage of a chest-piece.[4] The sexualization of female characters is more apparent in the game trailer, in online material from Blizzard, and on the game boxes, all of which show a half-naked female night elf, more sexualized and more inappropriately dressed than the in-game night elves, clearly indicating that sex sells. And as a debate over the appearance of the recently introduced blood elves indicates, the game designers use a rather traditional notion of masculinity and femininity to please the player community.

This discussion has so far considered all playable races as subject to a visual gendering. However, there are some interesting differences between Alliance and Horde races, in particular in the version of *World of Warcraft* before *The Burning Crusade*, as all the Alliance races have bodies similar to human bodies, while the Horde races are more monstrous, with features taken from fantasy creatures. Jessica Langer discusses in chapter 4 how the races of the two factions resemble a divide between the Alliance races as "familiar," seen from a white Western perspective, and the Horde races as "the Other," depicting Native Americans, black Caribbean folk, and the "pure" Otherness of the undead. Although the game lore tells a more complex story, it is not unusual for players to see the Alliance as the good side and the Horde as representing evil (Ducheneaut, Yee, Nickell, and Moore 2006; see also chapters 2 and 4).

Draenei and blood elves, the two races introduced in *The Burning Crusade*, distort this pattern. The draenei are a demonic race with cloven hooves, tentacles on males, pointed ears, and a tail, and they introduce a nonhuman look to the Alliance races. The blood elves, on the other hand, are descendants of night elves and share their bodily features, introducing a more human-like look amidst the Horde races. The balance is however restored through a presentation of the draenei, not as the evil version of demons also found as nonplayer characters in the game, but rather as "honorable," according to the game lore. The blood elves have a more motley history and are identified as the reason the draenei are stuck in Azeroth. Thus both the new races are introduced into the already established conflict between the Alliance and the Horde. The blood elves also have a prerelease history confirming this, explained by Blizzard on one of the official WoW Forums in October 2006: "In response to concerns that the Blood Elf male appeared to be too feminine, and after reviewing the model from a visual and conceptual standpoint, the decision was made to increase the body mass to give them a more substantial, masculine feel. It was also important that as members of the Horde...the Blood Elves gave the impression of strength and a more menacing presence." We do not have many insights into the designers' intentions, but Blizzard's note confirms that Horde races are supposed to be a bit more "menacing" than the Alliance races, as well as the close connection between "body mass" and masculinity.

Thus there are some general differences between the races of the two factions. However, the image of gender is not equally clear-cut between Alliance and Horde races, as femininity in some ways seems to be in conflict with monstrous racial features. Female trolls and orcs seem to have *more* in common visually with the human-like female Alliance races than with their corresponding racial brothers. They seem to be beautified and feminized in ways that draw their visual appearance away from race and toward a more generic femininity, both in their body shapes being shrunk and adjusted into stereotypical female proportions and their faces being beautified away from some of the more monstrous racial features. The two new races also fit in this scheme. The draenei in particular take the in-race gender difference even further than any other race. The demonic male draenei has a huge and muscular torso with

Figure 3.1
Female and male draenei.

an extreme shoulder width, tentacles around the neck, cloven hoofs, a big tail, and huge muscular arms. The female draenei has a thin female body with thin arms lacking visible muscles. Her tail is a tiny whip, her cloven hooves are stretched out and made less pronounced, and she has lost the tentacles and demonic mask worn by males. Instead she appears with a classically feminine face, conforming to the young fashion model image. Seen from the front she resembles a female night elf or human more than a male draenei.

It is primarily males then who define the generic races, while females of the most monstrous races are *more* female than race: the female features have preempted some of the racial features, as if they were in conflict. It seems we have encountered a limit of femininity, indicating that femininity has a much stronger resistance than masculinity toward features that, from a Western perspective, are perceived as monstrous and ugly. The exception to this pattern is the female tauren, who has kept more of her monstrous racial features than have females of other nonhuman-like races. Of all the females, she is the one most alienated from the traditional notion of femininity, but she is alienated using familiar cow-like features from the tauren's exterior rather than by features taken from monstrous fantasy creatures.

Even though it can be difficult to determine a character's gender on a heated battlefield, gender is always present in *World of Warcraft* and it always makes a difference in characters' visual appearance. In terms of the various feminist positions, the visual gender representations clearly build on an idea of gender as difference. However, the number of choices of bodily and facial expressions make a multitude of gender visualizations available, some more and others less coherent with gender stereotypes.

NPCs and Gender Distribution

Numbers do matter to questions of gender equality, as with the Parité movement's goal of equal gender distribution within French politics, which can be seen as a demand based on arguments of justice. The distribution of males and females in a field, an occupation, or in certain positions also influences the perception of these as male/masculine or female/feminine, which in turn also will make involvement in that field, occupation, or position signify gendered meaning that is more or less gender authentic (or inauthentic) to males and females (Faulkner and Kleif 2003, 310). The traditional male dominance in computer games is not only true for the game protagonists, but also for nonplayer characters (NPCs), even in games like *Tomb Raider*, where Lara Croft primarily fights men, animals, or robots. NPCs have a number of different roles in *World of Warcraft*. Hostile NPCs will attack player characters who come too close, while friendly or neutral NPCs have various positions and roles, like quest-givers, vendors, or trainers of various skills. NPCs are also an important part of the world's population, and they make an area seem inhabited, adding an impression of a living society. In this part we will explore the general gender distribution among NPCs of the playable races, as this tells us something about the general gendering of the universe of Azeroth. Playable races have designated starting areas mostly populated by NPCs of the same race, and we will primarily focus on the first villages that player characters visit, which are important places for a first impression of the NPCs inhabiting the game world.[5]

The gender distribution of NPCs in all the starting-area villages shows an average of one-third female NPCs. However, when we split the numbers we can see some variations. First, there are slightly more females on the Alliance side (34%) than on the Horde side (30%), a difference that also to some degree is represented among player characters, with an average of 34.4 percent female Alliance player characters and 24 percent female Horde player

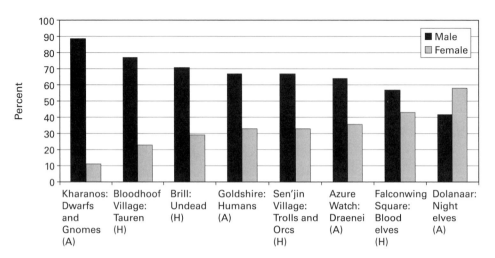

Figure 3.2
Gender distribution in starting-area villages.

characters (Ducheneaut, Yee, Nickell, and Moore 2006, 296). Second, as figure 3.2 shows, the distribution in the different villages and their matching races also shows some variation. The graph lists four Horde and four Alliance villages on a scale from least to most female NPCs, and the greatest variation is between the Alliance villages, which hold the extreme positions on both sides of the scale.

The most lopsided village is that of dwarfs and gnomes, with only 11 percent of the population female (although with 26 percent in their city). On the other side of the scale are the night elves, where females outnumber males with 58 percent female NPCs in the village, and even more in the night elf city, primarily due to a large number of female guards. The draenei village follows the general trend with about one-third females, but their city also has a high proportion of female guards increasing the proportion of females (55 percent). Within the Horde races, the distribution of males and females does not change significantly from one village to another, and the small differences here are compensated in the cities in such a way that the general distribution among Horde races is about one-third females and two-thirds males. The blood elves' village stands out among the Horde races with the highest number of females, and the introduction of this race in *The*

Burning Crusade increased the number of female NPCs within the Horde races from 27 percent to 30 percent.

It seems that the number of females is closely tied to the aesthetic appearance of races, as villages with more than the average number of females coincide with the races that have the most "beautiful" female characters according to Western stereotypes, with slim and well-proportioned bodies. Races with less attractive females, however, like the short and rich-bodied dwarfs and gnomes, have a lower proportion of female NPCs. The span between the female-dominated night elves and the male-dominated dwarfs is also reflected in players' choices of characters, which according to Ducheneaut, Yee, Nickell, and Moore are affected by "real-world stereotypes…with players clearly favoring the 'sexy' female Night Elves…to their perhaps less visually pleasing Dwarven counterparts" (2006, 296).

The Burning Crusade introduces not only new races, but also a new planet, The Outland, where Alliance and Horde troops unite in the battle against the Burning Legion. Shattrath City, the only large city in Outland, is faction-neutral, with more or less all of Azeroth's races, both playable and not playable, represented. Shattrath is clearly a city preparing for war. It is also a city markedly dominated by males, who make up more than 80 percent of the population. Male-only groups of soldiers march and train in Shattrath, and women are not only absent, but the female gender is also used as an insult by one of the trainers: "That was some pretty fancy prancin" ladies!…If we can't teach you to shoot, you'll have a career in the cantina to fall back on." The trainer's insult clearly mirrors how accusations of femininity are used as insults against men in Western society. In Shattrath it becomes clear that the act of warfare is a male thing: it requires "balls" and not "ladies," which might explain why the number of females in Shattrath is lower than the average representation of females in Azeroth.

The number of males and females says something about the overall gendering of the society created in the game, and Blizzard goes a long way in creating a society with room for both males and females. The gender distribution among the playable races of *World of Warcraft* can impress us with the fact that about one-third of the NPCs are female, that one race has a female majority, and two other races are close to 50 percent. This clearly represents a feminization of a computer game universe compared to the earlier trend of low number of female NPCs. But the gender distribution can also make us question the way this "world" of *Warcraft* is represented when it is nearly two-thirds male—and even moreso in Outland, where a large proportion of the female half of a normal society is left in the dark. In this way, *World of Warcraft* does reflect the real world in terms of females' visibility in public arenas. Males and females are not perceived as equals or totally interchangeable, or in terms of Parité, females have not reached a total abstraction as individuals in such a way that the game designers find it natural to construct an in-game world with an equal gender distribution.

There is, however, another side of the NPC gender distribution that is interesting, and that is the different roles NPCs have in the game—roles that are potentially perceived as gendered in our culture. There are a number of female NPCs holding positions that have, both in the real world and in earlier computer games, been held by men, like the female guards protecting a group's territory. And be assured, the female guards hit just as hard as male guards! Warfare and fighting are typical male activities, which puts a fighting female into a "gender-inauthentic" (Faulkner and Kleif 2003, 310) position, arguably making her a ground-breaking figure and provoking gender stereotypes by introducing another possible subject position for females. However, there is no special attention drawn to the fact that the guards are female; they share all the racial features of their sisters, and are simply guards who happen to be female. The gender-inauthentic positions these female NPCs have in the game are in a way naturalized or unquestioned, as if our real-world perceptions about gender do not apply—as if gender is ignored, resembling the ideas of the paritaristes: "that women could be abstracted from the cultural understandings of the difference of their sex" (Scott 2005, 126). The male and female guards in the gameworld reflect a notion of anatomically dualistic individuals who are ignorant of culture. However, they also act as potential signifiers for new meaning, challenging stereotypical ideas of certain positions as inauthentic for females.

Activities with Feminine Associations

Most activities in computer games have traditionally been actions, deeds, adventures, or storylines associated with men, male spheres, or masculinity (Jenkins and Cassell 1998). Some of these are also important in *World of Warcraft*, like fighting, warfare, and competition. You will not advance in the game without fighting. However, if we employ gender stereotypes from real life, there are also activities that are associated with women or femininity in *World of Warcraft*, like cooking, picking flowers, sewing clothes, and healing—all of which are skills a player character can acquire. The gender connotations of these activities also seem to be recognized by the game designers, as indicated by one of the females' jokes: "Why does everyone always assume that I know tailoring and cooking?"[6] Picking flowers and sewing clothes are, however, given labels that decrease their feminine associations: herbalism and tailoring, the last even pointing to a traditionally male-dominated craft. Healers can be associated with female nurses in war: present in the combat zone to bandage the warriors and get them back on their feet as quickly as possible. Healing is both a skill that every character can train in, and a class ability, most developed for priests, who also are cloth-wearers—another feature associated with femininity, according to Ducheneaut, Yee, Nickell, and Moore's study of players' choices in combining class and gender: "The gender distribution by class is interesting in that it seems to reflect stereotypical assumptions of those classes. For example, the classes with the highest female ratio are all healing or cloth-wearing classes.... Thus, real-world stereotypes come to shape the demographics of fantasy worlds" (2006, 296).

These are only a few of the in-game activities and skills a player character can acquire, and there are certainly also skills and activities with strongly masculine associations, like blacksmithing, mining, or engineering. Even though activities with masculine or less clearly gendered associations dominate, it is interesting to note the existence of a handful of activities with feminine associations, which means that *World of Warcraft* not only presents the traditional invitation to women to act like men, but also invites men to engage in activities associated with women or femininity. An open question though, is whether this means a feminization of male player characters through involving them in activities associated with femininity, or a defeminization of the activities themselves. On the other side, it is also interesting that the various activities that have feminine or masculine associations in our culture are seemingly unaffected by gender, just like the distribution of male and female NPCs in various positions. Or in other words, these activities and positions are only gendered through our cultural perception of them as gendered, and although my claim is that we always perceive the world, including the world created in a game space, through our cultural discourses, Blizzard seems to ignore some cultural discourses about gender.

Conclusion

The goal of this chapter has been to explore how gender is constructed in the designed game universe of *World of Warcraft*, and the analysis has pointed to diversity, multitude, and plurality as some of the most important keywords for describing gender constructions in this game. The feminist positions introduced earlier all say something about gender as a relationship between male and female: as pure difference, as equal to a masculine norm, or as a meaningless but always present dichotomy, and we find a mixture of all these positions in *World of Warcraft*. The game lore includes males and females in both traditional and untraditional gendered roles. Putting women into untraditional roles represents a challenge to gender stereotypes. However, the posttraditional woman is *expected* to make her career choices in opposition to traditional gender roles (Annfelt 1999, 77). Thus perhaps even more challenging to gender stereotypes is the seduced and used male in Aegwynn's history, replicating a position typically held by women in popular culture. The design of player characters also allows for a large degree of variations, from stereotypical images of "fashion model femininity" or "steroidal masculinity" to images that do not conform to Western stereotypes of gender. But we have also encountered some of the limits of gender, as monstrous racial features seem to be in conflict with femininity. For the most monstrous races, it is primarily males who define racial features, while some females are more female than they are members of their race. The relatively large number of female NPCs also indicates a willingness by Blizzard to break with traditional ways of gendering computer game universes. Reaching a critical mass is often assumed to make a male-dominated field less gender-inauthentic to women. Although it is not clear exactly how large a critical mass needs to be, Blizzard clearly contributes to reaching a critical mass of female characters in the game environment. However, while the limit of femininity seems to be tied to aesthetic considerations, the limit of masculinity is tied to power through representation and the continuous male dominance, indicating that females can not in general outnumber men, reminding us of Hanne Haavind's claim that "a woman today can do everything as long as she does it in relative subordination to a man" (referenced by Jónasdóttir and von der Fehr 1998, 13). And last, the introduction of activities with feminine associations, despite the low number and partial defeminization through use of less feminine labels, presents an interesting invitation to males to "do as women." It has been claimed that feminization of a previously male-dominated or masculine field involves the risk of a decrease in power or status (Salminen-Karlsson 1999), or for a computer game, the risk of losing male players. There is, however, no evidence supporting a loss of male players in this case.

Gender is present in *World of Warcraft* in many ways, but it is not necessarily insistent or obvious, and some times it is not even meaningful—or at least, it is not given meaning through the game design itself. In other words, gender is partly constructed in ways that can be understood in light of the Parité movement's arguments about gender as a meaningless anatomical dualism. The Parité movement did not suggest a quota of women, and they did not claim that women have either special needs or abilities. They demanded that political representation should reflect the always-present dichotomy of citizens as men and women, insisting on a gendering not only of women, but also of men, and simultaneously insisting on the meaninglessness of gender. In a way Blizzard does exactly that, as they seem to ignore many of our cultural images of gender, traditional gender stereotypes, and gendered storylines—a parité-like gendering of the universe where gender is present, but practically meaningless. However, the continuous construction of gender as a strict male-female dualism is clearly wasting the fantasy world's potential for playing with alternative gender labels, like the MUDish neuter, either, Spivak, egoistical, or 2nd.[7]

People are different, and while some women (and men) feel at home in gender stereotypes, others do not (Faulkner et al. 2004). Cross-gender computer games, targeting everybody, need to acknowledge diversity and plurality among their users, and thus recognize differences both between men and between women. The computer game industry has been criticized for not listening to worries concerning negative presentations of gender and race (Dovey and Kennedy 2006, 93; Leonard 2006). It is not difficult to find games supporting this claim. However, the ambivalence that grows out of variations in the gender constructions in the design of *World of Warcraft* seems to indicate that Blizzard is aware of women as an important group of gamers. The game is clearly moving away from the tradition of hypersexualizing female characters in a male universe, as well as away from one-dimensional presentations of gender within strict gender stereotypes.

Stereotypes still exist in *World of Warcraft*, but they are, as we have seen, also being challenged. Skjeie and Teigen claim that we tend to accept continuing gender inequality as long as we believe we are moving in the right direction (2003). The French Parité law was passed in 2000. However, it ended up a modification of the original proposal, not granting equal representation in elected positions, but rather on electoral lists, showing that it was difficult to reach a total abstraction of women as universal individuals. But the law did represent one step forward, increasing the number of women in elected positions (Scott 2005, 126–127). *World of Warcraft* is not—from a feminist perspective—perfect, but it does point toward a gender-inclusive design, proving game universes to be an interesting playground for challenging cultural perceptions of gender.

Acknowledgments

Thanks to Charlotte Hagström and Jøran Gandrudbakken for help with counting male and female NPCs in the game. Also thanks to all the contributors to this book for interesting discussions and comments during the writing process, and a particular thank you to Jessica Langer, Jill Walker Rettberg, and Janne C. H. Bromseth for reading and making comments which greatly helped to improve the chapter.

Notes

1. Even girls can have difficulties seeing other girls as gamers. In a study of female hackers in Norway, Nordli found that even female hardcore gamers did not really trust new girls to be "real" gamers, and saw them as a threat to their own hard-earned image as skilled female gamers (Nordli 2003). I have also found that women are not really expected to have fun with computers. During an interview with three female computer students, they simply laughed at my question about what they did to have fun with the computer, referring to boys as the ones who had fun with computers—before they told me about their own pleasurable experiences with computer games (Corneliussen 2005).

2. This claim does not imply that girls are encouraged to "become" male, or copy masculine behavior. It is rather a criticism of women's choices. Thus the lack of women in, for instance, computing, has been presented as a result of "women's (poor) choices," and can only change if women make the "right" choices (like men do) (Corneliussen 2003).

3. The official history of *World of Warcraft* can be read at http://www.wow-europe .com/en/info/story/. All quotes in this section are from this history.

4. It is also possible that the experience of hypersexualized characters vary between different choices of server and which faction to play with. My own experiences, after playing with both the Horde and the Alliance, on Normal, RP, and PvP servers, have however revealed very few examples of hypersexualized characters compared to the experiences reported by MacCallum-Stewart and Parsler in chapter 11.

5. All NPCs have been counted and registered as male or female in the villages. Large parts of all the big cities have also been counted, and unless a discrepancy is noted in the text, the results from the cities match the results from the villages.

6. The command "/silly" will make the player character tell a preprogrammed joke.

7. From a queer feminist standpoint this could be seen as an example of the heteronormativity of Western society, requiring gender to always be constructed within a heterosexual matrix (Bromseth 2006).

References

Annfelt, Trine. 1999. *Kjønn i utdanning. Hegemoniske posisjoner og forhandlinger om yrkesidentitet i medisin- og faglærerutdanning.* Trondheim: NTNU, Senter for kvinneforskning.

Annfelt, Trine. 2002. "More Gender Equality—Bigger Breasts? Battles over Gender and the Body." *Nora, Nordic Journal of Women's Studies* 10, no. 3: 127–136.

Bromseth, Janne C. H. 2006. *Genre Trouble and the Body That Mattered: Negotiations of Gender, Sexuality and Identity in a Scandinavian Mailing List Community for Lesbian and Bisexual Women.* Trondheim: Norwegian University of Science and Technology, Faculty of Arts, Department of Interdisciplinary Studies of Culture.

Carr, Diane. 2006. "Games and Gender." In Diane Carr, David Buckingham, Andrew Burn and Gareth Schott, eds., *Computer Games: Text, Narrative and Play.* Cambridge: Polity Press.

Cassell, Justine, and Henry Jenkins. 1998. "Chess for Girls? Feminism and Computer Games." In eds. Justine Cassell and Henry Jenkins, *From Barbie to Mortal Kombat: Gender and Computer Games*, 2–45. Cambridge, MA: MIT Press.

Castronova, Edward. 2005. *Synthetic Worlds: The Business and Culture of Online Games.* Chicago: The University of Chicago Press.

Core/Eidos. 1996. *Tomb Raider.*

Corneliussen, Hilde. 2003. "Konstruksjoner av kjønn ved høyere IKT-utdanning i Norge." *Kvinneforskning* 27, no. 3: 31–50.

Corneliussen, Hilde. 2005. "'I Fell in Love with the Machine'—Women's Pleasure in Computing." *Journal of Information, Communication and Ethics in Society* 3, no. 4: Special Issue: Women in Computing (WiC).

Corneliussen, Hilde, and Torill Mortensen. 2005. "The Non-Sense of Gender in Neverwinter Nights." Presented at Women in Games 2005, University of Abertay, Dundee, Scotland.

Dovey, Jon, and Helen W. Kennedy. 2006. *Game Cultures: Computer Games as New Media.* Maidenhead: Open University Press.

Downs, Edward, and Stacy Smith. 2005. "Keeping Abreast of Hypersexuality: A Video Game Character Analysis." Presented at The 55th Annual Conference of the International Association of Communication, New York, NY.

Ducheneaut, Nicolas, Nick Yee, Eric Nickell, and Robert J. Moore. 2006. "Building an MMO with Mass Appeal: A Look at Gameplay in World of Warcraft." *Games and Culture* 1, no. 4: 281–317.

Entertainment Software Association. "Home Page." Available at ⟨http://www.theesa .com⟩.

Faulkner, W., E. Rommes, K. Sørensen, H. Gansmo, L. Pitt, J. Stewart, R. Williams, P. Preston, C. McKeogh, and V. L. Berg. 2004. "Strategies of Inclusion: Gender and the Information Society." Final Report, Research Centre for Social Sciences, Edinburgh, Scotland.

Faulkner, Wendy, and Tine Kleif. 2003. "'I'm No Athlete [but] I Can Make This Thing Dance!' Men's Pleasures in Technology." *Science, Technology, and Human Values* 28, no. 2, 296–325.

Gansmo, Helen Jøsok, Hege Nordli, and Knut H. Sørensen. 2004. "The Gender Game: A Study of Norwegian Computer Game Designers." In Helen Jøsok Gansmo, *Towards a Happy Ending for Girls and Computing?*, Ph.D. Dissertation, Trondheim.

Graner Ray, Sheri. 2004. *Gender Inclusive Game Design: Expanding the Market.* Hingham, MA: Charles River Media.

Haines, Lizzie. 2004. *Why Are There So Few Women in Games?* Media Training North West.

Jenkins, Henry. 1998. "Complete Freedom of Movement: Video Games as Gendered Play Spaces." In Henry Jenkins and Justine Cassell, eds., *From Barbie to Mortal Kombat: Gender and Computer Games.* Cambridge, MA: MIT Press.

Jenkins, Henry, and Justine Cassell, eds. 1998. *From Barbie to Mortal Kombat: Gender and Computer Games.* Cambridge, MA: MIT Press.

Jónasdóttir, Anna G., and Drude von der Fehr. 1998. "Introduction: Ambiguous Times—Contested Spaces in the Politics, Organization and Identities of Gender." In Drude von der Fehr, Anna G. Jónasdóttir, and Bente Rosenbeck, (eds.), *Is There a Nordic Feminism? Nordic Feminist Thought on Culture and Society*. London: UCL Press.

Kennedy, Helen W. 2002. "Lara Croft: Feminist Icon or Cyberbimbo? On the Limits of Textual Analysis." *Game Studies* 2, no. 2. Available at ⟨http://www.gamestudies.org/0202/kennedy/⟩.

Leonard, David J. 2006. "Not a Hater, Just Keepin' It Real: The Importance of Race- and Gender-Based Game Studies." *Games and Culture* 1, no. 1: 83–88.

Moi, Toril. 1999. *What Is a Woman? And Other Essays*. Oxford: Oxford University Press.

Nordli, Hege. 2003. *The Net Is Not Enough. Searching for the Female Hacker*, PhD dissertation, NTNU, Trondheim.

Pratchett, Rhianna. 2005. "Gamers in the UK: Digital Play, Digital Lifestyles." BBC. Available at ⟨http://open.bbc.co.uk/newmediaresearch/files/BBC_UK_Games_Research_2005.pdf⟩.

Salen, Katie, and Eric Zimmerman. 2004. *Rules of Play: Game Design Fundamentals*. Cambridge, MA: MIT Press.

Salminen-Karlsson, Minna. 1999. *Bringing Women into Computing Engineering: Curriculum Reform Processes at Two Institutes of Technology*, Linköping Studies in Education and Psychology No 60. Linköping University Department of Education and Psychology: Akademisk Avhandling.

Schleiner, Anne-Marie. 2001. "Does Lara Croft Wear Fake Polygons?" *Leonardo* 34, no. 3: 221–226.

Scott, Joan Wallach. 1988. *Gender and the Politics of History*. New York: Columbia University Press.

Scott, Joan Wallach. 1996. *Only Paradoxes to Offer: French Feminists and the Rights of Man*. Cambridge, MA: Harvard University Press.

Scott, Joan Wallach. 2005. *Parité! Sexual Equality and the Crisis of French Universalism*. Chicago: University of Chicago Press.

Skjeie, Hege, and Mari Teigen. 2003. *Menn imellom: Mannsdominans og Likestillingspolitikk*. Oslo: Gyldendal Akademisk.

Sundén, Jenny. 2003. *Material Virtualities: Approaching Online Textual Embodiment*. New York: Peter Lang.

Taylor, T. L. 2003. "Multiple Pleasures: Women and Online Gaming." *Convergence* 9, no. 1: 21–46.

WomenGamers.Com. 2000. "Neverwinter Nights: Days of Open Hand." Available at ⟨http://www.womengamers.com/revprev/adv/pre-neverwinter.php⟩.

Yee, Nick. 2003. "Gender and Age Distribution." *The Daedalus Project: The Psychology of MMORPGs.* Available at ⟨http://www.nickyee.com/daedalus/archives/000194.php⟩.

The Familiar and the Foreign: Playing (Post)Colonialism in *World of Warcraft*

4

Jessica Langer

World of Warcraft, unlike Blizzard's earlier *Warcraft* offerings, requires players to choose between two factions and to dedicate large amounts of playtime and resources to the faction of their choice in order to have access to the highest-level content. The Alliance is composed of Tolkien-inspired races like elves and dwarves; the Horde is depicted as a ragtag batch of peoples whose belief systems and aesthetic senses borrow heavily from real-world cultures that have themselves been marginalized and colonized. As I will discuss, the most popular game servers are PvP servers, which allow all-out war with players of each faction encouraged to kill anyone who belongs to a hated race.[1]

Much has been made in discourse both in and out of the game of the assignation of the labels "good" and "evil" to each side in turn. Within the context of the game, of course, each side considers itself in the right and the other side the enemy; debates rage on the official Blizzard-sponsored forums, as well as on other major discussion websites like Slashdot.org, as to which side is *evil.*[2] However, I would argue that analyzing the Alliance and the Horde primarily within a dichotomy of good and evil is misdirected. Rather, the central space of tension between the two sides is that between familiarity and otherness. Despite the Alliance and the Horde being functionally equitable in terms of game mechanics, *World of Warcraft* carries out a constant project of radically "othering" the Horde, not by virtue of distinctions between good and evil but rather by distinctions between civilized and savage, self and other, and center and periphery. The assumptions of good and evil that derive from these characterizations are not direct, but are rather symptoms of a common Western cultural association of foreignness and insidiousness, an association that itself derives from Western colonial ideologies.

Therefore, in this chapter I argue first that the Alliance and the Horde are divided along racial lines not into good and evil but into familiar and other or foreign,[3] and that this division has consequences not only within the game but in the real world as well.[4] To this end, it is helpful to use aspects of postcolonial theory to conceptualize these divisions. Second, I suggest that the bodies and immediate home environments of both player characters and NPCs are often used as signifiers of familiarity or otherness, a theme which corresponds significantly with real-world debates as to whether race is biologically or socially determined. I argue that while race in the game is biologically determined, race in the real world is socially determined, which creates a significant rift in perspective. Finally, I discuss the idea that the game itself is a complex text in terms of race: at times it codes certain racial stereotypes in a straightforward manner, but at other times it follows a more sophisticated model in which it interacts with actual preconceptions and stereotypes, each shaping the other, so that it is racism itself—or rather, a race-based dialectical model—that is being critiqued.[5] Both of these impulses exist within the game, and both will be analyzed here.

Theory and Definitions

This essay will make use of some recent criticism linking cyberspace and multiuser in-game worlds not to a state of "race-blindness," as had previously been both hoped and claimed,[6] but rather to a shifted but still-present state of racism and marginalization. Lisa Nakamura's 2002 book *Cybertypes: Race, Ethnicity and Identity on the Internet* is particularly useful in this context. In her study of how race and other marginalized identities are constructed and played out online, Nakamura argues that the Internet does not erase racism and oppression based on identity, but rather constructs identity in a different but no less inequitable way. Maria Fernandez has also touched on this: she writes that "the lack of physicality and the anonymity made possible in electronic communication are believed to elide all differences. To admit that inequalities exist in cyberspace is for some tantamount to *authorizing* inequality" (1999, 63). As Nakamura, Fernandez, and others have shown, and as I aim to show, recognition of virtual modes of inequality is vitally important, both in conceptualizing the unique ways in which inequality and marginalization are played out in cyberspace in general and in MMORPGs in particular, and in attempting to find ways to interrupt and change those new and destructive patterns.

It is necessary here to clarify my use of the terms "familiar" and "other." By using these terms, I do not mean to imply an entirely or even primarily Western audience for *World of Warcraft*, nor do I mean to create a center-periphery model of players that mirrors the one in the game. Such a characterization would be both insulting and incorrect, as the number of *World of Warcraft* players in China, for example, reached over 3.5 million in January 2007, comprising half of all players.[7] Rather, I would suggest that the globalization of media access has combined with America's role as the world's most pervasive cultural producer to situate the Western cultural mythos as familiar to audiences worldwide. There is also the simple fact that Blizzard is an American company, which likely influences its tendency to construct its games' ethnocultural schema along the lines of Western—particularly American—social ideology.

I contend that in terms of correspondence with the real world, race in *World of Warcraft* functions thus: trolls correspond directly with black Caribbean folk, particularly but not exclusively Jamaican; tauren represent native North American people (specifically Native American and Canadian First Nations tribes); humans correspond with white British and white American people; and dwarves correlate to the Scottish. The other races, both Alliance and Horde, do not correspond so directly to real-world peoples, but they still represent the general familiarity or foreignness of their factions. For instance, certain cues such as hairstyles and body shape suggest that orcs represent colonial depictions of black people in general, and the undead seem to represent a sort of "pure" Otherness centered in Kristevan abjection (which will be discussed at length later). Blood elves, the newest Horde race, seem on the surface to upset the familiar/foreign schema of the factions, but I would argue that they are portrayed largely as analogues to drug addicts, particularly narcotics addicts, a class of people who are marginalized *within* white Western society rather than locked outside of it. Gnomes, draenei and night elves have similar sliding significations, with the night elves in particular seeming at times to represent a stereotyped East Asianness, with their Japanese *torii* gates and their "Darnassus Kimchi." East Asian people are often considered, condescendingly, by American society to be "model minorities" who remain somewhat outside of society but contribute to it positively rather than negatively.[8] This characterization echoes the role of the night elves within the Alliance faction. Nevertheless, all of the Alliance races are depicted as either Western or Western-approved, whereas the Horde races are depicted very much as Other.

My analysis in this essay will focus mainly on the Horde races, with some reference to the Alliance. This is for several reasons. One is that many discussions of otherness center on the normative group and discuss the Othered group only in relation to it, contributing therefore to the very alienation that they hope to undermine, a dynamic I wish to avoid. Another reason is that the Horde is more diverse than the Alliance: where the Alliance has five races that all, in their own ways, approximate whiteness, the Horde has five races that are all extremely different. These vast differences between the races, as well as the gathering together of these disparate races under the same flag, make the Horde a more fruitful site for discussion of otherness than the Alliance. This very structure, the relatively homogenous nature of the Alliance contrasted with the radical heterogeneity of the Horde, suggests that the game sets *itself* up as a center-periphery model, which I wish to interrogate and critique. Finally, the specific correspondences between real-life races and in-game races are far stronger on the Horde side than on the Alliance side; this makes the Horde a richer site for analysis.

Familiarity and Otherness

In her essay on gender and genre in video games Sharon R. Sherman writes that, in quest games such as the *Mario* series, "the appropriation of mythic and *Marchen* [folk-tale] content and form ensures the success of this arena of popular culture and perpetuates gender stereotyping" (1997, 245). I would extend this argument: these video games—of which *World of Warcraft* is one—perpetuate not only gender stereotypes but ethnocultural stereotypes as well. Though Sherman focuses on the Campbellian hero's journey narrative as the central structure around which this appropriation is built, I would suggest that the iconography itself is equally important, especially since advances in video game rendering and graphics abilities now lend unprecedented levels of detail and pseudoverisimilitude to the gaming environment. This is perhaps *more* important in a relatively open-play MMORPG such as *World of Warcraft*. The cultural appropriation that Sherman discusses functions as a cognitive link to societal tropes that have been repeated and inculcated into players from when they grew up on fairytales: the use of familiar iconography is as much a marketing decision as an aesthetic and formal one, since players are more likely to find compelling a world that mixes familiarity with novelty than they are to welcome a world that is entirely alien to their experience.

Included in that familiarity are constructions of power and hierarchy similar to those found in the real world: colonial subjects and other marginalized peoples—in this case the Horde—are cast largely as dirty, disorganized, primitive (in the cases of trolls, orcs and tauren), or greedy (in the cases of undead and blood elves), and with power that is activated either in physical strength or in abuse of magic. For example, trolls are described in the introductory voice-over as "cruel" and "barbarous," possessed of a "dark mysticism" and a "seething hatred for all other races," and on the official Web site as "vicious," "barbarous and superstitious," and "wily."[9] Orcs, while presented more charitably than are trolls, are "savage,"[10] and tauren walk the line between being "quiet and peaceful" and "implacable enemies who will use every ounce of their strength to smash their enemies under hoof."[11] All of these things are presented not on their own terms but in relation to a more familiar, more pseudo-Western culture—the Alliance. The Alliance is presented as the "self" to the "savage races'" Other, with power activated in reason and intellectual accomplishment. "Many players insist that the Alliance are the 'good guys,'" writes Leigh Schwartz, "and it's easy to see why: One look at the Alliance's bald eagle gryphon mounts is enough to show that the Alliance are 'us' in this war" (2006, 319).

The depictions of subaltern cultures to be found in *World of Warcraft* are not nuanced representations; rather, they are processed, generalized cultural memes, thrown in to give each race its own flavor. The purpose is to reinforce a particular feeling or atmospheric sense about the race in question. *World of Warcraft* does this by using aspects of those cultures, particularly spoken accents and visual cues, which are easily and quickly identified with them. This, like all stereotypes, has the effect of creating a narrative or aesthetic shortcut to the desired player reaction.[12] There are also echoes of Homi Bhabha's assertion that stereotyping is a method of making otherness "safe" and comfortable for the colonizer (1994). Of course, stereotypes are inescapable and sometimes inevitable, as some method of distinguishing people from each other is necessary to function in the world; as Terry Eagleton has written, "without stereotyping of some kind, social life would grind to a halt" (2006). The problem here is that Blizzard's use of real-world cultural inflection is often so simplified that it invites a similarly simplified view of the entire cor-responding culture.

Sherman's invocation of folktales and classic fantasy is especially significant to an analysis of *World of Warcraft*. To an extent unique among current MMORPGs, *World of Warcraft* takes its cues equally from real-world cultures and from a Tolkienic construction of orcs, trolls, dwarves, elves, and humans. *World of Warcraft* depictions of these races are therefore doubly familiar: they have *both* the Tolkienic underpinnings of Western fantasy discourse *and* ste-reotyped features of real-world cultures. The result is that they become hybrid stereotypes, with attributes from both sources. Both associations work to-gether to determine the identity of a character, and therefore both of these sites of otherness are bound up together in the avatar you see on the screen.

The structure of the game contributes significantly to the split between the Alliance and the Horde. The title is the biggest clue to what lies within: anyone who buys *World of Warcraft* expecting it to be about world peace is bound to be disappointed. The setting is one of constant war between the two factions, punctuated only by periodic, shaky partial alliances when both factions must work together toward a common goal, such as the opening of the gates of Ahn'Qiraj that began in the spring of 2006, or the ongoing battle against *The Burning Crusade* that began in earnest in January 2007. Certainly some of the animosity between factions is a direct function of gameplay. However, es-pecially on Role-Playing servers—those on which players are encouraged to stay in character in all public interaction—the conflict between the Horde and the Alliance becomes ideological as well. Schwartz, in her study of "Fan-tasy, Realism and the Other in Recent Video Games," writes that she "experi-enced the game on a role-playing server and observed that some players would role-play hatred and bigotry in order to make the game more real to them" (2006, 320). In my own playtime on an RP-PvP server, I have had the same experience and witnessed a similar dynamic many times: players eagerly ex-pand their conflicts with players of the opposing faction from play-fights dic-tated by game mechanics to emotionally charged in-character battles, using the familiarity/otherness code posited by the game and its lore, often extend-ing beyond the strict boundaries of gameplay and onto Blizzard's official forums or unofficial fan-built websites and chat areas. This practice, while a natural and even encouraged outgrowth of the richness of the virtual game-world, can have serious repercussions: the "hatred and bigotry" that both I and Schwartz have seen and experienced are directed not only toward players of the opposing faction, but players of an opposing faction *that closely represents a real-world marginalized culture.* Thus, such speech is far more loaded than it otherwise would have been.

Another key to the familiar/foreign dichotomy in *World of Warcraft* can be found in Edward Said's famous critique of what he calls "Orientalism," a critique central to postcolonial studies. For Said, Orientalism is an explicitly *political* and *systematic* discourse by which the Other, specifically the Easterner or the Oriental, is constructed in Western thought. This becomes a feedback loop: these artificial constructions, which may contain just enough accuracy to be seemingly plausible, inform Western scholarship about the East, and that scholarship then informs the next generation of scholarship, and so it goes. Myth and truth become indistinguishable. Said draws on Michel Foucault's causal link between power and knowledge to suggest that the reification of Orientalist scholarship in the West generated both the motive and the power necessary to spur Western colonialist projects.

Said's work has been critiqued, at times quite persuasively: there are those who find fault with his invocation of Foucauldian power/knowledge dynamics; those who believe the theory to be either too narrow, too general, or both; and those who think that Said's grasp of orientalist scholarship is simply wrong.[13] Said himself "reconsidered" his theories six years after *Orientalism* was published.[14] Regardless, many of Said's basic theories remain quite relevant, and can usefully be carried over to the study of *World of Warcraft.* The most helpful aspect of Orientalism in terms of *World of Warcraft* is the concept that Western scholarship—and, in this age of digital globalization, Western-based media—simultaneously idealizes and disparages Othered peoples.

One of the best-known examples of this paradox is the idea of the colonized as "noble savage," possibly the most famous backhanded compliment in existence, a concept applied by Western imperial philosophers to the larger discourse of Orientalism. The noble savage is simultaneously disparaged and idealized. He is uncivilized, but not because of his own moral failing. Rather, he is merely insufficiently enlightened, a result either of being too inherently different for enlightenment or of never having been taught the proper (read, in an imperial context, Western) way to live. He is also simple and pure of mind and heart in a way that is inaccessible to Westerners because of the sophistication of Western philosophy. Several of the Horde races fit well into this paradigm. According to Blizzard's official game lore, orcs started out as a relatively peaceful, loosely federated group of tribes, and their ferocity and warlikeness toward humans during the First War is attributed not to them but to a greater demonic power controlling them.[15] Therefore, their past violent behavior is excused by a lack of agency on their part. Tauren also fit into the noble savage mold: they are portrayed as gentle giants whose ire can only be raised by outside forces and who, unlike the more philosophically complex Alliance races, have no aggression of their own; however, they are paradoxically also displayed as war-beasts in game art. They are noble, or at least are not evil, by Western real-world moral standards, but they are also depicted as savages by those same standards.

Those Horde races that are not presented as noble savages are presented as the other side of the coin: the ignoble savage, if you will. Trolls' intelligence is often called "cunning," a word that implies bad intentions. Their spirituality, which is a simplified and Westernized version of the Afro-Caribbean religious tradition of Voudoun (often spelled "voodoo"), is presented as sinister, a theme I will expand upon later. The undead and blood elves, for their parts, are presented as the twisted foils of the Alliance's humans and night elves. The undead have decomposing human bodies and rasping human-accented voices, and are exclusively self-interested. Blood elves are the night elves' dysfunctional cousins: magic addicts in deep denial, whose self-interest and snobbishness is carried out with an addict's zeal.

For trolls, the orcs, and the undead, the player-controllable faction is in fact a small offshoot of the entire race. The Darkspear trolls, the Frostwolf clan of orcs, and the Forsaken are all groups who have been victimized both by the Alliance and by others of their own race, often because these groups have attempted to *stop* violence perpetrated by their compatriots, and have been marginalized thus. Tauren are allied to the orcs, and therefore the Horde, because the orcs offered protection against a group of violent centaurs who were attempting to perpetrate a genocide against the tauren in order to obtain control over their land. The blood elves have been driven nearly to extinction by the Scourge, which also destroyed the source of their power. Therefore, the common thread linking the playable Horde factions is not a mutual moral compass but rather a shared experience of colonization and oppression and a shared project of resistance.

Another possibility, one more charitable to Blizzard and suggestive of the game as a complex text, is that Blizzard deliberately obfuscates the good/

evil question in favor of a familiar/foreign construction because the game designers do not wish to totalize any of the races or tribes within the races. This suggests two desires: one, recognition of a social responsibility not to assign a single sense of morality to an entire populace, especially one that closely resembles a real-life group; and two, a desire to make the game as mimetically realistic on its own terms as possible, which would include moral and ethical variation within a populace as in the real world. This dynamic does seem to be at work in the game, and does lend it complexity, which will be discussed in more detail later on.

Regardless of motive, however, and regardless of ultimate outcome, it seems to me that a dichotomy of familiarity and foreignness is the most productive way to characterize the split between Alliance and Horde, for better or worse—or both.

Horde Bodies and Their Environments

In order best to analyze the racial dynamics of *World of Warcraft*, it seems necessary to detail the parameters on which the discussion is based. This section contains close, though by no means complete, analyses of the bodies and general environments of each Horde race.

Tauren

Tauren are quite literally cow-people, and are named as such. They are bipedal and their body shapes approximate those of humans, but are cow-like in their horns, snouts, hooves, and pelts. The cow is an interesting animal to use in this context, as cows are integral to Western society as both a source of meat and milk (symbol of plenty) and as an avatar of rage (angry bulls).

The resemblance between actual tauren character bodies and stereotypical depictions of Native American and First Nations (hereafter referred to for brevity's sake as Native) bodies is perhaps the least direct of the three. However, there are many tauren hairstyles and accessory styles available that echo those worn in many old commercial photographs, made for a white audience, of Native people. The near-ubiquity of Native American/First Nations styling suggests that the images of the tauren, like those old photographs, "open [them] up to real or imaginary appropriation as private property by non-Indians" (Marez 2004, 340). Their literal fusion of human and animal may

Figure 4.1
Tepees and totem poles in Bloodhoof Village, Mulgore.

also be a reference to the closeness with nature that Natives are presumed by white colonizers to have, or it may be read as a physical conflation of Plains tribes and the buffalo they hunted for their livelihood.

Most of the references to Native culture are situated in the tauren home environments of Camp Narache, Bloodhoof Village, and Thunder Bluff. All are peaceful places, with rolling hills and creatures such as wolves and big cats. Tauren dwelling structures are, in essence, giant tepees (see figure 4.1), modelled very closely on those sturdy but portable dwellings made by the no-madic, herd-following Native people of the American and Canadian plains. The painting on these structures also resembles closely the geometric and color schemes of the most well-known traditional Native art. There are also large totem poles scattered throughout tauren lands.

Tauren NPC names—which are part of the environment as they float above the heads of the characters by default, though this option can be switched off—are modeled heavily on stereotypically Native names. Many are called

"Braves," after the archaic American term for Native soldiers, and they have names like Leaping Deer and Windfeather. The music in Thunder Bluff is a concoction of breathy pipes, drums, and other stereotypically Native elements. All of these factors combine to make an environment that is stereotypically, but not authentically, Native: to borrow a phrase from Bhabha's theory of mimicry as method of colonial control, it is "*almost the same, but not quite*" [italics in original] (1994, 86).

Trolls

The implied troll resemblance to black Caribbean, particularly black Jamaican, culture is at its clearest in terms of accent and appearance. Jamaican voice actors perform the troll accent; NPCs say "Whatagwon?" and call the player characters "child," idiosyncratic Jamaican idioms.

At the same time, trolls are defined by their deviation from Western beauty norms, particularly troll women. Trolls, while humanoid, have nonhuman features such as tusks, a pronouncedly slouched stature, large two-toed feet, and blue or green skin. Although night elf and draenei females also have similarly nonhuman features like pointed ears, purple or blue skin, and glowing eyes, these features are geared toward a Western conception of beauty, while on trolls they are geared toward ugliness. Take the jokes told by the troll female: one is a sardonic "I feel pretty, oh so pretty," followed by the sound of spitting, and another is, "Strong halitosis be but one of my feminine traits." The latter joke has a counterpart in the troll male, who claims that "I like my women dumpy and droopy with halitosis," which not only presents the troll female body as disgusting but adds an extra layer of revulsion for the male's preferences. Troll females are presented as simultaneously hypersexualized (their dance is explicitly sexual and resembles Jamaican dancehall) and repulsive—this depiction echoes classic colonial representations of black Caribbean women, and even some contemporary ones.[16] This simultaneous approval and disparagement echoes again Said's Orientalist paradox.

The specifically troll home environment is not as extensive as those of the other Horde factions; like the gnomes, they have come under the protection of another faction after losing their own homeland. There is, however, Sen'Jin Village, which is highly Caribbean-influenced. The background music is clearly meant to refer to "tribal" Jamaican music. It is a town of open, thatched-roof wooden huts, decorated with masks that are extremely similar to those used in religious rituals in Voudoun, a religion that has historically been denigrated and ridiculed in Western cultural production.[17] Voudoun is also referenced in the "mojo" that drops from hostile trolls in the larger world, in the spoken NPC phrase "stay away from the voodoo, mon," and in some troll questlines. Similar architectural patterns are found in troll settlements elsewhere in the world, such as in Stranglethorn Vale and Zul'Farrak.

Orcs

Orcs, unlike trolls and tauren, do not clearly correspond with any specific real-world culture. Rather, they seem at times to represent colonial depictions of blackness, and at times to be a sort of sink category—not a specific racial type in itself, but a symbolic drain into which all sorts of negative stereotypes seep.[18] Orcs have dark (green) skin, fangs, stocky bodies, and wide, grimacing mouths: all symbols of aggression and unattractiveness in Western culture. Like troll females, orc females are particular targets of racist discourse, though less tied to real-world racism: they, like their troll sisters, are considered both unattractive and hypersexualized, putting them in the subaltern position in terms both of gender *and* race that has historically been imposed on women of color.[19]

Blood Elves

Blood elves, with their impossible beauty, express their bodily otherness in a different and paradoxical way. They can be seen to represent the unrealistic, airbrushed beauty standards of Western society, along with arrogance about that beauty and derision for the appearances of the other Horde races that occasionally slips into outright racism. (Whether this racism is presented as read or as a critique of itself will be discussed later.) Perhaps the best example is one of the blood elf female jokes: "So I went to this troll spa the other day and I wound up with dreadlocks and a freakin' *bone* in my nose! I mean, come on! Who PAYS for that?" The blood elf male's physical otherness, on the other hand, is presented through feminization and implied homosexuality, anathema to traditional Western masculinity.[20] All but two of the available blood elf male hairstyles are long, flowing locks, and the two exceptions are anime-style spikes. And again, the jokes contribute to this characterization: taking his cue from the girl group The Pussycat Dolls, the blood elf male coos, "'Don't you wish your girlfriend was hot like me?"

The blood elf environment is similarly paradoxical. Ethereal trees drop golden leaves while desperate magic addicts stumble around beneath them.

Creepy, ghostly Mana Wyrms abound in the midst of green grasses, and magical brooms sweep up dust in what is perhaps a nod to the classic Disney short *The Sorcerer's Apprentice*, a cautionary tale for those, like the blood elves, who believe that they can control magic without it controlling them.

Blood elves are also significant in that they are an expansion race, added in *The Burning Crusade* expansion in January 2007, and they, unlike any of the other Horde races, have the ability to be paladins, a trait formerly restricted to the Alliance. Even in this, though, the familiar/foreign dichotomy of the factions is at work. While Alliance paladins use the Light (their name for the source of magic), blood elf paladins *abuse* it—they are portrayed as junkies and addicts to the power of magic. The Light is a powerful force, but the Alliance paladins use it in a "civilized" way in religious rituals that are distinctly Western, whereas blood elves use it in a "savage" way: to find out how to gain access to the power of the Light, they kidnapped a Naaru—a sentient god-like being of pure Light energy—and tortured it until they figured out how to use it.

Undead

The Otherness of the undead functions differently from that of the previous four Horde races: a useful theoretical framework for the embodied Othering of the undead is Julia Kristeva's concept of abjection. The abject is neither subject—I—nor object, "an otherness ceaselessly fleeing in a systematic quest of desire." Rather, it is the place "where meaning collapses," the place "where I am not," not the opposite but the *negation* of subjectivity (1982, 1–3). One of Kristeva's most important examples of abjection is in the body of a corpse.

> The corpse (or cadaver: *cadere*, to fall), that which has irremediably come a cropper, is cesspool, and death; it upsets even more violently the one who confronts it as fragile and fallacious chance. A wound with blood and pus, or the sickly, acrid smell of sweat, of decay, does not *signify* death. In the presence of signified death—a flat encephalograph, for instance—I would understand, react, or accept. No, as in true theater, without makeup or masks, refuse and corpses *show me* what I permanently thrust aside in order to live. (1982, 3)

In this sense, the undead are the apotheosis of the Horde's foreignness. Their role in the game is one of constant negation. They are allied to the Horde not to contribute what they can to the faction but to take what they can from it. Their corpse-bodies are skeletal and spare, a paradox in their own impossibility. They belong to a larger category of undead creatures within the game, all of which are physically repulsive because their bodies are not how they should be: namely, they are incompatible with life, as what should be *inside* is on the *outside*. The desired player reaction to this reversal of bodily integrity is one of disavowal and disgust, and the fact that undead bodies are seen as more in line with Horde than Alliance bodies enhances the bodily Otherness of the Horde.

The Undead environment is similarly abject. The Undercity's waterway flows not with water but with toxic magical waste, inverting the source of life into a source of death. It is buried underground like a tomb and yet is populated, putting it in the same paradoxical category as its inhabitants. Like the undead themselves, the Undercity represents a space of abjection, "the place where I am not," the ultimate foreign.

Race and (Dis)Embodiment

Although online space has traditionally been considered in many ways disembodied, the inclusion of visual avatars in online interaction, especially video games, has re-embodied the player. The player's avatar, her or his virtual embodiment in the gameworld, is one of the main features of *World of Warcraft*. The state of the body has also been important in postcolonial theory as a key identity marker, both in terms of colonial oppression based on the physical differences between colonizer and colonized and as a site of anticolonial resistance. Virtual embodiment of the type available in *World of Warcraft* can be seen as the next step in online communication: instead of being a visual blank, as were players in earlier text-based MUDs and MOOs, the player has the capacity to decide on his or her own appearance to others. In the colonial, racist paradigm, it is the colonizer who has power relating to embodiment: he creates and maintains a power hierarchy based partially on unchangeable facets of physical identity such as skin color and face shape. In a virtually embodied space such as *World of Warcraft*, however, this power is given over somewhat to players: they can choose how to be embodied, which seems to create a structure in which players have the power, and in a sense they do.

However, as Thomas Foster writes, such virtual embodiment is a mode of play that "privileges vision as a mode of information processing, and visual perception remains inextricably linked to a history of racial stereotyping" (1998, 160, in Nakamura 2002, 34). There are two layers to the stereotype-based embodiment that happens in *World of Warcraft*: that of the players' own biases, brought into the gameworld from the real world, and that of Blizzard's own stereotypes, built into the gameworld itself.

The first layer, that of player-based stereotyping, has been discussed at length by Nakamura and by Jeffrey Ow. Nakamura writes of the "orientalized theatricality" of players in LambdaMOO, a text-based online role-playing game, in which several white male players go by nicknames which reference East Asian culture: characters from other video games and icons, such as samurai, from East Asian history (2002, 39). These players perform a role within the game that is deliberately constricted and guided by both real and imagined features of the stereotypical framework they have chosen. This sort of stereotyping is not dependent on visual cues; it can as easily be activated by a name or a textual description. However, it remains important, and perhaps takes on even more importance in games with a visual center. Nakamura posits a possible explanation for the preponderance of such frankly unimaginative play: "racial cybertypes," she writes, "provide familiar, solid and reassuring versions of race which other users can readily accept and understand since they are so used to seeing them in novels, films and video games" (2002, 40). This echoes again Bhabha's assertion that stereotypes are comfortable and "safe" spaces for the colonizer, or the group in power, to inhabit. Over time, however, and with the constant repetition and replication of pop cultural paradigms in today's media, these stereotypes are caught in a feedback loop: "seeing them in novels, films and video games," players take them up and solidify them, and are seen by others, which solidifies them further. Eventually the question of authenticity recedes as simplified depictions take over, in a feedback loop—a Baudrillardian catch-22.

Ow attempts to counter this by unmasking the player: he argues that players "neither know nor care" about the authenticity of their depictions of Oriental characters, and that they are "unwilling to truly transform" themselves, instead wearing "the digital skin to become superficially Oriental" (2000, 40) without giving thought either to the authenticity of their claims or—more importantly—to the impact that they may have on the actual people they claim to represent. Of course, the orientalizing white males of Nakamura and Ow's narratives are certainly not the sum total, or even the majority, of those who participate in online games. However, racist colonial stereotypes engendered by past and present Western colonialism continue to proliferate within online discourse.

The second layer of embodiment involves Blizzard's own in-game paradigms. In *Cybertypes*, Nakamura suggests that where self-identity is limited to a series of predetermined choices, "identities that do not appear on the menu are essentially foreclosed on and erased" (2002, 102). These "menu-driven identities" therefore act not only as erasures of the possibilities outside of them, but also as reinscriptions of the particular chosen identity types, and the repetition of these reinscriptions that happens in a game like *World of Warcraft* (in which images are reproduced indefinitely) adds magnitudes of strength to these depictions. Within *World of Warcraft*'s own version of this, I would emphasize two different aspects: one is the humanoid virtual bodies themselves, and the other is the environment in which they are embodied and the connections between the bodies and their surroundings. In each of these two areas, the Horde is depicted as foreign, while the Alliance is depicted as familiar. Indeed, the inclusion of real-world race in the equation along with folklore-constructed race further complicates this already complex dynamic. Nakamura writes:

Being raced in cyberspace is doubly disorienting, creating multiple layers of identity construction. While on the one hand people of colour have always been postmodern (and by extension "virtual"), if postmodernism is defined as that way of seeing subjectivity as decentred, fragmented and marginalized, on the other hand their lack of access to technology and popular figuration as the "primitive" both on- and offline (those virtual samurai and geisha are certainly not to be found in "modern," let alone postmodern, Japan) positions them simultaneously in the nostalgic world of the premodern. . . . The celebration of the "fluid self" that simultaneously lands postmodernity as a potentially liberatory sort of worldview tends to overlook the more disturbing aspects of the fluid, marginalized selves that already exist offline in the form of actual marginalized peoples, which is not nearly so romantic a formulation. (2002, xv–xvi)

There is a power imbalance at play here. On the one hand, you have the players, who are able to take on by proxy the identity (though, significantly, not the subjectivity) of a person from a marginalized group. This capability, taken further, may invite the dangerous idea that because one plays, for instance, a tauren, one knows in some small sense what it is like to have the *subjectivity*, rather than just the audiovisually indicated *identity*, of a member of the real-world group the tauren represent. On the other hand, you have the real-world people whose identities are being borrowed, some—but not all— of whom are actual players. Therefore, the people whose cultures are being appropriated in *World of Warcraft* are in a double bind of sorts. They are marginalized both in the real world—they are made "virtual" by virtue of their inclusion in popular discourse as stereotypes rather than individuals—and in the gameworld, where they are constructed as the exotic Other whose bodies—and, putatively, minds—any player can claim to inhabit.

Constructions of Race

Just as feminist theorists have argued for many years that gender is not a biological but rather a *social* phenomenon, postcolonial theorists have argued that race is determined by social rather than biological standards. A case in point is that of American Irish, Italian, and Jewish people, who were considered ethnically nonwhite in the early twentieth century when they were largely immigrants, but who gradually "became" white over the course of the century. E. L. Goldstein writes about Jews in particular: "Because white Americans saw Jews as racially different and yet similar to themselves in many ways, the image they attached to them tended to be much more ambivalent than the one fastened on African Americans and other more stable outsiders. . . . While the black-white discourse of race bolstered white Americans' sense of confidence and superiority, their image of the Jew reflected the doubts and anxieties they harbored about their own society, ultimately undermining the efficacy of their black-white worldview" (2006, 2).

One of *World of Warcraft*'s major themes, however, is that physical appearance is often determined by inner nature. That is, race is not only a biological feature, but is tied inextricably and physically to particular personality and intellectual traits. For instance, the satyrs—huge, hoofed beasts that guard the Dark Portal in the Blasted Lands—are former night elves who allied with the destructive Burning Legion and were thereby changed by demons from lithe, ethereal creatures into the monsters that they now are—ones that look more like tauren than night elves. A similar thing happened to the naga, who used to be upper-class night elves before their queen Azshara made a diabolical agreement with the Old Gods: their survival for service. They are portrayed as twisted and mutated; significantly, one major aspect of their "difference" is that they are matriarchal. This is not usually a question of morality, however: generally, appearance signifies familiarity or otherness rather than good or evil.

Interestingly, although trolls, orcs, undead, and the like are referred to as "races" in *World of Warcraft*, they actually function more as different species than as races. They are all humanoid but have racial traits that are biologically determined. This is true not only in terms of audiovisual embodiment but also in terms of game mechanics: each race has a set of particular "racial" abilities, such as the tauren war stomp or the blood elf affinity for enchanting.

As I have discussed, all of the Horde races, especially those that most explicitly correspond with real-world marginalized societies, are represented as less like the player (who is in all cases human) than are the Alliance races that have similar correspondences. In fact, if there's one thing that I think it's possible to claim about all *World of Warcraft* players, it's that they are all, unquestionably, human. By making "human" a specific category within the game, limited to avatars who have Caucasian features, whose skin darkens only to a very deep tan, and who speak in North American accents, the game excludes those real-world players whose cultural markers are represented by in-game non-humans *instead of* in-game humans. Implicitly, the game suggests that those players who have Jamaican accents, for instance, are humanoid—but specifically *not* human.

Furthermore, these bodies deliberately suggest not the actual bodies of people from real-world cultures but rather stereotypical representations of those bodies. Here, then, is the crux of the problem with Blizzard's cultural borrowing: if in-game races are closely identified with real-world races, and those same in-game races are treated as biologically distinct species rather than socially categorized races, then the implication is that real-world race is also primarily biologically determined—an outdated and destructive implication that belongs to a racist discourse.

Conclusions

There is a fine line to walk with cultural borrowing in video games. Many game designers have come down on the wrong side of it, regardless of their intentions. In an essay on the *Civilization* series of historical-simulation games, in which the player's empire must take over stretches of land populated by "barbarians" but considered "empty" by the game design and the official manual, Christopher Douglas writes:

though some might find the game's recognition of historical contingency progressive and liberating, I would argue that its ultimate effect is to reinforce the pattern of interaction between the colonizing power and the aboriginal. . . . The game has abstract radical potential, but it is circumscribed by how things really turned out. That radical potential thus works ideologically to reinforce the notion of cultural and maybe racial supremacy. That things might have turned out differently need not produce existential-national anxiety in Western players, in light of the imaginable histories that include the subjugation of those players on an alternative, virtual earth. Rather, the actual story becomes explicable, when faced with the endlessly replayable historical simulations of civilization, only through reference to a kind of spiritual or cultural rightness of European civilization. (2002)

Schwartz concurs with Douglas, writing that "game designers reinforce cultural meanings while appearing to challenge them" (2006, 319). It is this dynamic that *World of Warcraft* seems sometimes to fall prey to and sometimes to avoid. The game acts much of the time as a purveyor of straightforward stereotypes: this seems most in evidence, and most destructive, in *World of Warcraft*'s characterization of trolls. The game's relentless characterization of trolls as cunning, wily, barbarous, and vicious, coupled with the extremely close modeling of troll civilization on a pan-Caribbean cultural aesthetic, is racist. However, this very same racism and race-based worldview is critiqued in the blood elf female joke about the troll beauty parlor in which the blood elf and not the troll is implicitly ridiculed for her ignorance. *World of Warcraft* is a tricky, complex construction of cultural meaning in this way: it is both racist and antiracist, frequently at the same time. Of course, part of this complexity is because *World of Warcraft* is not a fixed text: it is a *game*. However, the game also mirrors the real complexity—and, often, ambiguity—of wider discourses about race and colonialism.

There is also the matter of appropriation of identity, which I touched on earlier: what Lisa Nakamura calls "identity tourism" (2002, 39). Those who play Alliance are slipping into a role that follows both Western fantasy conventions and video game fantasy conventions, but those who play Horde are appropriating an identity informed by otherness. This is, however, not necessarily a criticism: some may do this to experience the exoticism of otherness, but others may do so in order to fight, though virtually, against the very normativity that gives rise to this dichotomy. Just as *World of Warcraft* is complex in terms of race, it is complex in terms of identity. Thus, the inherently hybrid identity of the player/avatar has the potential not only to be used for identity tourism, but also for subversion of the expected norms.

We can see, therefore, the many layers of meaning that function in *World of Warcraft*. Though player-driven stereotyping and game-driven stereotyping are in a sense distinct systems, they affect each other significantly. Players give feedback to Blizzard on content development, and Blizzard's depictions of Horde bodies and Horde environments feeds the players' own ideas about the Horde races—and about the cultures on which those races are based. Again, we have a feedback loop between Blizzard and the players themselves: one that becomes more and more complex as time goes on, in which issues of race and colonialism are both reinscribed and subverted.

Notes

1. In making this assertion as to server popularity I draw my data from the official *World of Warcraft* Server Status page at http://www.wow-europe.com/en/serverstatus.

2. For a representative example, see the Slashdot discussion "Stereotyping the Horde" at http://games.slashdot.org/games/06/05/17/1642211.shtml.

3. For the purposes of this paper, I treat the terms "otherness" and "foreignness" as approximate synonyms, and they should be read as such in this context.

4. I use the term "real world" for the sake of expediency. Of course, video games are part of the real world; however, my use of the term should be read as referring to what Darko Suvin calls "zero world," the "empirically verifiable properties" (1972, 377) surrounding the player, as distinguished from the digitally realized world within *World of Warcraft*.

5. I am grateful to Adam Roberts for this way of phrasing this insight, and for his valuable assistance and input on this chapter in general.

6. See especially Fernandez 1999.

7. See Blizzard's official press release at http://www.blizzard.com/press/070111.shtml.

8. See especially Lee 1996 and Fong 2001.

9. http://www.wow-europe.com/en/info/races/ contains links to this information as well as the official write-ups for all other races.

10. Ibid.

11. Ibid.

12. See chapter 6 by Tanya Krzywinska.

13. See for instance Kerr 1980, Mackenzie 1995, Buruma and Margalit 2004, and Irwin 2006.

14. See Said 1985.

15. The official Blizzard backstory for the Warcraft universe can be found at http://www.worldofwarcraft.com or http://www.wow-europe.com. Another excellent, though unofficial, source is http://www.wowwiki.com.

16. Witness, for instance, the character of the sorceress Tia Dalma in *Pirates of the Caribbean 2: Dead Man's Chest*, in which black British actress Naomie Harris plays a sexually aggressive witch-in-the-woods whose straight teeth are blackened and whose hair is matted into a parody of dreadlocks. The male crew find her simultaneously alluring and disgusting.

17. Although Voudoun as a distinct religious practice is native to Haiti, it includes elements from several older African religious traditions and is practiced more or less throughout the Caribbean as well as by those of Caribbean descent living elsewhere. For more information see, for instance, Olmos and Paravisini-Gebert 1997.

18. I am grateful to Adam Roberts for this particular phrasing.

19. Hilde G. Corneliussen goes into greater detail regarding the interactions of gender and race in *World of Warcraft* in chapter 3.

20. For an interesting take on male blood elves' masculinity and details regarding Blizzard's treatment of same, see chapter 3 in this volume.

References

Bhabha, Homi. 1994. *The Location of Culture*. London: Routledge.

Blizzard Entertainment. "World of Warcraft Server Status Pages." Available at ⟨http://www.wow-europe.com/en/serverstatus⟩.

Buruma, Ian and Avishai Margalit. 2004. *Occidentalism: The West in the Eyes of its Enemies*. New York: Penguin.

Douglas, Christopher. 2002. "'You Have Unleashed a Horde of Barbarians!' Fighting Indians, Playing Games, Forming Disciplines." *Postmodern Culture* 13, no. 1. Available at ⟨http://www3.iath.virginia.edu/pmc/issue.902/13.1douglas.html⟩.

Eagleton, Terry. 2006. "Have You Seen My Dada Boss?" *London Review of Books* 28, no. 23 (30 November 2006). Available at ⟨http://www.lrb.co.uk/v28/n23/eagl01_.html⟩.

Fernandez, Maria. 1999. "Postcolonial Media Theory." *Art Journal* 58, no. 3: 58–73.

Fong, Timothy P. 2001. *The Contemporary Asian American Experience: Beyond the Model Minority*, 2nd ed. Upper Saddle River, N.J.: Prentice Hall.

Foster, Thomas. 1998. "'The Souls of Cyber-Folk': Performativity, Virtual Embodiment, and Racial Histories." In *Cyberspace Textuality: Computer Technology and Literary Theory*, ed. Marie-Laure Ryan, 137–163. Bloomington: Indiana University Press.

Goldstein, E. L. 2006. *The Price of Whiteness: Jews, Race, and American Identity*. Princeton, NJ: Princeton University Press.

Irwin, Robert. 2006. *For Lust of Knowing: The Orientalists and their Enemies*. London: Allen Lane.

Kerr, Malcolm H. 1980. "Orientalism" (review). *International Journal of Middle East Studies* 12, no. 4: 544.

Kristeva, Julia. 1982. *Powers of Horror: An Essay on Abjection*. Translated by Leon S. Roudiez. New York: Columbia University Press.

Lee, Stacey. 1996. *Unraveling the "Model Minority" Stereotype: Listening to Asian American Youth*. New York: Teachers College Press.

MacKenzie, John M. 1995. *Orientalism: History, Theory and the Arts*. Manchester: Manchester University Press.

Marez, Curtis. 2004. "Aliens and Indians: Science Fiction, Prophetic Photography and Near-Future Visions." *Journal of Visual Culture* 3, no. 3: 336–352.

Nakamura, Lisa. 2002. *Cybertypes: Race, Ethnicity and Identity on the Internet*. London: Routledge.

Olmos, Marguerite Fernandez and Lizabeth Paravisini-Gebert. 1997. *Sacred Possessions: Voodoo, Santeria, Obeah, and the Caribbean*. Chapel Hill, NC: Rutgers University Press.

Ow, Jeffrey A. 2000. "The Revenge of the Yellowfaced Cyborg Terminator." In *Race in Cyberspace*, eds. Beth E. Kolko, Lisa Nakamura, and Gilbert B. Rodman, 51–68. London: Routledge.

Said, Edward. 1985. "Orientalism Reconsidered." *Cultural Critique* 1, no. 1: 89–107.

Said, Edward. 1978. *Orientalism*. New York: Vintage.

Schwartz, Leigh. 2006. "Fantasy, Realism and the Other in Recent Video Games." *Space and Culture* 9, no. 3: 313–325.

Sherman, Sharon R. 1997. "Perils of the Princess: Gender and Genre in Video Games." *Western Folklore* 56, no. 3/4: 243–258.

Suvin, Darko. 1972. "On the Poetics of the Science Fiction Genre." *College English* 34: 372–382.

World

5

Espen Aarseth

Tom said to himself that it was not such a hollow world, after all. He had discovered a great law of human action, without knowing it—namely, that in order to make a man or a boy covet a thing, it is only necessary to make the thing difficult to attain. If he had been a great and wise philosopher, like the writer of this book, he would now have comprehended that Work consists of whatever a body is obliged to do, and that Play consists of whatever a body is not obliged to do.

—Mark Twain

What sort of a world is Azeroth, the "world" in *World of Warcraft*? This chapter investigates the notion of Azeroth as a crafted, fictional world, and questions the worldliness of this particular creative enterprise. If Azeroth is a place, what kind of place is it? What are the spatial and geopolitical logics behind it? This investigation will raise several issues and meta-issues connected to gameworld analysis. Is the shape of the world motivated by gameplay design needs, or does it have other motivations as well? The world limitations, especially the lack of user-modifiable content, are quite striking compared to many other MMOGs. Can this be a factor in the success of the game? To what degree can the gameworld structure be said to contribute to the game mechanics, and how does the gameworld design reflect the implied ideal player, according to Blizzard?

While the rich variety of landscapes and cultural references in Azeroth can be seen as proof that Blizzard has succeeded in creating their Warcraft world, it appears to remain essentially hollow, a multicolored shell with a hard, static surface and no inner substance to speak of. Instead of seeing this as a failed potential, however, I will argue that it is precisely this hollowness that constitutes the game's great and multicultural success.

The chapter also explores the general notion of a gameworld in comparison to fictional, filmic, and theme park worlds, as well as the world we live in. Servers, communities, "realms" and intellectual property "universes" are keywords that all point in different directions when it comes to understanding the notion of games as a genre of spatial practice, a concept developed by Henri Lefebvre in *The Production of Space* (1991). Are gameworlds ends in themselves, objects of desire rather than the terrain of gameplay, subject to game mechanics, and never to be understood in isolation, but always as a background to the gameplay design?

This essay will approach *World of Warcraft* through a combination of ontology and critical aesthetics. Game ontology is a discipline that seeks to identify general principles and formal models with which to describe games;[1] critical aesthetics can be described as attempts to interpret the production of meaning of particular games (the game as a work of art *and* cultural artifact).

Azeroth in Gameworld History

Computer games all tend to incorporate a coherent, accessible playing space; a continuous, reliant area or set of areas for the players to explore, conquer, and inhabit. From the earliest 2D or text-based arenas of *Pong* (1972) or *Adventure* (1976), the evolution has steadily been toward bigger, more complex, more detailed, and more pliable landscapes, a march lockstepped with the evolution of computer hardware.

With regard to MMOGs such as *World of Warcraft*, the landscape simulation is perhaps the only, and certainly the most significant evolutionary change; they have evolved from the text interfaces of the MUDs of the late 1970s and 1980s via the 1990s *Ultima Online's* isometric 2D to *Everquest's* (1999) first-person 3D perspective.

In terms of game mechanics, gameplay, and social aspects, not much has changed in three decades. Yes, where there used to be tens or hundreds of simultaneous players connected to a game server, now there are thousands. But players still play in small groups of between two and a few dozen members, and there are seldom more than a hundred players in the same local area at any given time. Although the scale of thousands on the same server creates interesting economic consequences, as Castronova (2001) has shown, in player to player everyday sociability, 2007 is not that different from 1984. We still use text to communicate, we still genderbend, we still have fun in most of the same ways, along with a few new ones. So while the semiotic layer afforded by the graphics and the physics engines keeps improving, it does not seem to have a profound effect on the gameplay.

How does *World of Warcraft* fit in this picture? Significantly, it does not up the ante in terms of better, more, or nicer. The technical graphics and physics details are significantly less ambitious than with competitors such as *Everquest 2*, which came out a few months before *World of Warcraft* in 2004 (see figures 5.1 and 5.2). The opportunities for personalization are markedly less: *Everquest 2* players can tweak facial details and furnish their own apartments, and instead of the slightly flat, cartoonish artwork of *World of Warcraft*, *Everquest 2* has almost photorealistic, higher-resolution graphics that can only be described as more accomplished.

Figure 5.1
A screenshot from *Everquest 2*.

Figure 5.2
A screenshot from *World of Warcraft.*

   This comes at a price: moving over longer distances through the *Everquest 2* landscape is not as fluent and continuous as similar movement in *World of Warcraft,* and Norrath, the world of *Everquest 2,* feels like a labyrinth of connected, different-sized game levels, not a semiunified, semiendless surface like Azeroth. While some MMOGs allow their players to create buildings and govern towns or districts, in Azeroth the player is a ghost-like guest on an uncaring, slick surface, a stranger in a strange land. The nature of the game dynamics can be compared to a theme park ride, the Fordist paradigm of assembly-line mass entertainment as pioneered by Disney: "Move along, please, more enjoyable monsters and sights await around the next corner." The flying transporter beasts on their fixed trajectories resemble most of all a scenic conveyor belt or a monorail train taking tourists or workers to the next attraction or work site. Letting the flying passengers see not only the landscape but also other players busy with their little quests is a stroke of world-design genius, a means of making the world come alive that foreshadows the player's own exploration and stimulates it immensely, since the route by which the transporter animal travels is seldom the same way as the player traveled to get to the start or stop locations.

Perhaps Taylorism provides an even better model for explaining what goes on: the careful, scientific art of balancing the players' progression, spreading them out across the artificial landscape to avoid production bottlenecks, and making sure the toil is optimized for efficient gameplay. Other chapters in this book will detail the social structures and consequences of the gameplay dynamics, such as the peculiar work ethic that forces a group of players to meet with a high degree of regularity if they want to progress efficiently in the game. Those who fail the group fail themselves in the quest for leveling up, and soon find themselves looking for another group. The automatic social cruelty of this mechanism is as elegant as it is unethical. Casual players must fend for themselves; disloyalty to the group and to the game is its own punishment. On a higher institutional level, the guilds function as player-policed assembly lines in an attempt to ensure that the most dedicated players receive all the rewards and benefits the game has to offer. The social pressures and tensions of these institutions are worthy of their own investigation (see chapters 9 and 10).

Still, by spending many years studying MMOGs before coming up with their own synthesized design, Blizzard avoided several of the poor choices made by its competitors: a typical example is the collective "experience debt" incurred when a member of a group dies in *Everquest 2*; this causes all members of that group to gain experience more slowly for a specific number of points, as a form of collective punishment. This mechanism causes heaps of frustration, distrust, guilt, and animosity between players, who are then much less inclined to team up with strangers. It was wisely not imported into *World of Warcraft*, where a much less severe death penalty is used (see chapter 7 for more on death in *World of Warcraft*). Comparing metascores at gamerankings.com, a site that collects and averages game review scores on a scale from 1 (bad) to 100 (excellent), we see that *World of Warcraft* gets 92, *Everquest 2* receives 83, and *EVE Online* and *Star Wars Galaxies* both score 74. So in important respects, like critical acclaim and popularity, *World of Warcraft* is the better-liked game.

However, *World of Warcraft* is not a bold, experimental step forward, since it does not pioneer MMOG design in any significant way, but rather consolidates it. The world it offers is less deep, less individually accommodating, but more safe and polished compared to other games in the genre. Instead, Blizzard has quietly observed and distilled twenty years of game evolution, and bound the landscape together in a seemingly seamless whole, a continuous surface that, by being continuous and labyrinthine, gives the impression of being a lot bigger than it actually is. Walking from north to south on one of the two continents does not take many hours, if one's avatar can survive the hostile monsters, and even if not, it is possible to do it as a ghost. So what are supposed to look like hemispheres are actually comparable to small islands, perhaps not unlike this author's current habitat, Amager, an island just south of Copenhagen. Amager is some eight miles long, and walking its length would take approximately three to four hours. Another, more famous island, Manhattan, is of similar size: between its southern tip and the north end of Central Park are 7.5 miles.

Using mapwow.com, a service based on the Google Maps software and interface, it is possible to calculate the size of Azeroth's continents fairly accurately. Starting with the assumption that the biggest farmhouse in Goldshire (Stonefield Farm) would be around twenty meters in length, and zooming gradually out while measuring distances between key landmarks, it is easy to calculate that the distance between the north and south tip of the Eastern Kingdoms is about thirteen kilometers, or eight miles, in fact just like Amager. So it appears that Azeroth does not have much room for a kingdom, let alone several. Except for a *magic kingdom*, that is.

So, the whole continent of the Eastern Kingdoms is the size of a small island, and the average zone in the game is much smaller than an average airfield. This unenchanting truth might be nothing so much as a reminder of the heavy cost of producing quality graphical content in today's demanding game industry. Clearly, while the simulation of physics and the graphical representation get better, the gameworlds, which used to increase in size from game to game, no longer do, but have started to shrink. This observation seems to hold not just for MMOGs but for other genres as well. *Ultima Online* (Origin, 1997) supposedly has a world that takes thirty hours to traverse. *Oblivion* (Bethesda Softworks, 2006), the latest installment in the Elder Scrolls series, has a significantly smaller world footprint than its predecessor *Morrowind* (2002), which was again smaller than the earlier games in the series.

The world of *World of Warcraft* is small, static, and quite phony if we want to compare it to any real-world standard, and even to some other MMOGs. The population of any one server "realm" is in the single thousands, much less than the population of Amager, even if we include all the monsters and animals of the former and none from the latter. Seen from above, courtesy

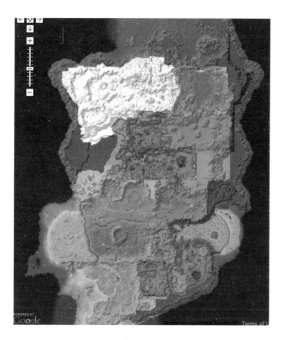

Figure 5.3
A map of the Eastern Kingdoms.

of mapwow.com, Azeroth, with its sharply distinguished zones, looks more like a quilt than a geological entity, even a fantasy-based one.

There are of course countless other peculiarities, all of which undermine the worldliness of Azeroth—interface functions such as e-mail, global chat channels, and radar; electronic auction houses; the aforementioned tireless and mechanically accurate flying transportation beasts; NPCs that reappear in due time after you kill them and give out the same quests over and over—the list is practically endless. Of course, all of these quirks are there for a simple reason: to provide more entertaining gameplay, like the pig in Valhalla that is cooked and eaten every night and reborn every morning.

Would a deeper, more real world provide better gameplay? Perhaps, but at a much greater game development cost. The nonreal-world aspects of Azeroth—the cartoonism, the lack of depth, and the ease of traversal—are no doubt a major part of the game's broad intercultural appeal. The transportation and communication devices and the possibility of player-initiated teleportation anywhere contribute to a functional gamescape that, precisely in its nonworld qualities (the way worldliness is negated by the game mechanics and the lack of real, boring distance) offers the players near-instant access to the attractions, very much like an amusement park, a carefully planned playground where the ludicrous is accepted simply because it is amusing and pleasant. Expansions to the gameworld work in the same way as expansions to theme parks: the map is expanded, and old customers will have a new reason to visit.

It's a Small, Small World, After All

Compared to a fictional fantasy world, the ultimate example of which is Tolkien's Middle-earth in *The Lord of The Rings* (1954), Azeroth is small and compartmental. In Middle-earth, the distances between major cities and places are more or less comparable to the medieval times of our world, as are the travel times between them. According to the *Lord of the Rings* in-book map there are 200 miles between Minas Tirith, the main human city, and Barad Dür, the stronghold of Sauron, the dark lord. Between Minas Tirith and Orthanc, home of the powerful wizard Saruman, it is another 450 miles as the crow flies. Enemy races and factions are separated by great distances as well as by natural obstacles such as mountain ranges, impenetrable woods, and rivers.

In Azeroth, however, the distances are surprisingly small, indicative of the fact that this is in fact no fictional world, but rather a *functional and playable* gameworld, built for ease of navigation. Between the human city Stormwind and the dwarf capital Ironforge, the direct distance is merely slightly more than a mile. The walking distance is longer, but there is also the Deeprun Tram, a two-station subway train that takes travelers between the cities in minutes. Undercity, the capital of the undead, lies about two miles to the north of Ironforge. Compared to distances between main enemy strongholds in Tolkien's fictional world, Azeroth's enemy cities are closer by a factor of 100. In fact, all of Azeroth could fit into a very small corner of Tolkien's Shire.

The reason for this geopolitical improbability is rather obvious and not at all irrational: Azeroth is all about playability. Tolkien's world is not designed for play, and fictional travel time can contain gaps where readers are spared the boredom of the main characters putting one foot in front of another for days or months without much else happening. In multiplayer games, space-time cannot be individually flexible, but is, in fact, objective and continuous. The players form an in-game community of social, localized agents, and this living structure cannot be overruled by the temporal lacunas and spatial montages common in works of fiction. Instead, the world designers must try to create a balance between individual and collective player needs in which the key design principle is enjoyment, not geopolitical or material realism.

We can observe this kind of discrepancy in other multiplayer games as well. In a recent study, Anders Løvlie (2007, 73) measured the speed of vehicles in *Battlefield 2* (DiCE, 2005) and found that the top speed of the virtual military cars was about half that of their real-world counterparts, while the Chinese fighter plane J-10, with a top speed of 1500 km/h, managed less than 200 km/h in the game. One obvious reason for this imposed speed limit is that the battlefield would have to be considerably larger if the planes flew at their real-world speed (or they would traverse the map in seconds), and this would affect other players negatively, such as those playing foot soldiers.

The *World of Warcraft* world, far from being modeled on fictional worlds or even on the real world, is a place where many different kinds of people come to have fun, play together and socialize, enjoy the scenery, and escape the boredom of real-world travel and travail. In other words, the design ideal for these kinds of worlds is theme parks like Disney World and Universal Studios.

The connection between games and theme parks has been made before, most notably by Celia Pearce (1997) and Angela Ndalianis (2005). However, while they (and the games they relate to) focus on individual rides and attractions, the world of Azeroth can more relevantly be compared to an entire theme park. If we were to imagine a fictional world of Azeroth connected to the other gameworlds of Blizzard's *Warcraft* series (I–III), a fictive universe where heroes and monsters fought to the death and changed the history of the world in doing so, it becomes clear that the *World of Warcraft* world is not that world, but rather a (virtual) theme park version of it. Of course, we don't have to invent this fictional universe, because it already exists in the form of novelizations such as Christie Golden's *Rise of the Horde* (2006), which chronicles the adventures of the orc Warchief hero Thrall. In the gameworld of Azeroth, we can visit, explore, playfight, and enjoy ourselves, moving from one attraction to the next while forgetting or ignoring everything about the fictional world of the same name. Or we can let the fictional and the ludic worlds enhance each other, just as we can ignore or recall the fictional aspects of Disney's universes when we enjoy our visits to Disneyworld or Disneyland.

Figure 5.4
Play between geozones: a sudden change of scenery, somewhere backstage in Azeroth.

In fact, if we compare the fifty square miles of Florida's Disneyworld to Azeroth, they not only serve a similar purpose, but are also quite comparable
in both size and layout. Both contain different thematic zones connected by
paths, roads, and rail-based transportation, which cater to differing tastes, age
groups, or levels.

Another indication of the *World of Warcraft* gameworld's careful design can
be found in an original and convincing analysis by Mattias Ljungström. Using
Christopher Alexander's architectural theory outlined in *A Pattern Language*
(1977), Ljungström identifies a number of Alexander's patterns in and around
the cities and regions of Azeroth and shows how they support the game's social infrastructure needs, such as good waiting and meeting places for players
(2005). Again, Azeroth has more in common with planned urban spaces than
with the wild natural world.

While the regional zones of Azeroth appear to make sense for a player in
the field who follows the quest instructions and explores the terrain, seen
from a bird's eye perspective they don't make much geographical sense. Not
only are the distances absurdly small, but the curious adjacency of glaciers,
marshes, jungles, deserts, and agonistic ethnic groups and wildlife challenges
the critical explorer to take the world seriously. The cartoonish feel does help

alleviate the worst pangs of unrealism, but only the artifical borders (for ex-ample, impenetrable mountains and oceans that cannot be crossed) and player level-based access restrictions (where the too-inexperienced avatar will be killed by too-challenging monsters, and the too-experienced avatar will find nothing of interest) keep us from seeing the absurdity of the constructed world as it really is. For instance, the hot, tropical jungle of Stranglethorn Vale is located just south of the dusty prairie landscape of Westfall, with a river running alongside both sectors. The distance from the northern border of Stranglethorn Vale to the settlement of Sentinel Hill in Westfall is no more than 500 meters. A razor-thin mountain range called the The Dagger Hills acts as a boundary between the two zones, making crossing impossible, like the Chinese Great Wall or the wall around West Berlin. But do players seem to care? Not at all! They will happily explore the world and its wonders while accepting the implausibilities therein in a way that should make fiction authors and filmmakers extremely envious.

What Kind of World is This?

The notion of "gameworld" is a tricky one, since it implies that what we are looking at is actually a world. Games have carefully constructed arenas opti-mized for gameplay, and their resemblance to real worlds is usually second to their function as playground and social channel. In the case of Azeroth, un-usual amounts of energy and care have gone into creating a rich platform for play experience to give players the impression of a continuous landscape, full of spectacular, pleasant, and yet challenging tasks, sights, and beings. As such, the resemblance to our physical everyday world is limited.

Rhetorically, to call something a world is to give it a privileged status as a self-contained, autonomous entity. As we have seen, the "world" in *World of Warcraft* is not a proper world, or even a fictional one, but a "world" in the theme park or zoo sense, a conglomerate or parkland quilt of connected play-grounds built around a common theme.

Azeroth has been constructed to withstand the pressure and tampering of millions of visiting players, who are allowed to see, but not touch—let alone build or destroy. The bears are over there, dinosaurs here, and wolves around the corner to the south. Like the robots in Michael Crichton's 1973 movie *Westworld* ("the vacation of the future, today") the monsters we kill for sport and glory are revived by the system minutes later, ready for the next hunter-visitor. Compared to many single-player worlds (for instance, *Oblivion's* Cyrodiil, where changes introduced by the player affect the gameworld permanently and have consequences for the remaining game experience), Azeroth is oblivious to its player inhabitants. They leave no lasting marks, monuments, or even grafitti, only what memories they may have instigated for the other players, their fellow visitors. Tom Sawyer would probably find it hollow. But his creator would recognize the business philosophy of work as play behind it.

Note

1. See Elverdam and Aarseth (2005) for an example.

References

Alexander, Christopher. 1977. *A Pattern Language: Towns, Buildings, Construction.* Oxford: Oxford University Press.

Castronova, Edward. 2001. "Virtual Worlds: A First-Hand Account of Market and Society on the Cyberian Frontier." CESifo Working Paper Series No. 618. Available at ⟨http://papers.ssrn.com/sol3/papers.cfm?abstract_id=294828⟩.

Elverdam, Christian and Espen Aarseth. 2007. "Game Classification and Game Design: Construction Through Critical Analysis." *Games and Culture* 2, no. 1: 3–22.

Golden, Christie. 2006. *Rise of the Horde (World of Warcraft).* New York: Pocket Star.

Lefebvre, Henri. 1991. *The Production of Space.* Oxford: Blackwell.

Ljungström, Mattias. 2005. "The Use of Architectural Patterns in MMORPGs." Paper presented at Aesthetics of Play conference, Bergen, Norway, October 14–15. Available at ⟨http://www.aestheticsofplay.org/ljunstrom.php⟩.

Løvlie, Anders Sundnes. 2007. *The Rhetoric of Persuasive Games: Freedom and Discipline in America's Army.* Department of Media and Communication, University of Oslo. Available at ⟨http://www.duo.uio.no/englishindex.html⟩.

Ndalianis, Angela. 2005. *Neo-Baroque Aesthetics and Contemporary Entertainment.* Cambridge, MA: MIT Press.

Pearce, Celia. 1997. *The Interactive Book.* Indianapolis: MacMillan Technical Publishing.

Tolkien, J. R. R. 1954. *The Lord of the Rings.* London: Allen and Unwin.

World Creation and Lore: *World of Warcraft* as Rich Text

6

Tanya Krzywinska

World creation has become a core feature of many recent digital games, and this fits hand-in-glove with the generic features of fantasy; the carefully crafted, extensive worlds found in massively multiplayer role-playing online games such as *Guild Wars*, *EverQuest II*, and *World of Warcraft* offer players the opportunity to inhabit such worlds wherein they play and interact with others in the guise of heroic adventurers. It can be said that most popular cultural artifacts are reliant on intertextual features for the generation of meaning and recognition. These are in part an outcome of genre production, but within certain genres, such as science fiction or fantasy, these are actively deployed to generate what Roz Kaveney (2005) called a "thick text;" in other words, a text richly populated with various allusions, correspondences, and references.[1] As such, any fantasy-based game draws on a range of preexisting sources relevant to the invocation of the fantastic to lend breadth and depth to a gameworld and to make use of players' knowledge. The inclusion of intertexual features is a ludic gambit as well as "a way of including the expert reader or viewer in a conspiracy of informed smugness" (Kaveney 2005, 4). For such reasons and more, aspects of myth and the mythic play significant roles in making the "World" of Warcraft. These are present in the register of narrative (the dimension in which myth is most visible): they have a structural function, play a role in shaping the experience of the gameworld and its temporal condition, and are also apparent in the registers of style, resonance, and rhetoric. Each of these contributes to the high-fantasy ambience of the game, even if at times more quotidian aspects come to the fore, and provides in different ways the means of locating players meaningfully in the game world. My aim in this article is to demonstrate how the game's textual structures and elements drive the logic that underpins *World of Warcraft*'s stylistic milieu and provides the context for and of gameplay. Some aspects of the game's mythic structures key into what might be termed classical myth, others are filtered through more recent renditions of mythic forms and structures in the context of "fantasy" rhetoric, and some are more tangentially derived through other forms of popular and game cultures. While players might engage with the game mythos in variable ways, it is nonetheless a core unifying feature of the design of *World of Warcraft*.

Since the publication of Bolter and Grusin's (2000) *Remediation*, it has been quite fashionable to focus on the ways that preexisting genres and forms have been used within digital games, and in many ways *World of Warcraft* can be said to remediate the mix of fantasy, myth, and heroic quests that characterize the genre of high fantasy into the specific context of the MMORPG. However, I have often felt that remediationist analysis generally does not come to grips fully with the numerous ways that intertextuality informs genre-based games at different levels and in different registers. What is crucial to understanding the intertextual aspects of a game like *World of Warcraft* is that the presence of multiple and deliberately planted intertexts encourages a certain type of depth engagement with the game, which extends beyond but also informs the types of gameplay tasks offered to players. Kaveney (2005) argues that certain types of genre-based popular texts actively encourage fan-type consumption by using consciously deployed intertexts. Their presence promotes close reading and an in-depth personal engagement. A fan's enthusiasm for a given text or franchise is marked by a broad knowledge of a text's generic resonances and narrative intricacies. Kaveney claims that such texts can be regarded as a "geek aesthetic" (this is not intended to be pejorative, but instead suggests that certain texts are designed expressly to appeal to those people who enjoy detailed and extended engagement). While it is the case that only a small number of players are fully versed in the lore that informs the "World" of Warcraft ("lore" is the term used by the game's designers), and indeed the game might be played without any real interest in accumulating such knowledge, the game nonetheless offers a vast array of textual features that justify regarding the game as a geek aesthetic. For even the most committed follower of game lore, these features are taken up by players in variable ways and times:

mythos is likely to slide into the background when a player is engaged in concentrated localized tasks or when indulging in certain chat room-style social activities, for example (see Mortensen 2006). To go some way toward opening up a more nuanced and expansive discussion of intertexts within *World of Warcraft*, this article focuses on the game's remediation of mythic forms and devices. In so doing I take account of the role of myth in the making of the gameworld's lore and investigate the relationships between mythic structures and the experience of playing the game.

Fictional worlds are common within genres such as fantasy, horror, and science fiction; examples include Lord Dunsany's world of "faery," J. R. R. Tolkien's Middle-earth, H. P. Lovecraft's Cthulhu mythos, Robert E. Howard's *Conan* novels, Frank Herbert's *Dune* novels, and Joss Whedon's "Buffy-verse." As is often also the case with classical myth, each of these imaginary worlds provides a blueprint formulation that is taken up and extended by others. As well as spanning a range of media forms and texts, each of these fantasy worlds (or perhaps more properly, universes, or in cases where different universes interconnect, multiverses) uses structures and forms derived from preexisting mythological cosmologies and follows in the world-creating footsteps forged in myth systems such as the Celtic, Greek, Native North American, and Nordic. As a form of narrative used to explain or allegorize a state of affairs, myth is, I would argue, intrinsic to the creation of a particular worldview in all these cases, whether that worldview is to be taken as real or as a form of make-believe. Playing a core role in the ontology of many myth systems is a particular cosmology that represents in literal terms some of the forces that affect the human sphere; these may be alien or supernatural, and they play important roles in the particular way the world, the worldview, and the ensuing state of affairs are configured and made coherent. Alongside the presence of cosmological forces, many myths and myth-based texts are characterized by the creation of extended imaginary terrains, which either intersect with the real world or bear a mixture of familiar and unfamiliar geographical features. Many of these mythical worlds extend beyond a single story, providing the basis for a range of interconnected stories.

Despite the fact that many mythological and fictional worlds make use of symbolism that extends beyond narrative (the use of the totemic symbol of the Minotaur's horns in Minoan culture, for example), the stories that underpin such cosmology and symbolism—and by extension worldview—are linear in nature. By contrast, the development of computing technologies that enable the construction of three-dimensional digital space within which a player character can move around and choose to do different activities shifts into the domain of the nonlinear. Because a player is an active choice-making agent within the gameworld, narrative becomes in this context more structurally complex. Unlike stand-alone games, or other media, *World of Warcraft* offers a persistent world in temporal terms that exists whether or not an individual player is playing. In this, the gameworld has a material presence beyond the sphere of the player that resembles in some respects the way that a so-called primitive mythologically based worldview functioned. The difference between *World of Warcraft* and a mythologically based worldview, however, is that we choose as consumers to inhabit the gameworld and understand, through a range of framing signifying factors, that this is a fantasy world designed for our entertainment rather than to be understood as reality. Despite the modal context of fantasy, we nonetheless do "real" things in that world as players have agency and interact with others; myth, fantasy, and reality meet and manifest in what we do and how we act and interact with others in the game. Although it is still the case that many game worlds make use of mythic structures (such as the hero quest,[2] frontier myths, and myths around the fall of a culture), the guiding framework, the mode of delivery, and therefore the nature of our engagement are altered. Nonlinearity and player agency therefore make for a significant material difference to myth-based narratives found in other arenas.

World of Warcraft uses a range of mythic structures to lend coherency and stylistic character to its overall design. These can provide a pattern (or archetype) that Raph Koster (2005) claims is core to the pleasure of playing games. The primary and highly recognizable mythic pattern that informs and structures the game is the epic hero quest, wherein various forces work to help and hinder the hero-player en route to achieving particular goals. According to Otto Rank's Introduction to *In the Quest of the Hero*, this format originates within early civilizations—Greek, Teutonic, Babylonian, Hebraic, Hindu, Egyptian—in stories and poetry aimed to glorify their princes and warriors, each filtered through the terms of their own cosmological traditions (Rank, Raglan, and Dundes 1990). The hero quest format has also become a staple of popular culture, partly through the widespread influence of Joseph Campbell's *The Hero with a Thousand Faces* (1969) on Hollywood scriptwriters. With ancient precedents and popular articulations, the hero quest figures strongly in the collective consciousness and thereby provides a shorthand way of setting expectations and a proven mode for encouraging identification. As well as enriching the text, I would argue that playing at or identifying with a hero, fictional or otherwise, affords a vicarious yet pleasurable sense of agency, the sphere of which is extended and exploited by many games.[3] Quests in *World of Warcraft* come in many different guises: they may involve delivering items or collecting objects—either from killing nonplayer characters or finding objects in the environment—or they might involve more unique actions such as jumping off a high cliff to prove one's bravery as in the Horde quest "A Leap of Faith," delivered by a shamanic Tauren located in Thousand Needles. Although such tasks provide experience and "loot" (items that have currency in the game), which are important as positive feedback to the generation of a pleasurable sense of progress through the game, they are nonetheless keyed quite closely to the state of affairs of the gameworld, and in certain cases into some of the major story arcs. Undertaking quests lends the player a sense that they are playing a role in the history of the gameworld. While this is important in stitching the player into the game's overarching narrative, it is however a form of "illusory" agency (Parsler 2006) because it is patently obvious to any player that they undertake the very same tasks already completed by others. If a player chooses to do the same quest more than once—for example, killing the dragon Onyxia (of which more later)—this repetition is balanced against, and in part masked by, the strong positive feedback provided by the game's various progress bars (experience points, skills, and the like) that increase as these tasks are undertaken.

To investigate the relationships between gameplay, player agency, and myth, it is important to understand what contributes to the creation of "worldness." Worldness in all its facets plays a core role in enriching *World of Warcraft* as text and the player's game experience. One of the primary ways that worldness can be defined (and has been by academics, writers, and game designers alike) is that the world should have a unifying consistency. This applies not only to spatial coordinates, style, and physics, but also to the past events that constitute the world's current state of affairs, to which the player character is subject. This means that the world has to have a history, and in the case of *World of Warcraft*, it is realized in using the rhetorics of myth. In accordance with this, the world's putative history (its lore and narrative), along with differences in the worldview of different groups and factions, are organized around certain core principles that work together to lend the world its integrity, vivacity, and dramatic gameplay possibilities. Mythic structures, forms, and rhetorics frequently provide informative sources for this history, and due perhaps to the multiauthorship of a gameworld that has evolved over a number of years, beginning with the first *Warcraft* game made more than ten years ago (*Warcraft: Orcs and Humans*, 1994), many different aspects of these are in evidence. Such mythic structures, references, and resonances play a central role in the creation of the game as coherent world, but they also have functional features. A number of playful, small-scale references to popular culture are also present—delightful for some players, yet for others they may well disrupt the sense of the gameworld as internally consistent. These nonetheless work intertextually and may function to demonstrate to players that the game authors share similar knowledge sets and tastes. Examples include a human lumberjack found in the Eastvale Logging Camp named Terry Palin, or the Champion of the Horde, who is called Rexxar (the name of Thulsa Doom's henchman in the 1982 movie *Conan the Barbarian*). There are also some references to widely known fairy tales (the Wolf and Red Riding Hood in the Opera House event in Kharazhan) and to other games (the barrels dropped by the large apes in Un'goro Crater, for example, refer to Nintendo's *Donkey Kong*). *World of Warcraft* is a direct extension of the events that occurred in the previous Warcraft games, and as result there are numerous intratextual cross-references. These intertextual references are internally consistent with the franchise's overarching mythos and, for those players who have played the earlier games, this coherence makes for thick text and a rich experience.

Like Tolkien's Middle-earth, the worldness of the game comes in large part from an assemblage of different—fictional—races and cultures; each has its own fictohistorical background (within which a variety of secondary myths and legends are found). As with the real world, particular myths inform the inhabitants' different worldviews, and they arise out of the putative historical experiences of each "race." These have a profound effect on gameplay and on the interpellation of the player into the game world, and also inform the ways players regard one another. Although putative histories inform the tensions and alliances between races, which have a significant impact on gameplay, the myths assigned to each race help to enrich and thicken the world by lending cultural diversity and—through diegetic and emergent conflicts arising from that diversity—dramatic tension. Many of each race's cultural indicators relate to myth and also inform both gameplay tasks and the stylistic designs of the gameworld's spaces. Each race and the places designated as their territories are informed visually by various symbols. The night elves, for example, worship the goddess Elune, and sickle moons, the totem of Elune, are carved on the walls of many of their buildings. Night elf characters have a range of voice emotes (activated by the player and heard in the game) that invoke the goddess Elune, such as their cheer, "Elune be Praised!" (accompanied by wild arm waving). It is only in those races aligned with a nature-based worldview, such as the night elves or tauren, that the druid class exists. The night elves are aligned with real-world symbolism relating to the moon and the use of nature-based magic, assigning the race its cosmological worldview and activating a mythologically resonant frame of reference.[4]

The game's numerous quests tie into mythic form through the rhetorical style in which they are spoken or written, their structure, and their content. Let's take one quest as an example: the Prophecy of Mosh'aru. It is delivered to players around level 40 by a factionally neutral nonplayer character troll who is located in Steamwheedle Port in the domain of Tanaris. It reads: "The ancient prophecy of Mosh'aru speaks of a way to contain the god Hakkar's essence. It was written on two tablets and taken to the troll city of Zul'farrak, west of Gadgetzan. Bring me the Mosh'aru tablets. The first tablet is held by the long dead troll Theka the Martyr. It is said his persecutors were cursed into scarabs and now scuttle from his shrine. The second is held by the hydromancer Velratha, near the sacred pool of Gahz'rilla. When you have the tablets bring them to me."

Although this quest text is clearly a call to action and a means of narrativizing gameplay events in diegetically historical terms, the language used is highly mythological in nature (filtered through the type of language often used in fantasy fiction): the use of the term "prophecy" evokes the supernatural world of mythology, and the names of the places are related to the race populating that terrain—trolls in the case of Zul'farrak, gnome engineers in the case of Gadgetzan. In practical terms, the quest encourages players to visit the "instance" or dungeon of Zul'farrak. The meanings of the quest's text are thickened by what players already know of the world; the narrative fragment deepens players' understanding of the gameworld's state of affairs, and in terms of the geek aesthetic, evokes the types of scenarios that players may be familiar with in their engagement with other fantasy-based texts. In addition, the mythological narrative "casing" of the quest (of which this is one of many) helps to disguise the game's technologically based mechanics, a point raised and explored by Eddo Stern (2002) in relation to the common presence of neomedievalism more generally in games. The presence of forms derived from myth and fantasy fiction provides a means of cloaking and making consonant with the world's high-fantasy milieu the way players are channelled by the game's infrastructure into certain activities and subject positions. This extends beyond the realm of individual quests. Quests are automatically deleted once completed, as the player's quest log can only show a limited number of quests at any one time. This rule demands that players make choices about their actions forced by the game's programmed infrastructure; it is an arbitrary rule but operates, along with many other features, to foreground choice and management as an articulation of player agency. As well as imparting fragments of information about the gameworld's fictional history, cosmology, and current affairs, instructions on how to undertake a quest must be read carefully as they contain sometimes less-than-obvious clues, thereby encouraging players to engage with backstory and helping dress up and contextualize in narrative terms the "grind" (a process that constitutes much of gameplay, involving "killing" multitudes of enemies to collect loot and experience points needed to level up characters). Doug Thomas (2005) has criticized the way that games such as these force players into mechanical grinding activities as a core and super-efficient feature of gameplay.[5] Such activity can work to curtail potential for diverse player-driven play styles, making gameplay seem, for some, overly repetitious and narrowly goal-oriented. Grinding for loot or experience points can be regarded as the type of agency that is very much geared by the game's statistically based progress mechanic. With this in mind, the designers of the *Burning Crusade* expansion spoke, in the "Making Of" DVD included in the collector's edition, of their concern to ensure that the new quests were tightly knit into the game's story.

Cues as to the state of affairs of *World of Warcraft* are also inscribed in the landscapes encountered in the game. In the case of the night elf homelands, for example (see figure 6.1), the woods and shores are littered with the ruins of once-splendid temples, and the various creatures that roam these lands have become corrupt, made aggressive by a supernatural force released by the unwise and decadent use of dangerous magics (a common theme found in high fantasy and myth). The night elf homelands speak of the history of the race, as is also the case with those of other races. Night elves are characterized along Tolkienean lines: they are an ancient race with an affinity with nature and regard themselves as superior to others, even though their civilization has been reduced by war and homegrown degeneration. As Walter Benjamin said of the cultural use of ruins, they cast an aura of mystery and

Figure 6.1
The ruins of a once-splendid and now haunted night elf city.

nostalgia, which in the context of the game lend atmosphere and drama
(2003). The ruins of once-splendid temples and cities act within the game, as
in real life, as in-memoriam signifiers of past glory, representing in romanti-
cized terms a lost object of desire (in this case, the loss of a balanced and
nature-friendly use of knowledge). The blood elves' homeland city, Silver-
moon, is also partly in ruin. The city's buildings were held up by arcane
magic, but the source of this power was destroyed by enemies and the blood
elves turned to less-powerful demonic magic to keep part of the city habitable.
There are many other ruins (the ruin of a culture signified through architecture) within the game, including those of the Azerothian orcs, who once had
triumphalist military architecture (as seen in Hellfire Peninsula, where they
had Roman-style grand monumental buildings), but, since being freed from
demonic enslavement, now live as exiles in more humble and makeshift conditions. All these ruins work with the "lost object" conditions governing desire investments, which are operative in both our engagement with myth and,

by extension, with the high-fantasy genre. The presence of ruined temples to lost gods is one of the ways that *World of Warcraft* makes use of myth to connect to the real world; for example, night elves draw on magical revivalism through new age culture's promotion of knowledge and beliefs that fall outside rationalism and Christianity or monotheism, within which myth is often valued as a lost way of seeing the world. Things of importance lost through war, greed, corruption, or degeneration play a defining role in the histories of other races, too, as well as underpin the core thematic logic of gameplay. And for some, the ability to play as a mythological hero in a world filled with myths and magics apparently lost to us in real life is one of the major attractions of this gameworld.

Within the context of fantasy fiction, a world is constituted by a set of imaginary landscapes that are connected in spatial terms. Most fantasy-genre worlds can therefore be mapped, and indeed many fictions of this type include maps to demonstrate graphically the relationships between spaces (for example, maps are provided as a kind of establishing shot in a preface to Tolkien's *The Lord of the Rings* and Robert Jordan's *The Wheel of Time* novels—aspects of these, among many, also provide *World of Warcraft* with intertextual sources). The geographical dimension of such fictional worlds lends itself extremely well to the creation of multiplayer game environments. It keys into the journeying component of the hero quest that forms the basis of games like *World of Warcraft*, as well as into the media-specific context of three-dimensional space provided by such games, through which the player is able to move quite freely. A variety of game scholars, including Henry Jenkins, Marie-Laure Ryan, and Janet Murray, have each argued that many types of digital games should be regarded as spatial narratives.[6] Although Markku Eskelinen argued against regarding the spatial aspects of games as inherently bound to narrative (2006), I would argue that it is important not to lose sight of the fact that the spatial features of a game such as *World of Warcraft* connect in generic terms with the particular qualities of many mythological systems and, following from that, with the fantasy genre. As George R. R. Martin noted, "J. R. R. Tolkien was the first to create a full realized secondary universe, an entire world with its own geography and histories and legends, wholly unconnected to our own, yet somehow just as real. 'Frodo lives,' the buttons might have said back in the sixties, but it was not a picture of Frodo that Tolkien's readers taped to the walls of their dorm rooms, it was a map. A map of a place that never was" (2001, 3).

The nature of *World of Warcraft*'s quest system forces players to be itinerant, traveling widely in the world to undertake the tasks required to progress. There is therefore a strong and highly recognizable sense of a journey structure in the game, working on the lines of the archetypal hero quest structure found in Homer's *The Odyssey* (circa 750 BC). Unlike Eskelinen (2004), I would suggest that it is common for players to understand the quest format in both narrative and other, more functional and experiential, terms (for example, as a means of gaining better equipment and experience points); one is not reducible to the other, but instead they create a gestalt that better reflects in conceptual terms the multifaceted experience of playing the game. Undertaking quests is for many players a core activity and can be regarded in mythological terms at both a semantic and structural level. The various maps available in the game aid travel and effective play; these might at times imply a narrative, but they also have other significant functions. They are part of the game's functional realism,[7] used in much the same way that one would use a map in the real world. The availability of in-game maps and online or paper-based atlases also promotes the sense that players are free to travel the world, either to take in the sights or to undertake localized tasks. It also contributes to the sense of the game as world by locating the player spatially and temporally (space has to be traveled in real time and is revealed chronologically, with some minor exceptions). But as becomes clear quite quickly, not all places shown on maps are hospitable, because they are populated by guards from the opposing faction; this presents to the player a localized issue, but also points backward to the mythologized events that comprise the contextual histories of the world. Players come to know these through a variety of means—including mininarratives, some of which connect to more overarching ones—but because players are located in the state of affairs of the world in the present tense, playing the game is not experienced solely in terms of narrative, but only inasmuch as narrative is a structure core to semantic engagement. The maps available are at first glance purely geographical and do not appear to show the effect of the state of affairs on territory, which determine where a player can or cannot roam without incurring unlooked-for trouble. For more experienced players, the given names of areas might however be read through their knowledge of the world's narrativized, lived, and embodied history (see Krzywinska [forthcoming b] for more on this). As with many other fantasy worlds, the world of the game and its representation in map form is not therefore simply spatial. Without the presence of conflicts between competing factions, which entails both history and differences in worldview, there would only be dead and undramatic—if admittedly pretty—space. Such conflicts are core to gameplay as well as to the more general experience of the game as world.

Complicating both linear chronology and the sense of being in the world in temporal terms, some aspects of the game have a rather complex recursive time structure; you may, for example, have killed the dragon Onyxia, but you will still find her alive in human form as Lady Katrana Prestor in Stormwind Keep at the side of the human boy-King, and encounter her repeatedly in multiple visits. In this sense, the game does not have a consistent linear chronology; as with retellings of myths, battles are fought over and over again, and in this there is a cyclical organization of time—a kind of "eternal recurrence," to use a phrase from Nietzsche (1961, 1). However, each time a battle is fought, it is likely to be done in a slightly different way, depending on the class and skill ability of a given group. It is also the case that ways of tackling a dungeon raid successfully are posted on the Web—as a result, battles are fought in similar ways, with patterns of battle handed down from more experienced players (there are player-made "master class" movies available for download on the Internet, some of which show how to tackle a given dungeon successfully). Although we might regard such repetition as an echo of mythic cyclical time, which might make for a successful raid (one which yields high-level items), the common practice of replicating proven techniques and strategies demonstrates how the game's design can be experienced as limiting player agency and creativity. Like the ancient Greeks, players are subject to the rules of the powers that be, and both modify their behaviors to keep those powers on side.

A further way in which the gameworld connects to mythological forms is through the inclusion of festivals, spread across the year, which many players find delightful and refreshing. The gameworld itself is a protean form in certain respects, with various additions and changes made by Blizzard through regular updates. Such updates include temporary festival-related material like quests, items such as fireworks and costumes, and decorations. The inclusion of festivals helps to tie the rhythms of real-world time to those of game time—both cyclical and linear—as they key into a number of real-world festivals. Winter Veil occurs at Christmas-time, as does New Year; the Lunar festival corresponds to Chinese New Year; Love Is in the Air aligns with Valentine's Day; Noblegarden is near Easter; and Hallow's End Corresponds to

Halloween. Others festivals have no direct real-world referent, such as Peon Day on September 30. These lend seasonal interest and provide fun things to do (such as quests that allow players to turn their mount into a red-nosed reindeer or receive a pretty dress to wear at festival celebrations), but more significantly, the annual festivals help to create a greater sense of a persistent and culturally driven real-time world and lend a greater sense of seasonal cycles within the world, which are not otherwise apparent in the visual appearance of the game's external environments. Up until recently there was no dynamic weather system in the world (an update given in March 2006 provided fairly limited changes to weather in most zones—although players can scale up and down the extent of the changes in the user interface), and neither is there evidence of seasonal change to vegetation—even though different terrains are assigned different climates in visual terms: as with eternally seasoned lands found often in myth and fairy tales, Winterspring is eternally snowy (see figure 6.2), the trees and sky of Azshara have perpetual autumnal hues, and

Figure 6.2
Winterspring, the land of the frost giants, perpetually cloaked in snow and ice.

Elwynn Forest is ever summer-green. Whereas festivals are cyclical and tie into both mythic and pastoral/agrarian time, they also work to some extent as a counterbalance against the pockets of temporal stasis found in the game, experienced in the unchanging environments and in the persistence of non-player characters that are killed over and over (death is not therefore final as it is in the real world, meaning that sacrifice—of which there are examples in the world—is to some extent devoid of meaning).

Although some of these festivals correlate in a high-fantasy mode with those of the real world and mythology, each of the festivals nonetheless ties into the gameworld's rich lore: the lunar festival is held by the druids of Moonglade (both Horde and Alliance) in "celebration of their city's great triumph over an ancient evil," and Peon Day is based on an "old" legend (which refers back to the earlier iterations of *Warcraft* games[8]) wherein, as described on the official Web site, "The leaders of the two races: orc and human each called upon a lowly worker and assigned him a great task.... Thus, on the anniversary of that day, we celebrate in honor of them and of all the peons and peasants everywhere."

Many of these festivals have a paganish aspect as befits the fantasy nature of the gameworld, with some drawing on intertexts derived from a combination of history (both in-game and that developed across the *Warcraft* series) and popular culture. One such example is the temporary inclusion during Hallow's End of a large burning Wicker Man in Horde territory (as in figure 6.3) wherein the forsaken (the undead) make sacrifice. Julius Caesar claimed that the Gauls made large wicker constructs shaped into human form within which sacrificial victims were placed and set on fire (1996).[9] This historical report may prove to be a fiction—a means of demonstrating to Roman citizens the barbarity of northern peoples—and is largely unverifiable, but the image of a barbaric (though possibly imaginary) past persists through European history. There are various woodcuts based on Caesar's account from the late seventeenth century; it finds its way into J. G. Frazer's *The Golden Bough* (first published in 1890), and more recently the image of the wicker man in the film *The Wicker Man* (1973). In the context of the game, Alliance players are offered a quest by a nonplayer character called Sergeant Hartman—a tacit reference to the film's main protagonist, who is eventually sacrificed, named Sergeant Howie—to go and view the horror of this spectacle, for which they gain a small reward. Witnessing this ritual event supports

Figure 6.3
A Wicker Man located outside Undercity in celebration of the festival of Hallow's End.

the diegetic cultural and historical antipathy between the Horde and the Alliance and provides perhaps a further justification for player-versus-player action. There are numerous examples of such intertexts throughout this multiauthored game, and their presence works along the lines of geek aesthetic, which in part enables players to express their knowledge and identity to others as a form of cultural capital, as described by Kaveney (2005). These, of which I have named but a few, are therefore important to constituting the game as a rich and thick text.

The presence of signifiers and narratives of a prehistoric and historic past, framed as they are within the rhetorics of popular culture, high and low fantasy, and myth, is one of the primary ways that *World of Warcraft* creates the illusion of a coherent world in cultural, stylistic, spatial, and temporal terms and, in addition, provides a rationale for the way that the player character is assigned a particular, predetermined, morally and emotionally loaded history and identity. As with the real world, the player character is born into this symbolic/mythological order, the game's lore, and its concomitant subject positions, even as players bring their own histories, interests, and goals with them.

Although players might choose not to engage with backstory, and it is not required to progress through and enjoy playing the game, playing as Horde or Alliance or a particular class does nonetheless affect the way the world is experienced and how players are regarded by others; this is often cued through reference to mythologically derived archetypes as well as through gameworld lore. Through a web of intertextual and intratextual signifiers, the game invites players to read the world and gameplay tasks as myth, and like myth these have allegorical and material dimensions. Although the mythological and magical/supernatural might be regarded as masking the game's technological underpinnings, I regard their primary importance as providing a symbolic language, constituting a sense for the player of being in a world, and providing a combination of otherness and familiarity for players, to "think about and through" (Kaveney 2005, 6). The mythological mode of creating a world and its concomitant meanings enables players, by virtue of drawing on archetypes, to live virtually in "once upon a time" and has a significant role in framing the conditions of play, beyond the programmed mechanics and rules. Having a material presence in this richly made fictional world alongside other players with whom we interact raises all kinds of questions of a philosophical nature about the relationship between fantasy and reality.

Notes

1. The precondition of reading or recognizing a thick text is that we accept that all texts are not only a product of the creative process, but also contain all the stages of that process within them like scars or vestigial organs (Kaveney 2005, 5).

2. See King and Krzywinska (2006) for more on the use of the quest format in video games.

3. "Mirror neurons" might go some way toward explaining in physiological terms why it is that we are able to identify or empathize with the actions of an onscreen avatar (as well as providing an explanation of human behavior, interpersonal interaction, and learning more generally). In watching another perform a certain action or experience a certain emotion, mirror neurons fire in much the same way as if we had performed that action or experienced that emotion ourselves—albeit in a somewhat weaker way, meaning we can potentially choose not to empathize with that action. For a fuller explanation, see V. S. Ramachandran's "Mirror Neurons and Imitation Learning as the

Driving Force Behind 'The Great Leap Forward' in Human Evolution," available at ⟨http://www.edge.org/3rd_culture/ramachandran/ ramachandran_p4.html⟩.

4. I argue in "Being a Determined Agent in *World of Warcraft*: Textual Practice, Play, and Identity" (Krzywinska, forthcoming a) that the mythologies, cosmological world-view, and concomitant iconographies that underpin the night elf race (as well as the tauren race, which is aligned in iconography and culture to Native North American culture) may well be designed to appeal to players attracted by so-called new age and pagan culture.

5. An abstract can be found at ⟨http://www.gamesconference.org/digra2005/viewabstract.php?id=139⟩.

6. From the highly variable viewpoints of formal narratology (Genette, Prince, Chatman), deconstruction, and experimental fiction, Jenkins's "spatial story" is a bit of a naive thematic construct; from the ludological perspective it is simply useless. Spatiality is an important factor in computer games, but that very fact makes architecture, choreography, sculpture, or even orienteering far more important to game scholars and designers than any travelogue or myth (Eskelinen 2004).

7. For extended discussion of "functional realism" in video games, see King and Krzywinska (2006).

8. Peons are the workers that in the real-time strategy context of the earlier *Warcraft* games are used by the player as builders and gatherers.

9. Caesar wrote that the Gauls are much given to human sacrifice and employ druids to do it. He went on to say, "Some of them use huge images of the gods, and fill their limbs, which are woven from wicker, with living people.... They believe that the gods are more pleased by such punishment when it is inflicted upon those who are caught engaged in theft or robbery or other crime" (1996, 127–128).

References

Benjamin, Walter. 2003. *The Origin of German Tragic Drama*. Translated by J. Osborne. London: Verso (Orig. pub. 1963).

Bolter, Jay David, and Richard Grusin. 2000. *Remediation: Understanding New Media*. Cambridge, MA: MIT Press.

Caesar, Julius. 1996. *The Gallic Wars*. Translated by C. Hammond. Oxford, UK: Oxford University Press. (Orig. pub. unknown.)

Campbell, Joseph. 1969. *The Hero with a Thousand Faces,* 2nd ed. Princeton, NJ: Princeton University Press.

Chatman, Seymour. 1978. *Story and Discourse: Narrative Structure in Fiction and Film*. New York: Cornell University Press.

Eskelinen, Markku. 2004. "Response to 'Games as Narrative Architecture.'" *Electronic Book Review*, September 1, 2004. Available at ⟨http://www.electronicbookreview.com/thread/firstperson/astragalian⟩.

Frazer, J. G. 1994. *The Golden Bough: Abridged*. Abridgement by Robert Fraser. Oxford: Oxford University Press. (Orig. pub. 1890.)

Genette, Gérard. 1980. *Narrative Discourse: An Essay in Method*. Translated by J. E. Lewin. Ithaca, NY: Cornell University Press. (Orig. pub. 1972.)

Kaveney, Roz. 2005. *From* Alien *to* The Matrix: *Reading Science Fiction Film*. London: I. B. Tauris.

King, Geoff, and Tanya Krzywinska. 2006. *Tomb Raiders and Space Invaders: Videogames Forms and Contexts*. London: I.B. Tauris.

Koster, Raph. 2005. *A Theory of Fun for Game Design*. Scottsdale, AZ: Paraglyph.

Krzywinska, Tanya. Forthcoming a. "Being a Determined Agent in (the) *World of Warcraft*: Textual Practice, Play and Identity." In *Videogame/Player/Text*, eds. Barry Atkins and Tanya Krzywinska. Manchester, UK: Manchester University Press.

Krzywinska, Tanya. Forthcoming b. "Arachne Challenges Minerva: The Spinning-Out of Long Narrative in *World of Warcraft* and Buffy the Vampire Slayer." In *Third Person*, eds. Noah Wardrip-Fruin and Pat Harrigan. Cambridge, MA: MIT Press.

Martin, G. R. R. 2001. "Introduction." In *Meditations on Middle-Earth*, ed. Karen Haber, 1–5. New York: St Martin's.

Mortensen, Torill Elvira. 2006 "'WoW is the New MUD': Social Gaming from Text to Video." *Games and Culture* 1, no. 4, 397–413.

Nietzsche, Friedrich. 1961. *Thus Spoke Zarathustra*. Harmondsworth: Penguin Books.

Parsler, Justin. 2006. "Understanding Agency." Essay written for Brunel University's MA Program Digital Games: Theory and Design.

Prince, Gerald. 1987. *A Dictionary of Narratology*. Lincoln: University of Nebraska Press.

Rank, Otto, Fitzroy R. S. Raglan, and Alan Dundes. 1990. *In Quest of the Hero*. Princeton, NJ: Princeton University Press.

Stern, Eddo. 2002. "A Touch of the Medieval: Narrative, Magic and Computer Technology in Massively Multiplayer Computer Role-Playing Games." In *Computer Games and Digital Cultures: Conference Proceedings*, ed. Frans Mayra, 257–276. Tampere, Finland: Tampere University Press.

Thomas, Doug. 2005. "2,443 Quenkers and Counting, or What in Us Really Wants to Grind? Examining the Grind in Star Wars Galaxies: An Empire Divided." Paper presented at Changing Views: Worlds in Play, Digital Games Research Association conference, Vancouver, Canada, June 16–20.

Wicker Man (The), directed by Robin Hardy. (1973, London: British Lion Film Corporation.)

7

What Makes *World of Warcraft* a World? A Note on Death and Dying

Lisbeth Klastrup

Which factors shape our experience of a gameworld and how do our expressions of these experiences, the stories we tell about them, reciprocally affect the living culture of this world? I have elsewhere argued that we need to begin to analyze particular and salient elements of gameworld experiences in order to better comprehend the relation between design choices, a specific gameworld culture, and the player's world experience (Klastrup 2003). If we want to understand a world like *World of Warcraft* in all its complexity, "death" is important as a pivotal design element and something that every player experiences several, if not many times during her time in a gameworld. In *World of Warcraft* (and many similar worlds), player characters do not disappear permanently when they die—they are resurrected shortly after death. Even though "death" is thus not a singular experience, nevertheless the reasons for dying and the accompanying penalty that, as part of the game mechanics, follows when a character dies, are generally the subject of heated discussions and many player stories—indicating that death is a feature which engages players. In this article, I seek to explore what the stories told about death and dying tell us about what behaviors and experiences in general matter to players in the world of *World of Warcraft*.[1] This is one approach to furthering the understanding of what makes *World of Warcraft* so unique and appealing a (game) world experience.

How to Study Death

In an online world such as *World of Warcraft*, characters in gameworlds die repeatedly, whereas the players playing them never (normally) die. The experience of "death" is thus not one of termination, though it may definitely cause a player grief. In most gameworlds, "dying" is an activity similar to a number of other repeatable activities that occur as part of the *everyday life* in the world and should also be studied in this context. Furthermore, since dying in an online world is a risk-free endeavor, it is subject to various forms of player testing that we would never attempt in "real life." Studying death therefore not only involves looking at how it concretely takes place, but also exploring the way players exploit this feature. Death and dying in a world like *World of Warcraft* can, as we will see, be playful and explorative, fun and entertaining, or merely be considered an unfortunate nuisance that obstructs the flow of playing the world as a game.

The study of the everyday "life with death" is here approached through a phenomenological perspective, situated within the framework of experience that the game *World of Warcraft* provides. This entails that my focus is on the *subjective* experience of death, as a player encounters it through his or her representation *in* the given world, the character. The stories told about the particular subjective experience with this character are significant objects of study, as they allow us a valuable insight into these experiences. Though the experience of the death of other characters and the experience of the death of players outside the gameworld are also narrativized and highly interesting to study, they do not tell us anything about the player's engagement with the world through her own character, and therefore lie beyond the scope of this study.[2]

In addition to observing practices and stories, I argue that a cultural study of death and dying in a world mediated and created by digital technology requires that "field work" includes a conscious exploration of the *experience design*: in this case how death is consciously staged and aestheticized (sensorially, interactively, emotionally)—to be, for instance, heroic, fun, or annoying—through the designers' choice of graphics, environmental staging, and through the design of the game system itself. As several studies have already shown, game design is never value free; game design in itself expresses values (see for instance Frasca 2001, Garite 2003, and Sicart 2006) and consequently also influences the nature of our experiences.

The experience and design of death in *World of Warcraft* is thus based on the author's self-observed death experiences in the world, supplemented by conversation with other players and guild members, and on a detailed analysis of how death and the punishment of death—the so-called "death penalty"—is implemented in the design of *World of Warcraft* as a game. Player stories about death and dying have been collected through the author's project survey at death-stories.org and supplemented by experiences described in various popular online fora on *World of Warcraft*, as well as by a study of player-created *World of Warcraft* machinima focusing on the subject of one's own character death.[3]

Designing for Death

If as a starting point we assume that all experience is subjective, it follows that game designers, or "experience designers," cannot design a specific experience that everybody using their system will have. They can, however, provide a framework of experience intended to provide a certain set of experiences (a game designed to be "fun" will hopefully not be experienced as "sad" by many players). Accordingly, gameworld designers cannot stage death in a way that guarantees a very specific experience of dying. But through their design, understood in a broad sense as comprising both game mechanics and aesthetics, they are able to *affect* people's experience of gameplay and death. In this way, they can teach players a lesson and exert a certain degree of social control, as T. L. Taylor also discusses in chapter 9.

From a game design perspective, the permanent destruction of a character the first time it dies is certainly an option and a possibility, but current MMOGs, including *World of Warcraft*, rarely employ it. It appears to be a de facto standard in most gameworlds that death happens at the point in time when a character runs out of "health points" (the quantitative measurement of life force), which as a rule, results in the character's removal from the place he or she died (most often the wilderness or a battleground). Since all characters inevitably run out of health points at some point during their life cycle, "death," therefore, not least to new players, serves as a punishment for not watching out for one's characters or for playing imprudently—for instance, taking a character into an area of the gameworld where the mobs are much stronger than the character can handle at its current level.

Thus from a general game design perspective the infliction of death can be seen as a way to teach players to handle the *game* aspect of the world in a more successful way—it is a method to force players to improve their play, whether they are playing the game alone or together with other players. In addition to the geographical displacement, dying is often punished by inflicting damage on the character's equipment or withdrawing a number of the character's experience points. The intended frustration is furthered by the player's experience of wasted time in general, as the player in many MMOGs, including *World of Warcraft*, has to spend some time reclaiming the dead character's body in order to continue playing. Furthermore, at the higher levels of the game, *World of Warcraft* players must spend both time and money to bring the character back to the state it was in before death ("buffed" by spells and in perfect armor). From these punishment strategies the concept of a "death penalty" has arisen. Death itself is not interesting; it is the punishment for dying that most often informs experience.

Before death as a concrete event is implemented as part of the gameworld mechanics, the game designers have to make some important decisions regarding both the short-term and long-term effects of death. In other words, they face the challenge of providing a form of death penalty severe enough that it results in a certain excitement, which forces players to take death seriously and play strategically to avoid it. On the other hand, they must not make it so harsh that players are scared away from the game at an early point in their gaming experience. As Rollings and Adams point out in their seminal book on game design, "death" is an essential game balance problem: "As with other games, character death must be accompanied by a disincentive of some kind, or players won't care if they die. The trick is to find a disincentive that is appropriately proportional to the likelihood of their dying—to put it in simpler terms, it's a balance problem" (2003, 525).

It appears that designers assume that death and its penalty will be considered an unpleasant aspect of playing, yet indispensable as part of the gaming experience, if designers want to enforce a more advanced engagement with the world and with the player's character.[4] Richard Bartle puts it bluntly in his book on virtual world design: "some of the more primitive and tedious aspects of the real world that players don't want to experience act, unfortunately, to set up some of the more advanced and enjoyable aspects that they do want to experience" (2003, 386).

The official FAQ on death in *World of Warcraft* on the worldofwarcraft.com Web site does indeed indicate that the designers of *World of Warcraft* align themselves with this perspective. It is clear from their argument that they consider a death penalty a necessity in the design of a balanced and ultimately challenging world: "One of the fundamental philosophies we have had throughout the development of World of Warcraft is to avoid overly frustrating elements used in other MMORPGs and make the game FUN. Of course, we realize that one cannot take this philosophy too far, since we also want players to respect the world, which is why things like falling damage, death penalties, and other elements exist. If players do not feel like they are overcoming obstacles, then the game does not feel rewarding enough."

Yet they also emphasize the aspect of fun, and the need not to frustrate players with overly serious death penalties. This might be done in the name of making a good game, but in a market situation where several MMOG producers are fighting for a share of the subscriber market, it is becoming increasingly important to make the experience of entering the world as successful as possible. Since *World of Warcraft* has also been created with the objective of attracting a new demographic of players who are not necessarily familiar with MMOG gameplay, a "soft" death penalty is likely to have been considered necessary to ease the new players into the more demanding levels of the game.

The Staging of Death in *World of Warcraft*

From a design perspective, various levels and variations of death need to be planned for in order to make the gameworld seem as contiguous and realistic as possible (this will be discussed in detail later). However, though dying can happen in a variety of settings and for a variety of reasons, death and the immediate consequences thereof are invariable. Thus, in *World of Warcraft*, the death experience is divided into several phases:

1. Dying (the player sees the character die and fall to the ground in third person perspective).
2. A red alert box appears, asking the player if she wants to resurrect the character.
3. The player is now provided with three options:

a. The player can wait for a member of her party or try to convince a character with healing skills to resurrect her on the spot (often at a cost).

b. The player can instantly click the button to "release your spirit" and the character wakes up ("respawns") in a nearby graveyard in ghost mode (the character is now transparent and the world is gray). As a rule, the character cannot interact with objects in the world while dead. The graveyard replaces what is in other worlds referred to as a "bindstone," a specific place in the world designated for resurrection. Graveyards and resurrection spots are normally placed in a safe area—for instance, close to a city.

c. The player can wait for six minutes, after which the character is automatically moved to the nearest graveyard, still dead.

If the player chooses b) or c), she again has three options:

1. The player can run back to where she died and retrieve the corpse of the character by clicking on it (the so-called corpse run).

2. The player can ask the "spirit healer" (an angel-like figure) in the graveyard to bring her back to life on the spot, at the cost of 25 percent damage to her equipment as well as resurrection sickness. Resurrection sickness reduces character attributes and damage dealt by 75 percent for a number of minutes, depending on level. From level 20 and upward, a character suffers for ten minutes.

3. The player can still be resurrected by a healer character.

The player's choices in the death situation can be considered a trade-off, depending on in which context the character dies. If the player has time and is "soloing," she is likely to choose the corpse run. If she is pressed for time, or has died in a place difficult to return to, she might be forced to choose the more expensive solution, the spirit healing. The additional possibility of being healed by a fellow player with healing abilities is a good example of the way in which design choices also inform social behavior; especially in instances, characters with resurrection abilities are almost indispensable even if they are easier to kill, and therefore players are forced to put together groups consisting of characters with different abilities, both fighters and healers. Finally, it is interesting to note that this implementation of death pretty much follows the death style of other MMOGs in the fantasy genre. These similarities seem to indicate that even though 3D-MMOGs are relatively new as a game form (if we count *Ultima Online* as the first modern MMOG, they came into being less than ten years ago), already certain generic conventions for death exist. As an

Figure 7.1
In between worlds—if the character tries to interact with an object in the world, the game system tells it "you are dead." This screenshot shows *World of Warcraft* being played with a third party user interface that has been modified by parties other than Blizzard Entertainment.

example, the spirit healer in the graveyard is *World of Warcraft*'s variation on the often-present NPC that, at a cost, will resurrect the player. *World of Warcraft*'s ghost state is however an original design element, though they might have been inspired by *Ultima Online* to a certain degree.[5]

The Ghost-World State as Penalty and Rite of Passage

One of my first and most memorable experiences in *World of Warcraft* was the first time I entered the ghost state. The experience of being set apart from the colorful happy "newbie" world of *World of Warcraft*, coupled with the eerie soundscape and the ghost-inspired aesthetics, left me in no doubt that I was dead.

Van Gennep, in his famous study of the "rites of passage" of different cultures, introduced the concept of the "liminal phase." The rites of passage are phases of social change members of a particular culture experience at important points in their life (from child to man, marriage, birth, death, and the like). Van Gennep divides them into three phases: separation, transition, and incorporation. In the case of death, in most cultures the rite of passage includes a separation of the dead person from the living, a transition from the world of the living to the world of the dead (for instance, crossing the river Styx), and finally incorporation into the world of the dead. In general, the rites of passage denote a period of transition from one phase of life (or death) to another, during which "Whoever passes from one to the other finds himself physically and magically-religiously in a special situation for a certain length of time: he wavers between two worlds" (Van Gennep 1969, 18). That is, the transition includes a period of "bracketing," where the person involved is placed outside the regular activities and space of society. The ghost state, or the period during which the character suffers from resurrection sickness in *World of Warcraft*, can be considered as such a transitional phase. However, in *World of Warcraft*, the ghost is luckily reintegrated into the world of the living, not the world of the dead. But I argue that ultimately the punishment and death experience lie not in death itself and the staging of it, but in the experience that follows, the experience of being separated from the world of gaming, of wavering between worlds and losing precious time while the player is a ghost. During this temporary removal from the world of the game, players cannot interact with anything or anybody in the world—and every minute they spend running back to their body is time taken from the world of gaming. Once back in the world, suffering from resurrection sickness provides much of the same experience. From a game design perspective, the ghost part of the death experience is not strictly necessary, but by briefly placing characters outside the game itself with no possibility for powerful action within the world, players are reminded that the world might close itself to them.

The Dynamics of Death Design

In many worlds, death penalties are adjusted over time. *World of Warcraft* notably has not changed their death penalty in any significant way since its launch in 2005. However, the designers seem to recognize a need for improvement in or change of the death experience. Thus, as an April Fool's joke in late March 2006, the developers announced the addition of a new playable race to the world, the wisp race (wisps are dead night elves). This race was remarkable in many ways, especially for its ability to detonate itself and thereby kill itself permanently, also taking down all bystanders in the explosion. Players quickly got the joke, though, and apparently the introduction of a permadeath character was one of the things that immediately caused suspicion.[6]

Perhaps also as an attempt to provide a new experience of dying, the *Burning Crusade* expansion introduced the possibility of dying by falling into the abyss from the edge of the Outland Territory. If a character goes over the edge, a long free fall follows. Then the normal death procedure ensues and the character ideally respawns at a graveyard somewhere in the Outland.

The Aesthetics of Death

Visual aesthetics are another important design element in *World of Warcraft* and the visual aesthetics of death are indeed omnipresent: each major town or battlefield has a graveyard nearby where characters respawn, and on journeys through the continents the player constantly encounters the corpses or skeletons of other characters. They also encounter NPCs in the form of, for instance, skeletons, or zombies. Occasionally the player will come across dead people adorning the landscape just for decorative purposes, such as the dead people in the gallows at Dalaran, or go on a quest that ends up in a graveyard or pays homage to a dead in-game character, such as the quest "Until Death Do Us Part." In this quest the player is asked to place a pendant on the grave of a departed beloved. When the pendant is placed and the quest thus completed, the grave opens and the character is allowed to read the epitaph on the grave.

Death Aesthetics as Reminders of Mortality

The existence of death as part of gameworld life is enforced by the way designers have chosen to implement and visualize death throughout the world—ways that continuously make the players aware of its presence. In *World of Warcraft*, the corpses of dead player characters are first visible as normal bodies, but they then quickly decompose into skeletons and bones. When players walk or run past the corpses of other characters, they are constantly reminded that other players also die and will die: death happens to everybody. The visibility of corpses can partly be attributed to the game mechanics (healer characters need to see corpses in order to resurrect them), but I believe that any player who has made their way through a world strewn with corpses would agree that these corpses, which often belong to players the player has no group relation with, also convey the concept and existence of mortality.[7]

The gothic aesthetics of death as it is implemented in the world thus serves a function in and of itself: there is more to the *World of Warcraft* than just gaming it.

Death Aesthetics and Mythical Narratives

What is the purpose of this aesthetization of death? It reminds the player of the mortality entangled with life in *World of Warcraft*, but in addition the visual aesthetic itself functions as storytelling. The corpses found at specific places in the world will tell us a tale of great battles recently fought at the site, or of characters struggling to complete a difficult quest (see, for instance, figure 7.2). The specific ways in which death has been visualized in the world therefore help us tell stories about what may have happened and will happen to us if we undertake certain difficult tasks; this creates a shared feeling of existing in a world where the border between life and death is fairly fluid.

Figure 7.2
The *champs de mort* after a battle between the Horde and the Alliance outside the desert city the Crossroads. Pictures posted to the official screenshot forums indicate that some players might even consider themselves war photographers. This screenshot shows *World of Warcraft* being played with a third party user interface that has been modified by parties other than Blizzard Entertainment.

Death, one might argue, is also part of the potential narrative architecture of the world, the myths that help enforce our experience of worldness, which Tanya Krzywinska discusses in detail in chapter 6.

Death Aesthetics and the Undead

In many settings, the death aesthetics in *World of Warcraft* have an overtly gothic style. The gothic flavor applies not only to the landscaping of *World of Warcraft*, but is also manifest in the design of characters, both player characters and NPCs. There is a particularly close link between the gothic dead aesthetics and the undead race (a humanoid variation of undead people also known as "The Forsaken," available to players on the Horde side). When choosing the look of an undead character, the player can go for a decidedly undead look, with hollow eye sockets and visible cranium (see figure 7.3). The death theme is emphasized further, as the undead character enters the world from a graveyard and is "born" inside a Draconian crypt. The first

Figure 7.3
The character selection and world entry screen for the undead characters presents them in an unmistakablly gothic graveyard setting.

levels are spent in an area replete with forlorn graveyards, graves, and zombies. The undead are also the only race given the option to replete their energy level ("health") by "cannibalizing" (eating) dead corpses. We only see the character making eating movements with its hands, but can clearly hear loud eating noises. Thus morbidity in *World of Warcraft* can be stretched to its very limits for those players who do not mind living life in the constant and near presence of death.

Living with Death

In the previous sections I have explored the ways death and dying are staged through the choices the designers have made in terms of the game mechanics, as well as the visual aesthetics and world population. From a perspective within the framework of experience this design offers, what do players think of death in *World of Warcraft* and which stories do they tell about dying?

Living with the World Design

Players might grudgingly accept death, but they are certainly not always happy about it. In an early "topic of the week" discussion of the death penalty in the *World of Warcraft Vault* forum (wowvault.ign.com), the player ChrisyTina expresses her frustration at what she sees as an unnecessary impediment to her gaming experience: "While I have respect for the risk vs. reward concept in a game like this, I also want for there to be as little dissatisfaction from my gaming experience as possible. The more and more I play MMOs, the more and more I don't understand why I *need* to suffer such penalties and restrictions where the result is nothing but lost time and ultimately being frustrated. It is just a game after all" (accessed February 28, 2007).

Other players, though, accept the death penalty as an inevitable and integrated part of the gaming experience. A young respondent in the death-stories.org survey puts it very simply: "Everything dies. Accept your failure" (S25, M, 10–15). However, even if *World of Warcraft* has the reputation of having a very soft death penalty, the survey indicates that *World of Warcraft* players do not agree on whether death is trivial or not. One respondent addressed the issue quite angrily: "I'm writing because I am certain that this is a typical 'death experience' in World of Warcraft—99.999 percent of deaths are utterly unremarkable. This death story is therefore typical. The other death stories you receive will most likely be atypical. Do not attempt to generalize from these 'death stories' to create any sort of academic paper. They're edge-case nonsense that doesn't reflect the simple fact that there's no story here—for the typical player, it's just a game and character death is a non-event" (S38, M, 26–30).

It should be noted that this player's comment must be seen in relation to the fact that he focuses on battleground deaths. On the battlegrounds, death has no penalty and it is followed by immediate resurrection somewhere on the battleground itself, much as in traditional first-person shooter games, where death lasts no longer than the blink of an eye.

However, in the death-stories.org survey players repeatedly emphasize that whether death is experienced as trivial or nontrivial depends on the context. It appears there is a marked difference between death experienced in relation to group play (death as part of a joint battle) and death during solo play (death as, for instance, the result of explorative mistakes). This supports one of the arguments that T. L. Taylor makes in her discussion of the study of online worlds in chapter 9—that as researchers we need to always make close studies of what actually happens on a particular server in a world in order to realistically understand "culture." When it comes to understanding dying as a cultural experience, we might need to zoom in even closer, and compare differences between death in battlegrounds, instances, and the general wilderness of the world. Additionally, we might need to distinguish between solo death and group death. That the issue of death is indeed complicated is suggested by another (older) female player, who notes, "Generally I believe it [death] bothers players a lot more than they let on" (S15, F, 46–50).

If we approach the experience of death from a contextual point of view, what forms of death does the player actually experience?

Death Experiences and the Exploitation of Death

On a general level, it seems important to make a distinction between two forms of in-game deaths. The first is combat death—that is, the result of a lost battle against other characters (also known as PvP, or player versus player) or NPCs (in the shape of either humans or mobs). The second is natural death, such as when the character falls from the top of a cliff and loses all her health points when she hits the ground, or when the character dies from fatigue when swimming, or lack of air when diving (the latter form of dying falls into the category often referred to as "Player versus Environment" play, which includes encounters with NPCs). Both combat deaths and natural deaths can be chosen consciously or happen by accident; players might choose to commit suicide, either in battle or in nature, as a way of getting quickly out of an area or in order to explore the landscape in which they are moving in ghost form.

That one can use the ghost form to explore an area without risking being killed is an example of how in-game death can be an expression of strategic play—a strategy to explore and stretch the borders of a game ("how far can I fall before I die?") and a way to skillfully exploit possibilities in death that the designers did not necessarily foresee. In the survey, a Chinese *World of Warcraft* player lists four ways she can die in the world, and comments on the fourth: "Fourthly, that's me myself who look for the death! I would like to suicide just to obtain one precious object. In *WoW*, in Tanaris (one game zone in Kalimdor Island), if I swim far far away to the center of the sea, I'll be dead of tiredness, but at the same time I can find a precious blue weapon profondly under the ses. So to get it, i must suicide myself" (S41, F, 26–30—quote unedited).

At its most extreme, in solo play a player can willingly engage in a lengthy death loop (dying just to be immediately killed again by an NPC) as a way to gradually move her body out of a dungeon that the player has ventured into to fulfill a quest or get a valuable object. This is a strategy that might work well when playing a character whose level is too low to game that particular dungeon.

Death and the Body

An interesting difference between the experience of combat death and natural death seems to be that players are more emotionally affected by those forms of natural death that are closest to a death one could imagine happening in real life. I personally hate drowning, which happens when a character's air ratio runs out before it can make it to the surface of the sea, and informal inquiries amongst fellow players confirm that they feel the same way.

This might indicate that when death becomes a bodily experience the player can relate to, or easily imagine, it has a stronger impact on the player than when the player experiences a form of death she cannot relate to (very few of us have ever engaged in man-to-man combat). However, from a designer's perspective, the strong focus on the body in the staging of death can be seen as an attempt to create a stronger identification with the death experience; in principle, we do not need to see the body fall to the ground and to hear the "cry of death" (all characters briefly wail at the moment of death) when we die in combat. Designers therefore seem to consciously try to cue players into some form of bodily identification with the death of their character. There is no natural reason why we should see our own body in third-person perspective just when the character dies if we are playing in first-person perspective.

It is interesting that stories about "natural" death rarely seem to be told by players, apart from those stories that depict extreme attempts to conquer nature. Perhaps one reason is that death in nature is sometimes caused by downright stupid behavior or embarrassing mistakes that the players do not want to share with others, such as falling off a bridge because the character tries to run too quickly across it, or falling off a mountainside because the player miscalculated its steps. Stories about successful or "fun" death are probably more likely to be circulated in public fora. However, the anonymity offered players in the Death-stories Survey has been an attempt to encourage players to tell also the less amusing and painful stories about death, and a few embarrassing stories have in fact been submitted.

Death and Sociality

The stories I have studied seem to indicate that most stories told about dying are stories in which other players are somehow involved. A Death-story Survey respondent relates and reflects: "I have found that I take the PvP deaths outside of battlegrounds much more personally than PvE deaths or deaths in WSG [Warsong Gulch; a battleground]. My first experience was having gotten flagged PVP during a raid outside of Tarren Mills. I was running back to town and was spotted by two much higher level characters. I was killed after a brief melee and then corpse camped. I was still very new to *WoW* and found the experience quite frustrating because there was no element of a fair fight. In addition, at that time I couldn't see any way out of the situation. Eventually I just sat until my PvP flag ended (S14, F, 36–40).

Her experience of PvP death as being the most "personal" may be due to the fact that it is much more difficult to foresee the end of PvP play, whereas the outcomes of encounters with NPCs are to a certain degree foreseeable. Player combat, especially in Horde against Alliance fights, involves not only death, but corpse camping and persecution, until the player finally escapes to a safe area or logs off. Death in this case might be experienced with a high degree of annoyance; it matters that the player's character is killed not just by the game system, but by another player.[8] The emotional experience of death in this case is different than that of the experience of death in nature. Where natural death might upset the player because of the bodily identification with the experience of death, death due to PvP combat upsets a player for social reasons or because it puts the player in a situation where she is completely disempowered.

In the survey, another player recounts one of her first PvP experiences and sees it as defining her general focus in the world experience. As a new player, she was attacked and mocked by a group of Horde players, but got help from the high-level character that had introduced her to the game:

I died. I felt awful; that I must be horrible playing this game. My friend assured me this is not normal. He then took control of the computer and with several messages into the general chat I suddenly had 5 level 60s surrounding me as they hunted the horde down. I stood back in satisfaction as I watched the horde try to flee from the wrath of Epic Alliance. . . .

Sweet, sweet vengeance. It is because of this experience at the beginning of the game that I now go out of my way to kill horde for honour. Currently 2400 kills of the enemy at level 20. *That one death at the start changed my whole playing experience* from Player versus Environment to Player Vs Player (S 26, F, 21–25, my emphasis).

This story demonstrates that experiences of unfair deaths caused by other players can also lead to follow-up stories about group vengeance. In this case, it is particularly interesting that the penalty for causing death is carried out by players themselves.

The Social Death Penalty

If death is caused by players within a player's own community or group, the death penalty can indirectly be carried out by players themselves and take the form of social separation. When a character, by dying or by blundering in a group combat situation, causes the death of others (in cases where the entire group is killed, this is referred to as a "wipe"), this might lead to a temporary or even long-term isolation from the group or from desirable guilds in the world:

Unsuccessful playing will result in not being able to group with the better players which will do the harder better parts of the game and succeed. It is a good enough punishment not to be able to experience the good stuff in the game (S 16, M, 21–25).

Well, the group you're with can get really angry with you if you die or bring upon the death of someone else. They can treat you poorly during the rest of the instance, or they may even kick you out for being stupid (S 16, F, 16–20).

In this case, the player character who has been isolated will have to explicitly make amends with the rest of the group, perhaps paying for other characters' armor repair. In general, if the blunder was of a more serious nature, he or she will have to work hard to earn the trust of the group or the guild—in other words, earn the right to be reincorporated into the community of players. An experienced player told me that another form of social punishment is simply to let a player die though she could have been saved by the group: in this way, the player is punished for not adhering to group dynamics and playing strategies.

A Brief Typology of the Stories about Death

Which stories do players generally tell about death and dying? Combining analyses of the stories submitted to the death-stories.org survey, a study of stories currently (as of late 2006) available on the *World of Warcraft Movie* site (warcraftmovies.com), and the videos on the Web site YouTube reveals that stories dealing with one's own character's death (or the death of a party) fall into several categories:

- stories about successful group play (a player sacrifices her own character, or watches other players finalize a raid successfully after she died in initial combat)
- stories about unexpected death (humorous deaths, or surprising deaths, such as when a player is unexpectedly killed by a mob after having successfully killed several others)
- stories about death caused by a technical glitch (such as server breakdown or overload)
- stories about revenge after death (such as the story by S 26)
- stories about corpse camping (frustration and disempowerment)
- stories about death as a lesson (the result of unsuccessful group play or personal blunders)
- stories about challenging death (extreme sport activities that might cause death).[9]

A closer study of these stories reveal that though the theme varies, they can be divided roughly into three basic categories: stories about heroes, stories about fools, and stories about the accidental nature of life in the gameworld. In order to examine more closely the relationship between death and sociality, I will briefly look at the stories about heroes and fools.

One of the opportunities that life in a virtual fantasy world (still) offers a player is the opportunity to make the character a hero and protagonist in a hero story, even if just for a moment. As a character gains levels, and corpse runs and death penalties start to cost the player more wasted time, self-chosen death can be glorious, a way to show dedication to the group (typically the guild) to which the character belongs, or a means of demonstrating that the player is a courageous and bold player. In his book on *Heroes, Villains and Fools*, sociologist Orrin E. Klapp enumerates five different types of heroes: the winners, the splendid performers, the heroes of social acceptability, the independent spirits, and the group servants (1962). If we apply this typology to the heroes of the *World of Warcraft* player stories, these gameworld heroes seem to mostly fall into either the first or last categories. They can either be cast as "winners" who, through a combination of strength and skills, are able to slay dangerous mobs, or as "group servants" who are willing to offer their lives in order to save the group of which they are part.

The combination of the players' codependence in big raids or battles (where dozens of players need to fight together to slay elite monsters or characters of another realm or faction) and premass destruction war culture seems conducive to the creation of heroes.[10] In the battles of the *World of Warcraft*, it is still possible to appear as the heroes of the wars of olden, golden times when valorous man-to-man combat was still an essential part of the war experience. Some players' attitude to death in fights intriguingly resonates with some of the ideals of glorious death that could, for instance, be found in the early writings about World War I, during which it was still considered heroic "to die young, clean, ardent; to die swiftly, in perfect health; to die saving others from death..." (Vachel cited in Cannadine 1981, 236).

A salient example of a hero story of this nature can be seen in the machinima movie *My Life for the Horde*, a staged story that types the main character as a hero who is both an independent spirit (setting out to kill a boss monster in only the company of a faithful friend) and a hero willing to give his life to serve the group, in this case "his people," the Horde. Several other player stories emphasize this aspect of sacrifice, such as in the story a respondent relates about the sacrifice of his hunter character in a dragon decoy.

Stories about fools, such as players who caused the death of a group, can likewise be found in many variations. This story by a survey respondent is quite typical:

One day, we were heading to an instance called Black Fathom Depths. In order to get into the instance itself, we had to fight our way through tunnels, killing naga and satyrs. Anyway, we were fighting our way through, and our tank all of a sudden rushes off, aggroing about 10 of these creeps. We could barely take 4 at a time. What we didn't realize was that our tank had rushed off into the instance entrance—a place where the creeps couldn't follow. However, he never informed us that the entrance was just around the corner. The creeps' aggro then turned on us, and I, being a warlock and a cloth class, died very quickly. These 10 creeps then quickly killed our druid and our pally. Our tank, the warrior, survived when he was the one who caused all the problems to begin with. Needless to say, we were all very angry with him.

This story has become a famous story in our group of 4. We will never let our warrior forget his stupidity (S17, F, 16–20).

One particular story about a very special fool has made its way into the shared lore of *World of Warcraft*. It is a player-made film of a guild raid involving a player referred to as Leeroy Jenkins. As the story goes, Leeroy is AFK (away from keyboard) while the group plans a raid, and when he returns to the screen, he simply charges into the dungeon. The other members follow and the entire group is wiped out.[11] It is still debated whether Leeroy's famous last words were "at least I have chicken" (he was out for chicken) or "at least I ain't chicken" (at least he is not a coward).

Leeroy Jenkins has since got his own Wikipedia page, his own card in the *World of Warcraft* card series, and "pulling a leeroy" (charging blindly into a fight, causing mobs to attack the entire group and kill it) has become a term used to describe this particular kind of foolishness, as this survey story demonstrates:

We had been progressing steadily through the instance, communicating constantly on Teamspeak, when one of our number *pulled a Leeroy*—that is to say, suddenly ran off on his own and engaged a number of monsters in another room, without mentioning it to anyone else.... We cursed, and complained, and berated the player responsible over Teamspeak, however this has become an enduring lesson for the group—that player has never repeated his actions, and we're all a lot more careful about wandering off on our own. And we still joke about it from time to time ;-) (S27, M, 31–35, author's emphasis).

The wipe caused by Leeroy Jenkins is an outstanding example of a fool story that teaches players how *not* to behave. It also demonstrates how specific fools can become part of the popular culture of a world, enforcing stereotypical group behavior in both positive and negative ways.

Why Dying Matters in *World of Warcraft*

In instance runs in WoW it is very important not to die because your group is depending on you to do a job as a member of the group. If you're the healer and you die then no one else will get healed anymore and the whole group will die. However, when you are running around by yourself questing and leveling skills, I think character death is much more acceptable because you're learning, making mistakes and progressing (S29, M, 21–25).

In this article, I have examined how a concrete gameworld feature at a given point in time informs the world experience and the appropriation of the culture of *World of Warcraft*. Do my studies indicate that players want this feature, "death," to be different? If we take the responses in the Death-Stories Survey as an indication, a majority of players seem to agree that the death penalty in *World of Warcraft* works well, and the fact that the designers have not found it necessary to change the death penalty in any significant way since *World of Warcraft's* 2004 launch seems to support this observation. It appears that the social penalty for dying at the wrong time or for causing the deaths of others makes up for what some consider a relatively soft death penalty.

This exploration of the design, aesthetics, and postfacto stories about dying in *World of Warcraft* has revealed that multiple character deaths are experienced as an intrinsic part of the gameworld experience, and that "death" is considered as both trivial and nontrivial depending on the context. A lesson learned from this project is to always study a particular gameworld feature in a variety of contexts. Thus we have seen that when death is nontrivial, it can lead to both humiliating as well as heroic undertakings.

The visual aesthetics of death, encountered in landscaping, characters, and NPCs, serve as a constant reminder that death and life are intrinsically interwoven, and that death is part of life in *World of Warcraft*. The temporary liminal existence that the death penalty forces the player into, as well as the humiliation that dying might cause in a social context, is a penalty that teaches the player to play better—when to be prudent and when to be brave. In addition, the way designers have implemented the death penalty—its opening up to various forms of strategic exploitations such as a handy removal from the battleground, the relative immunity of the ghost character, or strategic respawning on battlegrounds etc—teaches us that death, perhaps contrary to design intentions, need not always be an impediment, but can actually turn out to be an advantage or a way to exploit the world in entertaining ways.[12]

The Function of *World of Warcraft* Death Stories

In a discussion of the function of social types, Orrin Klapp states that the general function of the hero is "to stimulate people to do better" (1962, ix). According to Klapp, "social typing"—the casting of other people or oneself in the role of heroes, fools, or villains—is needed "in a mobile society where status is insecure, identities are uncertain, and people do not know each other well," because social typing "provides us with a convenient precis of the one with whom we wish to deal" (1962, 4). Klapp's description of the need for social typing seems oddly fitting for online worlds. Much like the stories that anthropologists have studied in small hunter societies (see, for instance, Bruner 1986), the heroic or foolish approach to life with "the tribe," as it is indirectly and directly enforced by, for instance, death stories, may serve as a guide to new players, teaching them to be better players and gamers by teaching them "collective values" as well as "socially necessary sentiments" (Klapp 1971, 18). Thus, the stories, aesthetics, and language referring to death help create the social player and teach her how to perform her character successfully in interaction with other players.

In order to understand the nature of gameworld experience, we need to explore the interplay between design, meaning-making, and culturalization. In this study, this endeavor has included exploring what aspects of death and dying designers and players emphasize and determining which death events are, ex post facto, considered "tellable" stories and which are not. The analysis has aimed to demonstrate that the function of death and death stories within the culture of a gameworld like *World of Warcraft* is to create and share a variety of experiences including both solo play and group play. The stories about these experiences help form the experience of the world as a social site by enforcing certain social practices. Thus gameworld death, just like death in real life, has the power to "either galvanize or corrode social systems and to either stimulate or neutralize the social participation of their members," as sociologist Michael C. Kearl argues in his book on the sociology of death in modern society (1989, 9).

Studying the experience of death and the death penalty should therefore be a pivotal element, not only in the design of game mechanics, but also in the social and visual design and analysis of worlds like *World of Warcraft*.

Notes

1. It is important to make a distinction between behavior and experience here. Experience is an active and reflective engagement with something that has happened; behavior is what you do in a concrete situation. The anthropologist Edward Bruner phrases it aptly: "An experience is more personal, as it refers to an active self, to a human being who not only engages in but shapes an action.... It is not customary to say, 'Let me tell you about my behaviour'; rather, we tell about experiences, which include not only actions and feelings but also reflections about those actions and feelings" (1986, 5). Experience is what we tell stories about.

2. However, it should be noted that death in the outside world sometimes interferes with the gameworld. In-game wakes are reported to have been held to commemorate dead players, or victims of disasters.

3. The death-stories.org survey collects basic demographic data about the players' gender, age, and country. It asks which MMOGs the players play (a drop-down list of the most popular MMOGs in 2006 is provided, but players might add other worlds.) Having provided this basic data, players are asked to submit a death story. It is emphasized in the introduction to the survey that it can be any kind of story: "Tell or retell your story about the character death experience which has affected or annoyed you the most, the grind of everyday gameworld death, the death experience that has become part of your community lore, the unremarkable deaths that you have already forgotten." After having submitted their story, players can then voluntarily comment on more general aspects of death in MMOGs, such as whether they consider it trivial or not, and whether death should have long-term repercussions. At the time of writing (February 2007), 43 players have responded (the survey is still open). Of the submitted stories, 26 take place in *World of Warcraft*. To preserve anonymity, responses quoted in this article are referred to by their submission number (Sx), gender of respondent (M/F) and the age range in which the respondent has placed him or herself (for example, S25, M (male), 10–15 (age range 10–15).

4. In relation to character engagement, it should be noted that the care for one's character is much more developed in game genres focusing on continuous character advancement, such as role-playing games (where information about character level and character stats are saved in between gaming sessions). "Character" does, for instance, not really matter in games of the first-person shooter genre, where characters are largely iconic and have no personal characteristics.

5. In *Ultima Online*, the character turns into a ghostly gray presence when it dies, also in the inventory window. It remains a ghostly figure until it is resurrected or the corpse retrieved.

6. In a discussion of the new wisp race at the Quarter to Three forum, a player wrote: "Actually for a second I did think it was real and think 'Oh god, not MORE elfiness.' Then I saw 'Permanent death' and knew it was fake. Whew." Available at ⟨http://www.quartertothree.com/game-talk/archive/index.php?t-25332.html⟩.

7. This feature does also provide the player with some rather absurd experiences, such as being able to make a newly resurrected character look at its own decaying corpse!

8. The potential for humiliation by another player is even more emphasised in duels, when the player character automatically falls to her knees to beg for mercy when she is defeated.

9. These stories are exemplified by movies about the Teldrassil death slide, where the player has to slide down a very long and very steep mountainside without dying, or the gnome death race, where a group of level 1 gnomes compete against each other in a race from the city of Ironforge (Horde territory) to the City of Stormwind (Alliance territory). The gnome who survives the race without dying wins. However, the race stories primarily focus on the various ways in which the gnomes die.

10. For a further discussion of the preworld war aesthetics and content in *World of Warcraft*, see chapter 2.

11. The Leeroy Jenkins raid was apparently not very well planned in general, but rumor has it that entire thing was staged, and was in reality a very sophisticated guild commercial.

12. The research for this article is in itself an example of how death can be entertaining. To test death in the Outlands, a small group of Truants players, the author included, had much fun throwing themselves from the edge in a number of variations.

References

Bartle, Richard. 2003. *Designing Virtual Worlds*. Indianapolis: New Riders.

Bruner, Edward M. 1986. "Experience and Its Expressions." In *The Anthropology of Experience*, ed. Victor W. Turner and Edward M. Bruner, 3–32. Urbana: University of Illinois Press.

Cannadine, David. 1981. "War and Death, Grief and Mourning in Modern Britain." In *Mirrors of Mortality: Studies in the Social History of Death*, ed J. Whaley 187–241. New York: St. Martin's Press.

Frasca, Gonzalo. 2001. "The Sims: Grandmothers are Cooler than Trolls." *Gamestudies.org*, 1, no. 2. Available at ⟨http://www.gamestudies.org/0101/frasca⟩.

Garite, Matt. 2003. "The Ideology of Interactivity (or Video Games and Taylorization of Leisure)." In *Digital Games Research Conference 2003*, ed. Marinka Copier and Joost Faessens, CD-ROM. Utrecht: Utrecht University.

Kearl, Michael. 1989. *Endings: A Sociology of Death and Dying*. New York: Oxford University Press.

Klapp, Orrin. 1962. *Heroes, Villains, and Fools: The Changing American Character*. Upper Saddle River, NJ: Prentice-Hall.

Klapp, Orrin E. 1971. "Heroes, Villains and Fools, as Agents of Social Control." In *Social Types: Process, Structure and Ethos*, 12–18. San Diego: Aegis Publishing Company.

Klastrup, Lisbeth. 2003. *Towards a Poetics of Virtual Worlds—Multi-User Textuality and the Emergence of Story*. PhD thesis. Copenhagen: IT University of Copenhagen.

My Life for the Horde. Machinima by BannermanProductions.com. Available at ⟨http://www.warcraftmovies.com/movieview.php?id=9508⟩.

Rollings, Andrew and Ernest Adams. 2003. *On Game Design*. Indianapolis: New Riders.

Sicart, Miguel. 2006. *Computer Games, Players, Ethics*. PhD dissertation, IT University of Copenhagen.

Van Gennep, Arnold. 1969. *The Rites of Passage*. Chicago: University of Chicago Press.

Quests in *World of Warcraft*: Deferral and Repetition

8

Jill Walker Rettberg

One of the first things you will see in Azeroth is a quest-giver: a nonplayer character with a bright yellow exclamation mark above his or her head. Right-click on a quest-giver, and a tiny story will appear in a window on your screen, such as this one from Marshal McBride, one of the first characters you see if you play a human: "Hey, citizen! You look like a stout one. We guards are spread a little thin out here, and I could use your help...." The quest-giver will give you a brief background story and a request for help, all contained in the same window on your screen: "Your first task is one of cleansing, Esmerita. A clan of kobolds have infested the woods to the north. Go there and fight the kobold vermin you find. Reduce their numbers so that we may one day drive them from Northshire." This is the in-character version of the quest, the version within the fictional world. Below it you can read a brief summary that one might imagine is narrated by the game interface or a narrator standing outside of the fiction: "Quest Objectives: Kill 10 Kobold Vermin, then return to Marshal McBride." Next, the rewards for the quest are specified: "Rewards: You will receive: 25 copper," and finally, at the very bottom of the quest window, two buttons provide you with a choice: Decline or Accept? If you accept the quest, you go and do what you have been asked to do and, if you succeed, return to receive your reward.

Quests in games are tasks that the player is asked to perform, and are one of the ways in which gameplay is structured in *World of Warcraft*. Many games contain quests, and quests come in many varieties, from the compact missions of *Grand Theft Auto* to the lengthy puzzles and riddles of interactive fiction[1] or adventure games. Different games and different genres have different kinds of quests. I propose that studying the structure and dominant patterns of quests in a game gives us access to some of the basic patterns of the game itself.

This reading of *World of Warcraft* is centered on the ways in which its quests work. I find that the quests and thus the game are characterized by two complementary rhetorical figures: deferral and repetition.

Reading Quests

A rhetorical figure or scheme is "a departure from standard usage" that is "not primarily in the meaning of the words, but in the syntactical order or pattern of the words" (Abrams 1993). Examples of rhetorical figures are repetition of words or phrases, alliteration, rhythm and rhyme, or inversions of an everyday word order. The *trope* is a counterpart to the rhetorical figure and its syntactical patterns: a nonliteral use of language that plays with semantics instead of syntax. Tropes deal with meaning, not with word order. If I call my love a rose, I use a metaphor, a comparison of my love to a rose. This is a semantic move (I combine the meanings of "rose" and of "my love"), and thus it is a trope. If I call my love a red, red rose, I add repetition to the metaphor by repeating the word "red." Repetition plays with syntax, and so is a figure, not a trope.

Quests in *World of Warcraft* have a very clear syntax. The basic parts of a quest do not vary: quest-giver, background story, objectives, rewards. Occasionally the quest-giver is replaced by an object (a treasure map found on a dead monster; when you click it it starts a quest), but even in these cases the quest itself plays out in the same manner, showing if anything that the role of the quest-giver is singularly inanimate. The player's role is likewise very fixed: you can accept or decline a quest, you can complete it or discard it. Objectives do vary, but most quests pose the same basic objectives of traveling, killing, and collecting (Walker 2006). This limited syntax means that certain patterns appear in the course of questing. These patterns are what this chapter is about.

Previous genres of computer games and other digital artifacts have also been found to be characterized by particular rhetorical figures. In his reading of the classic hypertext fiction *afternoon, a story* (Joyce 1990), Espen Aarseth proposes linking and jumping as the "master figure" of hypertext. Further, he sees hypertext fiction's main tropes as *aporia* and *epiphany*. In rhetorics, an aporia is the expression of doubt. In hypertext fiction, or at least in *afternoon*, Aarseth argues that doubt is an integral part of the reading experience. The reader is only given parts of the story in each node, and it is not clear whether following a given link will help the reader to figure out the story. The epiphany is the aporia's companion trope, found when the solution is obtained and the puzzle solved (Aarseth 1997). Aporia and epiphany may also be characteristic of most puzzle-based games, like interactive fiction (Montfort 2003), but are rarely found in *World of Warcraft*, where quests are straightforward, directions purely geographical, and the challenge lies in finding the object and killing the opponents, not in solving puzzles.

In their analysis of quests in the single-player game *Diablo*,[2] Wibroe, Nygaard, and Andersen identify two main types of quests in the game: simple exchanges and breaches of contract (2000). A simple exchange is a quest where the player is asked to fetch something and is given a reward for doing so. A breach of contract occurs when the quest-giver refuses to give the player the reward, and the player thus has to fight the quest-giver to get it. Simple exchanges are standard fare in *World of Warcraft*, but there are very few, if any, breaches of contract. This is partly due to the grammatical structure of quests in *World of Warcraft*, which is coded into the game and shapes the ways in which the game designers can write quests.

Simple exchanges and breaches of contract are closer to examples of narrative structure such as those proposed by Vladimir Propp and later narratologists than they are to the more conventional rhetorical techniques of the ancient Greek orators. In 1928 the Russian Formalist Propp outlined a "grammar" of Russian folktales that included a list of "functions" by which all folktales could be described (1968). For instance, early in a story, a member of a family will leave home and become the hero of the story. Next, the hero is given an interdiction; something is forbidden. Later, the hero is certain to breach the interdiction and do the thing that is forbidden. Not all stories contain all functions, but they always appear in the same order.

Joseph Campbell's subsequent analysis of the structure of myths follows a similar pattern, and is frequently referenced in discussions of quests in computer games (Tosca 2003; King and Krzywinska 2006, 49) as Campbell more explicitly than Propp uses the term "quest" to describe the hero's objective in a myth or narrative and the journey made to obtain those goals. It is clear that these simple functions of narratives and myths are also used heavily in games, as is also discussed by Tanya Krzywinska in chapter 6. However, my reading of quests in *World of Warcraft* will focus less on narrative functions and more on the rhetorical figures. My analysis will thus be more akin to Aarseth's reading of *afternoon* as characterized by aporia and epiphany than to Wibro, Nygaard, and Andersen's analysis of *Diablo* as characterized by simple exchanges and breaches of contract.

Before delving deeper into the rhetorical figures of deferral and repetition, I will take a look at other recent research on quests in games, and look more closely at how quests in *World of Warcraft* work.

What Are Quests?

There are several ways of defining quests in games, just as quests are different in different kinds of games. When Ragnhild Tronstad, who was studying text-based MUDs at the time, wrote her influential discussion of quests as performatives (Tronstad 2001), she saw them as puzzle-based structures. She used an example of a player trying to open a locked box. The player realizes that she needs to find a key to open the box, but she doesn't know where the key might be or even whether whatever is in the box will help in solving the quest she is on. Clearly, this kind of quest has much in common with the play between aporia and epiphany that Aarseth describes in his analysis of hypertext fiction. Both genres are in a sense puzzles or, as Nick Montfort suggests of interactive fiction, riddles (2003). While Tronstad doesn't explicitly define "quest," she uses it as players of MUDs and puzzle-based adventure games generally do: a quest is a task that is explicitly assigned to the player and that involves some level of challenge. As in literature, a quest in an adventure game can be large or small, and as in literature, quests in games tend to be used to set the plot in motion. If Odysseus didn't want to get home there would be no *Odyssey*. If King Arthur and his knights weren't looking for the Holy Grail there would be no stories about them. If the player of *King's Quest 1* wasn't asked to recover the kingdom's valuable treasures (a missing magical mirror, shield, and chest) there would be no game. Or rather, if there were still a game, it would be a very different kind of game.

In *World of Warcraft* the player is not assigned a single, grand, overarching quest such as these. Quests that announce an all-encompassing ultimate goal suit games with clearly defined ends, and *World of Warcraft* is designed to be endless. Even when you reach the maximum level there are always more things to do. You can fight more battles, gain more honor and reputation, or do that raid one more time. Quests are an important part of playing *World of Warcraft*, but instead of the player attempting to resolve a single, large quest (find the Holy Grail, bring peace to Azeroth) the player instead picks and chooses from a vast number of very small quests.

Espen Aarseth's proposed definition is far broader than that which Tronstad implicitly uses: "the player-avatar must move through a landscape in order to fulfill a goal while mastering a series of challenges. This phenomenon is called a quest" (Aarseth 2004). This definition would certainly include the quests we meet in *World of Warcraft*, but as Susana Tosca points out in her essay, "The Quest Problem in Computer Games" (2003), it is also so broad that it can cover almost any game imaginable. While quests in *World of Warcraft* are sometimes designed as episodes in a longer quest chain, individual quests in *World of Warcraft* are on a far smaller scale than Aarseth's definition suggests.

Tosca notes that designers and gamers are less interested in defining "quest" than academics have been. The game design manuals Tosca discusses don't define "quest" at all, but simply take for granted that the reader knows what is meant. Tosca proposes a definition that distinguishes between the player's and the designer's perspective: "For the player, [quests] are a set of instructions for action, as they give her a goal that needs to be solved. For the designer, they provide a structure to plan for events and describe object interaction within a comprehensible framework" (2003). This definition easily maps onto quests in *World of Warcraft*, although neither the manual nor the online help files for *World of Warcraft* explicitly defines "quest," either, and the word isn't listed in the glossary a player can consult on the official game Web site. Instead, it's explained implicitly, as in this advice for "Your First Few Levels" in the Game Guide on the official Web site: "Find a Quest! Quest givers have exclamation marks over their heads. Go talk to the quest giver by right-clicking on them. Go around to every NPC with a "!" above their head and see what they want you to do."

In practice, quests in *World of Warcraft* follow a very rigid structure. They are very clearly discrete entities. A quest is always received from a quest-giver, who is clearly marked as such by the yellow exclamation mark above his or her head. The quest pops up in a box on the player's screen with well-marked sections representing the words spoken by the quest-giver, the objectives, a summary of what the player is expected to do (this being a more mechanical and pragmatic set of instructions for action), and a list of rewards that will be offered to the player on completion of the quest. The player can have up to twenty-five active (in other words, noncompleted but available) quests at a time, and they are displayed in the Quest Log, a window that color-codes active quests according to their difficulty level and sorts them by which zone they are in and by whether they are connected to a specific class or profession. By shift-clicking a quest, the player can display an even more compact set of quest objectives on the edge of her screen, tracking information in a brief summary that is continually updated: "Bloodsail Swashbucklers slain: 4/10."

Tosca suggests three variables that describe quests, while noting that her list does not form a complete quest typology. These variables are linearity (are quests fixed or open?), duration (long or short?), and single-player versus multiplayer. In *World of Warcraft* quests are strictly linear and they are very fixed. There are never alternative ways of achieving a goal, unlike the quests Tosca discusses in the game *Blade Runner*, where the player's objective of getting rid of the replicants can be achieved by killing them or by making friends with them (2003). The objectives specified in *World of Warcraft* are mechanistic and unequivocal: kill ten kobolds, bring me Van Cleef's head. Each individual quest is very clearly defined and of brief duration, though quests are often linked together in quest chains, where a player has to complete a number of quests in sequence in order to achieve an ultimate goal. Such quest chains can take a long time to complete and often require help from many other players. Quests also vary between being suitable for a single player or requiring several players. The color coding of quests indicates whether a player is strong enough to be likely to succeed in a quest alone (or "solo"), or should group with other players or leave the quest until he or she has attained a higher level.

Does the Content Matter?

In practice, most players probably don't pay a lot of attention to the narratives of quests. *Wired* reporter Lore Sjöberg captures the emptiness of many quest narratives with his satire of *World of Warcraft*, where he rewrites a sequence from the game as though it were a text adventure game. As in the text adventures of the 1970s and 1980s and the interactive fictions of the 1990s, the words after the > sign are imagined as typed by the player.

There is an elf with an exclamation point above her head here.
>Talk elf
"Alas," she says. "There is a great darkness upon the land. Fifty years ago the Dwarf Lord Al'ham'bra came upon the Dragon Locket in the Miremuck Caverns. He immediately recognized the..."
> Click Accept
"Hey," the elf protests. "This is important expository. Azeroth is a rich and storied land, with a tapestry of interwoven..."
> Click Accept
"OK, fine. Bring me six kobold tails."
> Shout "Where are the Kobolds?" (Sjöberg 2006)

In fact, most quests are not solved or resolved by studying the narrative for clues but by asking other players how they resolved the quest, as in Sjöberg's parody, or by consulting online game guides such as Thottbot, Questkeep, or Allakhazam. The biggest challenges in resolving a quest are navigation and combat. Despite geographical descriptions such as "south of Crossroads" or "in the ruins," it can often be hard to find a given object or opponent. Even when the object of the quest is not to slay monsters, it is likely that the landscape you need to traverse is monster-infested so that you have to fight anyway.

While Sjöberg's satire is tongue-in-cheek, its strictly utilitarian approach is mirrored by most quest guides and databases. Here is a quest guide from Azzor.com describing the most efficient order in which to complete quests in the Darkshore zone: "Before heading to Ameth'Aran, grab the For Love Eternal, Tools of the Highborne, The Fall of Ameth'Aran, and the Red Crystal quests. Before entering Ameth'Aran, finish the Red Crystal quest. It was faster to do this than it was the Bashal'Aran quests, and the reward is pretty good. It takes two trips, but before the second one, be sure to get the water from the moonwell" (Kiggles 2005).

Where walk-throughs of interactive fiction (be it classical works like *Zork* (1981) or *Adventure* (1976), or newer ones like Emily Short's *Galatea* (2000) or Nick Montfort's *Book and Volume* (2005)) provide careful hints and prods to help the player figure out the puzzle, walk-throughs of quests in *World of Warcraft* go straight to the solution. Worrying about spoilers is completely irrelevant. There are no puzzles to solve—the only challenges here are navigation and strategy. You need to find that which the quest asks you to find, and you need to work out how to kill mobs you encounter. Should you bring a group? Should you work around the edges? Should you stealth? Do you need special potions or buffs? Experienced players may also select quests according to the rewards they'll give in terms of experience points, gold, and objects, and may work out which quests are worth the time spent.

Instead of walk-throughs, then, there are Web-based databases of quests, objects, mobs, and quest-givers. Droprates—how often a needed item will be found on a killed mob—are listed, and precise location coordinates are shared. Players post comments to listings of individual quests stating at what level they successfully completed the quest, and they let future readers know whether the quest was worth the effort or not in terms of experience points and other rewards earned. Though some quests must be completed to unlock areas of the game or to acquire particularly good equipment, no player is likely to complete or want to complete all quests he or she finds.

Many quest databases cite the words spoken by the quest-giver and give information about locations, but most leave out any other narrative information given in the game. For instance, TenTonHammer.com's "Guide to Onyxia" notes in a slightly annoyed tone that "[t]o get this quest you must listen to all of Warlord Goretooths story before you can access the quest. He will not have a question mark over his head even when you hit a level high enough to access the quest." There is in fact no description of the content of Warlord Goretooth's story in the major quest databases, although this is the first quest Horde players must complete in a long chain leading to one of the most prestigious raids of the game.

An example of a dissection of a quest that takes out almost every hint of narrative can be found at bookofwarcraft.com, where quests in the level 12 to 20 night elf zone Darkshore are listed in a table that only gives the bare essentials. In some ways it gives us more information about the quests than is found in game; for instance, by specifying location coordinates, the number of experience points and reputation ("rep") earned, and some very specific numbers describing attributes of the equipment the player earns on completing the quest. Notably, the listing also leaves out much of the narrative information given in the game itself.

Quest Name: Washed Ashore II
Quest Giver: Gwenneth Bly'Leggonde
Start Coords: 36.45, near the hippogryphs
Level: 14
Action Required: Recover Sea Turtle Remains

Destination Coords: 32.46, skeleton of a sea turtle at the bottom of the ocean, west of Auberdine
XP: 975
Rep: 100.25
Reward Item: Clamshell Bracers, mail 57a / Dryweed Belt, leather, 38a, +2 Intellect / Sandcomber Boots, cloth, 17a

Even in the game, this is an example of a quest with minimal narrative qualities. It is the second in a series that has you collecting beached animals on the coast for Gwennyth Bly'Leggonde, a quest-giver in Auberdine. The first time you meet Gwennyth, she asks you the following:

Majestic sea creatures are known to launch themselves at the Darkshore coastline, beached there until they die. Lately, these beasts have been washing ashore in ever-increasing numbers. I've been sent here by the Temple of the Moon to investigate, but the presence of murlocs along the water has made my research difficult.

There is a giant creature washed ashore just south of Auberdine that is ringed by the foul Greymist murlocs. Could you go there and retrieve bones from the creature for our study? (Washed Ashore)

Your quest log also gives you some additional information in the objectives for the quest, namely that the beached animal you're looking for is a turtle: "Recover the Sea Turtle Remains from the Skeletal Sea Turtle in the waters west of Auberdine, and then speak with Gwennyth Bly'Leggonde back in Auberdine." On the beach you find you have to fight hostile murlocs until you find the remains of the turtle. Moving your cursor over it, you'll see that the cursor turns into a cogwheel, the sign that if you click on it, something will happen. Clicking gets you the object that you're supposed to bring back to Gwennyth. At that point she asks you to go and collect more beached creatures, but more briefly: "That beached creature is not an isolated incident here in Darkshore. There are more along the coastline and even in the water. I would like for you to investigate another one that we know of; this one was reported to be in the water due west of Auberdine, close to a sunken vessel. Return to me with anything that you may recover that would aid our research" (Washed Ashore, part 2).

Although this quest is thin on narrative content, it is one of many quests dealing with environmental destruction, a recurring motif that Esther MacCallum-Stewart discusses in some detail in chapter 2. Night elf zones and druid quests are particularly involved in this motif as the care of nature is part of their ethos, but deforestation and signs of impending environmental disaster can be found throughout Azeroth: in the corrupted plants of Fel-wood, in the sickly gazelles of the Barrens (which the NPC Ruul Eagletalon describes as "unwitting victims of a greater taint and corruption that is spreading all throughout the land"), by the toxicologists on Dreadmire Peak, and so on. This motif is in many ways a natural corollary to the exploration theme evident in almost all quests. Although players may not read the quest for narrative details, as suggested by Sjöberg's satire and by the lack of narra-tive elements in Web-based quest databases, these motifs and structures are repeated so steadily that they do help to shape the world.

Deferral

When a quest giver asks you to complete a quest, you are shown the rewards you will be able to choose between when you have finished. In this way, a quest is a promise—I will give you this, if only you do that. Each promise is graded by difficulty and sorted by zone so that the player's quest log contains a collection of possible activities and possible rewards. You have only to choose between them—if you are able to kill all those monsters and find all those places, items, and people.

Quests reward patience. Quests are more organized than most to-do lists, providing automatic crossing-off of completed items. They are as endless as to-do lists as well—perhaps in that way encouraging the tireless quest for per-sonal betterment that Scott Rettberg, in chapter 1, proposes is at the heart of *World of Warcraft.*

In his dissection of narrative desire, Peter Brooks writes of the "*anticipation of retrospection* as our chief tool in making sense of narrative" (Brooks 1984, 23). We read with a certainty that there will *be* an end, and that when we have reached it, we will be able to look back and see the whole. Quests tell us the end straight away, and provide an extremely clear structure for anticipating retrospection.

In a sense, *World of Warcraft* is evidence that we humans have finally suc-ceeded in creating something that we can desire endlessly, have entirely, and never consume. This game has no end; it is an endless deferral of an end. Brooks describes the paradox of narrative: we read because we desire the end, but when we reach the end, of course there is no more narrative to con-sume (52). "Desire comes into being as a perpetual want for (of) a satisfaction that cannot be offered in reality," Brooks writes, referring to the psychoanalytic tradition of Lacan as well as to his own concept of narrative desire (55). The gamer's desire in *World of Warcraft* is simple and endless: we want more. Always more.

Ragnhild Tronstad writes of quests as seductive, using Baudrillard's theory of seduction in a way similar to Brooks' analysis of narrative. She argues that "[c]ompleting the quest turns it into a product, a finite entity that no longer contains any secrets or exercises any seductive power over the player" (2004, 160–161). There are no secrets in the quests in *World of Warcraft*. Or if there are, they are simply the secrets of having a sufficiently powerful group to combat the mobs and of possessing both sufficient willingness to travel and a sharp eye for details. While the player in the MUDs Tronstad writes about "counters this seduction by insisting on replacing it with final meaning" (164), the *World of Warcraft* player must quickly realize that quests in this game have no final meaning.

Pragmatically, quests are generally means to an end. You have to complete quests in order to gain access to an area or to a new skill or item. You complete quests to get more experience points than you would through simple grinding (killing monsters mechanically without role-playing or quest motivation). Because quests generally give more experience points than simply killing monsters, players will try to collect as many relevant quests as possible before entering an instance with a group of players. In all these cases, rewards are promised, but can only be received after waiting.

In addition, quests are used to guide a player through gameplay and toward higher levels. When a player reaches an appropriate level, quests will appear that require travel to new zones, where more challenging quests await, constantly enticing a player to continue to explore the world. At lower levels, exploration quests often also include tutorial elements, such as the quests given around level 10 that teach new players to use flight masters to fly from place to place rather than running everywhere, or the quests given to warlocks and paladins at level 60 that lead to their learning the spell required to summon a special mount. For warlocks, for instance, obtaining their Dreadsteed (the epic mount for warlocks) requires a long quest chain involving shady deals with goblins; finding, fighting for, and purchasing expensive materials for complicated rituals; and finally summoning the Dreadsteed and killing the demon that owns it.

Some quest chains are very long and time-consuming. The Warlock quest chain is one example, but there are many others. The Onyxia quest chain is probably the most famous in the game, at least prior to the release of *The Burning Crusade* expansion pack in 2007. Onyxia is a fearsome dragon, the daughter of Deathwing. (Those who have read the novels about the Warcraft world or read the lore on the official game Web site or WoWwiki.com will recognize Deathwing as the nemesis of Horde and Alliance alike.) Dragons in this world can also appear as humans, and Onyxia herself poses as Lady Katrana Prestor, advisor to the child king of the humans, in Stormwind. One of the toughest raids in the game before the release of the *Burning Crusade* expansion was slaying Onyxia, and it was also one of the most prestigious and visible feats for a player or guild to have participated in. When a group has succeeded in slaying Onyxia (it takes forty people to do so) they can turn in her head to the leaders of Stormwind if they are Alliance, or Orgrimmar if they are Horde. The head is displayed in the city so all other players there can see it and bystanders are granted a buff that shows up on the screen (for Horde players) as "Warchief's Blessing" ("+10% crit with spells, +5% crit with melee, +140 attack power for 120 min," according to Allakhazam.com). On new servers, players discuss whether or not anyone has killed Onyxia yet, and there is considerable pride in knowing that your guild or even your faction (Horde or Alliance) was the first to kill Onyxia on your server. Many guilds specialize and do the raid again and again, practicing avidly and posting videos of the best, funniest, or most unusual fights with Onyxia to YouTube and other sites.

Before you actually fight with Onyxia, you have to complete a lengthy quest chain to acquire the Drakefire Amulet, often simply referred to as the Onyxia Key because it is required to gain entrance to Onyxia's Lair. The quest chain is different for Alliance and Horde players, but in both cases a player can start in their mid-50s but cannot complete the chain until level 60. The quest chain not only involves the usual killing of monsters, gathering of materials, and entering dungeons, but also requires the player to travel to Stormwind or Orgrimmar, depending on the player's faction, to give a message to the leaders there. Horde players thus speak directly to Thrall, the orc warlord, who is concerned about the dragon, while Alliance players, in an interesting twist, talk with Lady Katrana Prestor—who, as you remember, is actually Onyxia herself in human form. Much further traveling and battling is also required before the long-coveted Drakefire Amulet is finally given to the player.

Tastes of the Onyxia storyline are available for lower level players, too, foreshadowing future possibilities. In a simple three-quest chain set in Brackwell

Village, players around level 40 to 45 are first asked to kill nearby dragon whelps and hatchlings and take their searing tongues and hearts back to Draz'Zilb in Brackenwall Village. Draz'Zilb is an ogre who, despite his two heads and rude companions, is surprisingly well spoken. When you have brought him the body parts, he casts a spell over them to identify their origin. He pronounces them "The brood of Onyxia!" In the next quest Draz'Zilb gives a little information about Onyxia, too: "Stonemaul Village was invaded by the brood of Onyxia. But why would the daughter of the black dragonlord, Deathwing, descend upon our lands?" (The Brood of Onyxia). Draz'Zilb asks the player to notify the village leader, Mok'Morokk, of this threat, but Mok'Morokk refuses to act, and so it is left to the player to return to the area where the dragon whelps and hatchlings are and destroy Onyxia's eggs.

The main purpose this quest serves is to introduce the idea of Onyxia to the player and to show the player Onyxia's Lair, implicitly promising that more is to come. This quest chain is an excellent example of how the quest leads players into situations that mean more than the narrative embedded into the quests. As we saw earlier, most players probably won't really read the quest narratives, though they may recognize the name Onyxia and therefore be more likely to pay attention. However, there are almost always high-level characters in this area of the world, on their way to Onyxia's Lair. If the player has not already spotted the Lair, the sight of high-level players riding past will likely draw his or her attention to it. The lair, which is close by the eggs, is a very impressive cave with an entrance shaped like a huge, fanged jaw. It has the green whirling entranceway that by level 40 the player will know signifies an *instance*; that is, a dungeon meant for a group to fight their way through on their own. If the player attempts to enter Onyxia's Lair, the message "You must be part of a Raid Group, at least level 50 and have the Drakefire Amulet in your inventory to enter" is displayed. It is the situation that has been set up that is memorable, moreso than the narrative as told by the quest-givers.

Quests like these are thus structured both as promises that there is more to come and as deferrals of those goals. Onyxia is here, these quests say, look, right here, but you can't touch her—yet.

Repetition

Repetition is the complement to this deferral. Before she can actually fight the dragon, the player will hear about Onyxia again and again, in chat, by seeing the head, and in many quests. Repetition is present in *World of Warcraft* from the moment you create your character. The fixed set of options you have to choose from brings home the fact that your experience here may be a unique combination of options, but that the possible combinations are limited. Before too long you will meet another character with the same hair as you, or perhaps even an identical twin.

This basic rule actually encourages player effort. For instance, when I saw that a friend just a level above me had a wonderful new axe, I asked her where she got it. She described the quest chain she had completed to earn it, and I had a new goal: copy her quest to achieve the same axe. Not only were the challenges in the quest chain identical for me as they had been for my friend, the reward was literally the same item, with exactly the same properties and appearance.

The repetition of items emphasizes that code is the foundation of this world. Wearable items, such as armor or clothing, can be worn by any race and either gender, but will look different according to the size and shape of the character wearing the item. Esther MacCallum-Stewart and Justin Parsler mention a striking example of this in chapter 11, the Black Mageweave Leggings and Vest set, which appears as a black shirt and trousers on a male character, but as stockings and suspenders with a basque top on a female character. Likewise, there are items that look different on different races. Plato's theory of the Ideal forms that have faint copies on earth seems to suit this world well. The Ideal is the code, and the Actual is the way it looks on different characters. The properties or game mechanics of the item remain the same no matter how it is expressed visually on different genders and races.

Stranger still is the repetition of events that according to the terms of the fictional world should occur only once. It is understandable that when you kill generic monsters (wolves in the Barrens, for instance) new ones appear, but the suspension of disbelief is extreme when the fictional world asks us to accept that named characters we have killed reappear a few minutes later. This happens at all levels of play, but perhaps most notorious is the culmination of the game (prior to the release of *The Burning Crusade* expansion pack), the killing of Onyxia. Although each quest and all programmed events can be infinitely repeated, each individual player will experience them differently each time they happen. Most quests can only be performed once by each character. Once I have chased Mok'Morokk out of Blackenwell Village, I can't chase him out again, because I will have already completed that quest[3]—and the ogre will only respond to my challenge if I'm on the quest. However, I can help a friend chase him out of the village, and I can watch other people try to chase him out—or I can revisit the village and note that he appears to still be—or is again—the ruler of the village. Nothing ever really changes in Azeroth.

There is, however, a ritual quality to such repetitions. Westfall, the 10 to 20-level zone closest to the human starting point, has an unusually densely woven network of quests, the culmination of which involves the player successfully going through The Deadmines instance with a group of other players and killing Edwin VanCleef, the leader of the Defias Brotherhood. Whenever someone completes this final quest, Gryan Stoutmantle, the leader of the People's Militia and quest-giver in this chain, yells out congratulations so every player in Westfall can hear it: "The People of Westfall salute [name], a brave and valiant defender of freedom."

The first times a new player hears this she might not understand the significance of the yell, but as she continues working through the quests in Westfall—there are six in The Defias Brotherhood chain alone before one gets to the Deadmines—she will hear it again and again. When she finally gives VanCleef's head to Gryan Stoutmantle, thus completing the quest, she will hear him yell *her* name to all of Westfall. This repetition will be very different from the dozen other times she has heard the yell. The meaning of the yell shifts completely because this time it tells *her* story.

In this way, the repetitions of *World of Warcraft* could be likened to those rituals of our lives that have been honed through millennia: birth, coming-of-age, weddings, anniversaries, and deaths are all marked in ritual ways. Being present at the rituals of our friends and families prepares us for our own life course. These rituals mark the most important events in our life stories, enabling us to make sense of our lives *as* stories and as meaningful wholes. Many quests give players visible signs that they have been through that specific rite of passage. For instance, a player who completes The Defias Brotherhood quest chain may choose Chausses of Westfall (chain armor trousers suitable for warriors), the Tunic of Westfall (suitable for classes who wear leather armor, such as hunters), or the Staff of Westfall (suitable for magic users). For characters of this level, these are fine items that other players will notice. Most such items are "soul-bound," meaning that they cannot be sold or given away. The only way to receive these items is to complete the rite of passage of a specific quest. Just as many of our traditional rituals have temporary or permanent visual signifiers, such as wearing a wedding band after the ritual of marriage, the quest rewards worn by a character tell other players something about the character's history, experience, and status.

Ritual repetition has in many ways always been the function of literature, and of other narrative forms as well. Novels end in death or wedding bells, repeating again and again the basic events that make up a human life. In *World of Warcraft* the repetitions are simply that much more explicit.

Conclusion

These rhetorical figures of deferral and repetition are solutions to the problem of how to construct a game played by many people at once that needs to accommodate group play, solo play, and players who are at every possible point in the game (from newbie to highly experienced, from level 1 to level 70)—in the same game system and game world.

Might there be other solutions to this problem? Or will we find that repetition and deferral are the primary rhetorical figures for all MMOGs? It is at least clear that the tropes of previous games cannot simply be transferred to *World of Warcraft*. The quests of *World of Warcraft* are not like the puzzles of *Myst* or of interactive fiction, and they are not built around the aporia and epiphany Espen Aarseth identified as the primary tropes of hypertext fiction. The seduction Ragnhild Tronstad found in the puzzle-quests of Tubmud is related to the deferral of the quests in *World of Warcraft*, but the seduction, if seduction there is, is of a very different nature.

A cynic could no doubt see repetition and deferral as major figures in everyday Western lives and media. Judging by the popularity of *World of Warcraft* today, it at least seems fair to conclude that these patterns appeal to many players.

Notes

1. Interactive fiction is a text-based adventure game genre that began with Will Crowther's *Adventure* in 1976 and blossomed throughout the 1980s. After graphical home computer games made the genre unsuccessful commercially, interactive fiction has developed as a noncommercial genre with a very active community of independent authors and players (Montfort 2003). Early interactive fiction was a clear predecessor of MUDs, the first multiuser online games of the early 1980s, and MUDs are an obvious predecessor of MMOGs.

2. *Diablo II* supports multiplayer play, but Wibroe, Nygaard, and Andersen (2000) were referring to an earlier version of the game, released in 1996.

3. If a player creates an additional character, the player can replay quests with the new character. There are also some repeatable quests, particularly at higher levels where some quests are repeated to gain reputation with a faction.

References

Aarseth, Espen. 1997. *Cybertext: Perspectives on Ergodic Literature.* Baltimore: Johns Hopkins University Press.

Aarseth, Espen. 2004. "Beyond the Frontier: Quest Games as Post-Narrative Discourse." In *Narrative Across Media: The Languages of Storytelling,* ed. Marie-Laure Ryan, 361–376. Lincoln, NE: University of Nebraska Press.

Abrams, M. H. 1993. *A Glossary of Literary Terms,* sixth ed. Fort Worth: Harcourt Brace.

Brooks, Peter. 1984. *Reading for the Plot: Design and Intention in Narrative.* Cambridge, MA: Harvard University Press.

Joyce, Michael. 1990. *afternoon, a story.* Watertown, MA: Eastgate Systems.

Kiggles. 2005. "A Guide to Darkshore." *Azzor.com.* Available at ⟨http://wow.azzor.com/108/darkshore.php⟩.

King, Geoff, and Tanya Krzywinska. 2006. *Tomb Raiders and Space Invaders: Videogame Forms and Contexts.* London: I.B. Taurus.

Montfort, Nick. 2003. *Twisty Little Passages: An Approach to Interactive Fiction.* Cambridge, MA: MIT Press.

Propp, Vladimir. 1968. *Morphology of the Folktale,* second ed. Translated by L. Scott. Austin, TX: Indiana University.

Sjöberg, Lore. 2006. "WoW: The Text Adventure." *Wired.com,* March 8, 2006. Available from ⟨http://www.wired.com/news/columns/0,70348–0.html?tw=wn_index_3⟩.

TenTonHammer.com. "Guide to Onyxia." Available at ⟨http://wow.tentonhammer.com/index.php?module=ContentExpress&func=display&ceid=343⟩.

Tosca, Susana. 2003. "The Quest Problem in Computer Games." In *Proceedings of Technologies for Interactive Digital Storytelling and Entertainment,* eds. Stefan Göbel, Norbert Braun, Ulrike Spierling, Johanna Dechau, and Holger Diener. Stuttgart: Fraunhofer IRB Verlag. Available at ⟨http://www.it-c.dk/people/tosca/quest.htm⟩.

Tronstad, Ragnhild. 2001. "Semiotic and Nonsemiotic MUD Performance." Paper presented at COSIGN 2001, Amsterdam, September 10–12. Available at ⟨http://www.kinonet.com/conferences/cosign2001/pdfs/Tronstad.pdf⟩.

Tronstad, Ragnhild. 2004. "Interpretation, Performance, Play, and Seduction: Textual Adventures in Tubmud." PhD diss., University of Oslo.

Walker, Jill. 2006. "A Network of Quests in *World of Warcraft*." In *Second Person: Role-Playing and Story in Games and Playable Media*, eds. Pat Harrigan and Noah Wardrip-Fruin, 307–310. Cambridge, MA: MIT Press.

Wibroe, M., K. K. Nygaard, and P. Bøgh Andersen. 2000. "Games and Stories." In *Virtual Interaction: Interaction in Virtual Inhabited 3D Worlds*, ed. L. Qvortrup. London: Springer-Verlag.

Play

Does *World of Warcraft* Change Everything? How a PvP Server, Multinational Playerbase, and Surveillance Mod Scene Caused Me Pause

9

T. L. Taylor

In the past I have written about things like the relationship between off- and online experience, age diversity in MMOGs, and the positive potential of productive players. But *World of Warcraft* has challenged several of my previously held beliefs about massively multiplayer online games. While I continue to find resonance with these themes within my *EverQuest* (EQ) research, my time in *World of Warcraft* has only brought home for me even more the imperative for reflective analysis on the specificities of not only particular games, but particular servers and specified contexts.

Ethnographers, and indeed qualitative researchers in general, are always aware of the ways their method is tied up with the specificity and context of a field site. Close, in-depth case studies, although they can sometimes be used to help illuminate broader processes, find their core strength in the ability to tell a nuanced story of actual practices and meanings of local cultures and participants. And yet I see now we have a fair number of studies that have focused on a very small number of MMOGs, through which we are beginning to get an implied generalized theory of online games. I want to propose caution and case study diversity before we too quickly settle on the meaning of these gameworlds and the processes that occur in them.

I moved out of the United States in 2003 and when I found myself in February 2005 taking up *World of Warcraft* to play alongside some of my students, I was relegated to a European English server. Because I was also playing with people I knew offline I followed their server preferences and ended up on a player versus player (PvP) server. These two factors—a European English and PvP server—were dramatically different from my time in EQ (or, for that matter, any of the other MMOGs I had played in the intervening years) and I would argue significantly affected several phenomena I had previously discussed. Although I do not want to overstate my claim and suggest that the following are completely new and unique to *World of Warcraft*, I do want to highlight that the following consideration is strongly informed by the specific context of a particular European PvP *World of Warcraft* server as my field site. In part what I want to argue is that we need to renew our efforts to understand the role systems of stratification and forms of social control play in these gameworlds. Rather than simply identifying "emergent culture" as a prime property of MMOG life and stopping there, we also need a better understanding of the complex nature of player-produced culture and its relation to technical game artifacts.

The Complex Status of Emergent Culture

One of the innovative things in *World of Warcraft* is the malleability of its user interface (UI). Much like how previous games such as *Asheron's Call* allowed users to modify the UI, Blizzard has constructed their game system so that player-developers can dramatically change not only the way the game looks, but indeed how it is experienced and played.[1] This means that UI modifications (mods) are not simply cosmetic but can provide core functionality, even altering the nature of play itself. Some of the mods currently available allow you to do things like add special timers to your game window so you can see when spells are fading, easily swap out gear and equipment with one click, and even instantly heal people if they fall below a certain prespecified damage threshold (see also chapter 11).[2]

This kind of development is compelling for those of us drawn to the notion of productive player communities and the organic relationship between the system and participants. But I want to also issue a bit of a reminder that emergence should not be equated with free, utopic, nonhierarchical, or unfettered. Neither should we assume that players have any clear or uniform opinion about such interventions and may, even if deploying them, hold somewhat ambivalent feelings. To illustrate this more complicated picture I will briefly look at two particular mod interventions—damage meters and high-end raid tools.

Damage meters are, as one might guess from their name, tools that calculate the amount of damage individual players are doing to opponents (either other players or nonplayer characters). They then typically visually represent this information in real time within the UI and can also be output as text, complete with statistics and rankings.[3] Damage meters can be a useful tool for players by showing them how they compare to others in their group or raid, often acting as a notification system in case the player is doing too little or too much damage to an opponent. They can either be used privately—as when someone has one running and simply watches the tally to see their and others' performance—or collectively, by publicizing the results in text to a chat channel (as in figure 9.1).

Figure 9.1
A screenshot from a raid on Molten Core with the damage meter shown on the far right listing all players' names. This screenshot shows *World of Warcraft* being played with a third party user interface that has been modified by parties other than Blizzard Entertainment.

Damage meters occupy an interesting position as a sociotechnical object. Many players find them helpful in managing their gameplay and providing incentive or reassurance. For some groups they can also be playful objects, letting people tease each other and engage in friendly competition by sharing the rankings. Yet there are also instances in which this tool seems to incite frustration and evoke ambivalence. Because of the way they work, the proper use of meters needs some care (they need to be reset, they may not catch all the actual damage happening, and their results are often more accurate if several people run them simultaneously and synchronize the outputs). They are, however, often used much more casually, and so people can be left feeling that the meter is not correctly reporting information. This sentiment is tied to a deeper ambivalence about their use. As a game modification they are quite interesting in the kind of social work they attempt to do and the symbolic power they can hold. Because they present their findings within the UI and as quantifiable data, they can seem part of the core game system, and the seamlessness of their integration can hide the way they are actually grafted onto the game, potentially imperfectly. But while damage meters quantify and rank a particular player's contribution to a fight, they can only capture one aspect of that contribution. Since there is also no way to quantify all the other nondamage labor players contribute to a group, some can feel that their contributions are not meaningfully accounted for or, just as important, represented.[4] The graphical or statistical recounting of damage data can dwarf all other aspects of play and group participation. Thus damage meters can act as a powerful stratification tool.

Although it is not unusual to find people dumping damage meter outputs to pick-up groups as a way of either touting accomplishments or trying to get others to do better, within guilds the use of damage meters is often much more regulated. For some guilds they can be used as incentive devices, promoting both individual refinement of skills and in-group competition. But just as many guilds prohibit their use or the distribution of their output to chat channels. For some guild and raid leaders damage meters are seen as promoting unhealthy competition that is detrimental to the group. Individual (over-)achievement (seeking to be top of the damage meter) can be seen as jeopardizing the group's success. For example, racing to the top of the damage meter can often result in overnuking—excessive spell damage in a very short period—thereby disrupting the tactics and security of the entire raid. Sometimes guilds restrict meter output so that it can only be done after a raid, or only by certain members. One important lesson we might take from this is the

way the damage meter as a technical object can only be meaningfully understood within specific social contexts. For the pick-up group, who is focused on
one specific time-bounded task, it can present some immediate feedback on
performance and efficacy. Such a group may be less concerned with evaluating
in any holistic way the value of individual players. But for the guild (or a
group of friends), the data it reflects may be troublesome, as it does not
account for the full range of contribution the participants may bring to the
collective.

Without many of these mods a player's performance must be interpreted in
total. Aspects cannot be separated out and quantified. While impressions certainly form about who is skilled, particularly powerful, and helpful, they are
not visually represented within the system or broken down into numbers. In
most situations there is much more breadth to the construction of accomplished play, and people come to be thought of as good players and valuable
members to have around because of a variety of factors, actual damage output
being only one. But this holistic approach (often involving the nonquantifiable) does not translate well into a mod. There is an interesting tension between play becoming sharply rationalized, not only in its execution but in its
evaluation, via these tools and the more qualitative assessments of players that
emerge over time within groups. The tool becomes an actor involved in the
ongoing construction of play in a particular form.[5] And to do this kind of
work—for the system to be instrumentalized in this way—there must be in
place a method to watch.

One predominant trend that has arisen in *World of Warcraft* through mod
development—a system that promotes active productive engagement by the
players in shaping their game experience—is an extensive network of tools
and functions that consistently monitor, surveil, and report at a micro level
a variety of aspects of player behavior.[6] Worth critically noting here is that
these developments are instigated, promoted, and adopted by participants
themselves. While a fair amount of work and concern about technology, the
Internet, and surveillance has focused on either (1) the role of the state or
institutions watching individuals or (2) the gaze of individuals turned in on
themselves and the coercive effects of such (see, for example, Brignall 2002,
Forester and Morrison 1994, Jordan 1999, Lyon 1994, Penny 1994, Poster
1990, Zuboff 1988), we might meaningfully distinguish between those modes
and (3) one of coveillance in which there is lateral observation between community members (Andrejevic 2005, Lianos 2003, Mann, Nolan, and Wellman
2003).[7] The use of these tools in a game setting, in which co/surveillance may

at times intersect with playfulness and a desire for efficient action, further complicates things. We generally think of this kind of monitoring as pernicious, with evocations of Bentham's panopticon from Foucault (1979). Mark Poster suggested that the perfection of means of surveillance through new technologies creates a "superpanoptic" moment in which we are not only disciplined to surveillance but to "participating in the process" (1990, 93). But within the context of games and play, being watched (or watching) might actually be fun (Albrechtslund and Dubbeld 2005). How do we understand "participatory surveillance" within games? We have to consider the ways these tools do important work in assisting collaborative play, especially at the high end of the game. Again, the social context in which the tools are deployed matters greatly as, with the case of damage meters, they can be used in a variety of modes and are therefore understood by players in quite diverse ways. The challenges this poses to the interpretive work we do when analyzing games should not be understated.

To illustrate (and complicate) this further I will pull in another example from one of the most widely used high-end UI mods, CTMod (CT) and its companion, CTRaidAssist (CTRA). Each of these are an impressive collection of tools that provide some very helpful game functionalities. They allow you to control the interface to a much greater degree than the basic UI (see figures 9.2 and 9.3).

Mods like CTRA also provide extensive help to the organization and management of groups, allowing players easy access to important information about others in the raid and details in any given fight. But what it gives to the raid leader is also powerful.[8] I was alerted to this one day while running the Molten Core instance with my guild. Someone happened to wander a bit too close to a nearby mob, thereby drawing them to our entire group and nearly killing us all. Once we had killed off the creature and gotten back in formation, the raid leader said on our Ventrillo voice chat channel, somewhat severely, "I am going to be watching his [the next monster's] target and if I see one of you agro him you are getting minus DKP [dragon kill points, a cumulative reward system guilds often use]."[9] I was fairly new to using CTRA at the time and had not quite thought through the implications of the tool and how much it allowed us to watch each other and be watched. Even though I had not been the one to attract the last monster I immediately felt a knot in my stomach. It was almost as if I had done something wrong already. It was not just that suddenly my experience of the encounter became one in which there

Figure 9.2
Standard interface for a ten-person raid with no raiding mods. This screenshot shows
World of Warcraft being played with a third party user interface that has been modified
by parties other than Blizzard Entertainment.

was no room for error, but that I was somehow being scrutinized (or at
least potentially so) in a way I had not anticipated. Without the "view target's
target" function, figuring out who may be in error in such a situation is
much less precise, possibly unknowable in any concrete way. But this tool
was allowing our leader to watch, at a very micro level, each of our perfor-
mances. Certainly other guilds are much more forgiving in how they handle
such things and I do not want to claim that this attitude is ubiquitous. Many
guilds act much more playfully and casually. I do however want to point out
the ways that these kind of tools can not only foster and support this kind
of approach, but may under the right circumstances evoke it. Within some
contexts, such tools become powerful social actors worth taking a closer look at.

At its heart CTRA is very much a surveillance tool. Leaders can issue commands to review how much damage a player has taken to their armor and
what they are carrying in their bags.[10] It is difficult to use the notion of

Figure 9.3
Typical raid UI using mods. This screenshot shows *World of Warcraft* being played
with a third party user interface that has been modified by parties other than Blizzard
Entertainment.

surveillance in this context without automatically triggering an implicit negative connotation. Because of mods' incredible usefulness in facilitating play we
need to shade our understanding of surveillance a bit and consider the ways
players readily adopt and enjoy what these tools afford. I have spent some
time interviewing high-end raid leaders, and there is near-universal consensus
that this is an invaluable tool for the execution of high-end raids, which require significant coordination and cooperation. In fact, Tucker Smedes, one
of CTRA's developers, is himself a high-end guild leader and the tool's production has been directly tied to his experience of the difficult work involved
in leading these events. He noted what I have heard from many, that "The
amount of time I'm able to save using various commands and setups
makes my 'job' much easier as a raid leader" (personal communication
with the author, March 11 2006). The use of things like damage meters and
co/surveillance tools must also be considered within the specific context of

game play. Most computer games (especially MMOGs) involve the system monitoring, quantifying, and ranking the player's progress. Indeed, some suggest that computer games are in large part always about disciplining players into particular modes (Garite 2003). In that regard these functions speak a familiar language and therefore may call for a less normative critique.

But what happens when additional layers to play—in the case of mods, which are not only user-created but may be deployed unevenly—become grafted onto given systems? Does the member of the group who has no damage meter stand on the same footing as the one who does? Where does the player who chooses not to install something like CT fall? I want to juxtapose the common language of emergence and productive engagement with game systems—which I think often carries with it an implied notion of positive and "freeing" interaction—with the development, by players, of tools that stratify, surveil, quantify, and regulate their fellow gamers.[11] There is a bit of a double-edged sword to these tools (something I think guilds often acknowledge with the ways they moderate use). On the one hand they assist play and even make group coordination better. Yet through their rationalization and quantification of action they also strongly inform (and potentially limit) what is seen as "good play" or what is viewed as reasonable.[12] In this regard I am also particularly interested in the ways these tools dynamically shape our understanding of what is thought possible and playful within a game system. There is a complex relationship between the development of a tool and how it alters our notions of what we can, and should, do. In the case of things like CTRA, high-end encounters come to be seen as nearly undoable without the tool, and indeed all of the high-end guilds I have encountered require players to use the mod if they join. Because these tools have been refined through repeated use and iterative development and are widely adopted, they also act as strong normative agents.

When thinking about the ways these technical objects work, I was reminded of the power-gamers I previously interviewed and I began to wonder if in fact these functions are mainstreaming the focus on quantification we saw in that play style. In my work with power-gamers I saw them as inhabiting a space that might on the surface appear contradictory to some—the pleasures of instrumental and (hyper) rationalized play. In EQ this style was only one of many that players could select, even at the high end of the game. But if the adoption of these tools and the play styles they bring becomes mandatory, must we start to deal more concretely with notions of emergent coercive systems?

Using the language of coercion must be done cautiously within computer games, given that they are always already forcing particular choices and indeed that "coercion" is not antithetical to pleasure and play. It is certainly also the case that what we might think of as "soft" social coercion is always present and working to normalize players. And as we have seen, some of the tools are powerful assistants for high-end play, which gamers willingly and happily adopt. But since mod use emerges organically within the community, we need to turn to those moments in which all players are confronted with this new tool and look at how they deal with it. Can players opt out of using something like CTRA? Yes, but that typically means opting out of the raiding guilds, and thus the high-end content, entirely. The tools, and the way they script encounters, have become so normalized that choosing to not participate in that system is a strong signal. We can also consider the ways these objects circulate in diverse contexts and among diverse players. In many ways the "world" of Warcraft is not one single space open to all, and the play within it is fairly divergent. If we think of some of these mods as high-performance tools we can see how they at times uneasily intersect "average" players. Norms produced within raiding guilds sometimes get exported out to nonguild/nonraid encounters. For example, when the high-end player joins a pick-up group, they bring with them not only the experience and training gained from their play but the interface that supports it. There can then be quite different norms and expectations at work. And indeed, the technological artifacts each player is dealing with shape their experience of that play session.[13] This is a story then not simply of how forms of control and normalization emerge within player culture (that we have seen before in many other games), but the complex role our technical artifacts can have in the construction of such. Things like user-produced mods are sociotechnical actors and are always involved in reshaping the game space—and indeed what play is—in powerful ways.

The final thread I want to pursue briefly in this consideration of emergence speaks to this dynamic of malleability and what happens when our mods start to alter how we understand play. There at times seems to be an uneasy relationship between all these add-ons and what constitutes legitimate action in the game world.[14] The line between simply improving the UI and cheating or creating unfair advantage can be tricky. Blizzard (2006a) itself nods to this in their "Exploitation Policy" FAQ where they state: "We definitely want people to create their own UIs utilizing custom menu configurations, graphics, and even sounds. Anything that can be coded to modify the style and the look of the UI is fair game, as long as the modifications are done to the sanctioned internal files of the game. However, anything done to the UI to gain any sort of an unfair advantage over other players is unacceptable."

The developer community is certainly aware of the balancing act on this line. As Tucker Smedes (personal communication with the author, March 11, 2006) noted of their work, "CTRA as I said is one of the most used mods in all of *World of Warcraft*, so we've tried to ensure that the functionality is in place to make raids more enjoyable. Raiding can be stressful and tiresome, and we try to alleviate some of that stress by assisting the player. We've avoided using any code that will basically play for the user, but we try to do what we can that allows players to feel like things are smoother with CTRA in use."

But certainly having a mod that allows you to see precisely when your spells are fading while in combat against a player who may not have the same ability constitutes some kind of advantage. And the guild that relies on the admittedly useful timers that come with CTRA for various high-end bosses has a better hope of defeating them than does the guild that knows with much less precision when events will occur. My point is not to enter into a thorny discussion of cheating, or advocate for Blizzard to take any particular action. I primarily want to highlight the ways these player-produced artifacts force participants to confront their own categories of fair play and indeed may even shift them at times. Rather than just seeing these mods as simply functional overlays, I want to argue they are strong agents in reshaping what constitutes the game and legitimate play. And as sociotechnical actors, they are part of an ongoing dialogue within the community (of designers and players) about how the game is changing over time.

Conclusion

My goal with this chapter is to try and situate a larger conversation about emergence and virtual worlds within the specific context of *World of Warcraft*. Emergence should not be simply equated with the utopic or nonhierarchical, and is more a process than an outcome. As we can see from this brief case study, systems of stratification and control can arise from the bottom up and be strongly implemented in even player-produced modifications.

I also hope to have highlighted that we need even more case studies before we settle on any major lessons this genre brings us. For myself I have found the move to a both European and PvP context incredibly illuminating. The ways *World of Warcraft* provides a particular set of technological affordances and intervention possibilities for players in turn brings a host of critical questions relevant to not only gamespace, but to our consideration of sociotechnical artifacts. Rather than be disheartened by or dismissive of the shifting landscape of MMOGs, we should embrace the partial stories, the partial truths we are finding in the collection of work that continues to emerge in the field.

Acknowledgments

This chapter is a modified version of an article originally published in the journal *Games and Culture* 1, no. 4 (2006): 1–20. Reprinted here with permission.

Notes

1. See Rhody (2003) for a fascinating discussion on Asheron's Call and the use of player mods.

2. Since the original publication of this article, *The Burning Crusade* expansion was launched and with it some severe limitations on the functionality of mods were introduced. This only serves to highlight the ongoing process of negotiation at work between the modding community and Blizzard.

3. There are also healing meters which act similarly, calculating how much healing a person is doing.

4. For some players healing meters are the offset, but again, as anyone who has done a complicated raid (especially those that lead them) knows, actual damage and healing are only two components for overall success.

5. Mark Poster argued that "the structure and grammar of the database *creates* relationships among pieces of information that do not exist in those relationships outside of the database" (1990, 96). I find this particularly compelling in that it suggests the generative power of systems in not only providing data but formulating particular associations and sets of meanings for it.

6. It is not just that individual player action is cataloged, but it becomes aggregated. So, for example, mods like Auctioneer or Enchantrix take small data points (how much an item sold for or what it disenchanted to) and feed the info back into the game for players to then use. There is discussion in the literature of the notion of "surveillant assemblages" and in many ways the collections we see operating in the game

seem evoke that language (for more on this idea, see Haggerty and Ericson 2000 and Hier 2003).

7. There is actually a fourth position to be taken, that of *sousveillance*, a term coined by Mann, Nolan, and Wellman (2003) to describe instances in which people watch those above them (*sous* being the French word for below and *veillance* for watch). In this case, we could discuss a guild member watching the raid leader's position on the damage meter as one form of sousveillance.

8. Analysis of these tools requires a shift from a purely individual frame (what it affords a player) to one that takes into account group affordances.

9. For those familiar with the Mordot.com site and the now somewhat infamous recording of a raid leader berating his group for agroing the whelps in Onyxia, this description is all too familiar and probably happens more than we expect.

10. Since the original publication of this article I have now found another mod that actually watches what CTRA does and alerts the player if a raid leader is issuing a command to look through their bags—a mod that watches another mod.

11. Surveillance techniques in World of Warcraft extend beyond what players implement to assist their gaming sessions. Blizzard itself makes constant and covert use of tools that allow them to watch for people trying to hack the system. Its anticheat FAQ notes their use of a utility that scans the computer's Random Access Memory and watches for "unauthorized third party programs or computer code has been attached to the World of Warcraft process" (Blizzard 2006b). And on the scholarly side, the PlayOn Project at XeroxPARC deploys extensive data-mining techniques for their social science research on player communities within the game (http://blogs.parc.com/playon/). Piggybacking on the same open structure the rest of the mod dev community uses, they gather data on everything from how many players are in guilds to how frequently they play. I find Ien Ang's (2000) discussion of the "innovations" (and limitations) for measuring television audiences is provocative if shifted to the game context. In the same way that she suggested the act of "watching television" is not a neatly contained moment which can be easily measured, I wonder if we might say the same of playing computer games (and of socializing in them).

12. This can be seen most dramatically in the ways high-end encounters have now become so scripted—indeed to the degree that mods may automate many functions previously held by players such as calling out timed actions—that they normalize particular forms of play and action such that alternate modes appear not only unthinkable but downright stupid to many players.

13. Although this is often not a problem, sometimes high-end players in pick-up groups can feel things are going too slow or their mods let them see (and critique) their fellow player's performance in particular ways. I think there is a fairly common trend at the high end for players to operate in smaller and smaller social spheres—where

grouping outside of one's guild or with players of a less accomplished rank (often informally noted by guild tags) is done infrequently. In many ways progressing in the game is about moving up through levels of stratification that are not only formally built into the system (via levels) but emerge around skill (how good a player you are; in other words, not all level 60s are as accomplished as each other) and social status (which guild you belong to and how it is seen in the community).

14. This is not an unfamiliar issue as Pargman (2000) notes it as well in the world of text-based multiuser dungeons.

References

Albrechtslund, Anders and Lynsey Dubbeld. 2005. "The Plays and Arts of Surveillance: Studying Surveillance as Entertainment." *Surveillance and Society* 3, no. 2/3: 216–221.

Andrejevic, Mark. 2005. "The Work of Watching One Another: Lateral Surveillance, Risk, and Governance." *Surveillance and Society* 2, no. 4: 479–497.

Ang, Ien. 2000. "New Technologies, Audience Measurement, and the Tactics of Television Consumption." In *Electronic Media and Technoculture*, ed. John Thornton Caldwell, 183–196. New Brunswick: Rutgers.

Blizzard. 2006a. "Exploitation Policy." Available at ⟨http://wow-europe.com/en/policy/exploitation.html⟩. Accessed April 3, 2006.

Blizzard. 2006b. "Anti-Cheat Policy." Available at ⟨http://wow-europe.com/en/policy/anticheat.html⟩. Accessed April 3, 2006.

Brignall, Tom III. 2002. "The New Panopticon: The Internet Viewed as a Structure of Social Control." *Theory and Science* 3, no. 1. Available at ⟨http://theoryandscience.icaap.org/content/vol003.001/brignall.html⟩.

Forester, Tom and Perry Morrison. 1994. *Computer Ethics: Cautionary Tales and Ethnical Dilemmas in Computing.* Cambridge, MA: MIT Press.

Foucault, Michel. 1979. *Discipline and Punish: The Birth of the Prison.* New York: Vintage Books.

Garite, Matt. 2003. "The Ideology of Interactivity (or, Video Games and the Taylorization of Leisure)." Paper presented at Digital Games Research Association conference, Utrecht, The Netherlands, November 4–6. Available at ⟨http://www.digra.org/dl/db/05150.15436⟩.

Haggerty, Kevin D. and Richard V. Ericson. 2000. "The Surveillant Assemblage." *British Journal of Sociology* 51, no. 4: 605–622.

Hier, Sean P. 2003. "Probing the Surveillant Assemblage: On the Dialectics of Surveillance Practices as Processes of Social Control." *Surveillance and Society* 1, no. 3: 399–411.

Jordan, Tim. 1999. *Cyberpower: The Culture and Politics of Cyberspace and the Internet.* London: Routledge.

Lianos, Michalis. 2003. "Social Control After Foucault." Translated by David Wood and Michalis Lianos. *Surveillance and Society* 1, no. 3: 412–430.

Lyon, David. 1994. *The Electronic Eye: The Rise of Surveillance Society.* Minneapolis: University of Minnesota Press.

Mann, Steve, Jason Nolan, and Barry Wellman. 2003. "Sousveillance: Inventing and Using Wearable Computing Devices for Data Collection in Surveillance Environments." *Surveillance and Society* 1, no. 3: 331–335.

Pargman, Daniel. 2000. *Code Begets Community: On Social and Technical Aspects of Managing a Virtual Community.* Linköping, Sweden: Linköping University.

Penny, Simon. 1994. "Virtual Reality as the Completion of the Enlightenment Project." In *Culture on the Brink: Ideologies of Technology*, ed. Gretchen Bender and Timothy Druckery, 231–248. Seattle: Bay Press.

Poster, Mark. 1990. *The Mode of Information.* Chicago: University of Chicago Press.

Rhody, Jason. 2003. "/Em speaks, Or Textual Practices, Online Communication, and Asheron's Call." Paper presented at the Association of Internet Researchers conference, Toronto, Canada, October 16–19.

Zuboff, Shoshana. 1988. *In the Age of the Smart Machine: The Future of Work and Power.* New York: Basic Books.

Humans Playing *World of Warcraft*: or Deviant Strategies?

10

Torill Elvira Mortensen

Innovative ideas and behavior are often seen as deviant until they change society, while ideas that have been left behind by progress appear deviant in the present time. One innovation that is currently seen as sufficiently deviant to invite a diagnosis and a treatment is computer gaming. From an innocent pastime, computer gaming is popularly presented as a deeply disturbing activity, and the media brand gamers as addicts in need of treatment, antisocial deviants.

For those of us who argue that games are just another cultural expression, it is important to look at what they can teach us about human society. This article addresses what games can teach us about social norms and deviance. In order to understand this we need to look at "games," "norms," "rules" and "deviance," and the relationship between these concepts. If games can teach us about human society, perhaps they can teach us something about human behavior, innovations, and deviance.

Deviance From What?

In order to deviate, there must be a norm. In general society, the function of norms is to define acceptable behavior. In games this function is covered by rules. Players may defy rules through breaking them or avoid them by finding loopholes, but the rules still say how the game is to be played.

There is a tension created by the gap between norm/rule and practice, and tension is at the heart of gaming (Huizinga 2000, 11). I wish to look at gaming practices that do not adhere to the rules of the game. Some of these practices create miniature games within the game, while some threaten the game itself. The examples I use are all from players and play in *World of Warcraft* by Blizzard (2004).[1] *World of Warcraft* is a rich, varied, and generous computer-generated digital world. Through looking at the issues of rules and deviance from these in games, I hope to bring other viewpoints both to the practice of gaming and deviance as a concept.

In order to discuss the issue of deviant strategies, I need to spend time on some main concepts. Deviance demands a discussion of norms, rules, and social acceptance; strategy begs a discussion of the connection between rules and practice, or tactics. They are connected through the rule.

Code is Rule

When playing games human beings make up rules and stick by them. Johan Huizinga explains: "All play has its rules. They determine what 'holds' in the temporary world circumscribed by play" (2000, 11). Their constructed nature and the voluntary act of player obedience is what constitutes gaming. Obedience to rules is not a universal human trait, and while some players excel at mastering rules, others enjoy changing, subverting, redeveloping, and avoiding them altogether. This is not all that hard, as all it takes to break a game rule is making up your mind. This may result in game dysfunction, social sanctions, or exclusion, but such a disturbance of the play followed by a response and restored peace is part of the game. What takes an effort is to circumvent, reinterpret, or avoid the rules while still being perceived as playing the game.

The programmers of large multiuser games endlessly "tweak" the code: the rules are changed to obey the inevitability of the game design. This happens on a regular basis in *World of Warcraft*. Through countless "patches" programmers change the code, fix errors in how it works, and change the parameters for play. With the launch of *The Burning Crusade* in 2007, the code went through a major update. This meant that the rules of the game changed. The update shows that code is rule in computer games, and that rules are obviously as flexible as social norms: subject to change. Baudrillard describes it like this: "The Endless, reversible cycle of the Rule is opposed to the linear, finalised progression of the Law" (1990, 131). In our case the law is the development plan of *World of Warcraft*. The game designers create the law through their plans for how the game is to progress. The programmers interpret the law into rules. Rules are the practice of the law: changeable and fluid, as the code is adjusted to meet the demands from the design process.

This disagrees with a popular computer axiom. Lawrence Lessig observed that "Code is Law," and claimed that code is what regulates the digital universe (1999). Since the code creates what stands for natural laws in a game, this seems to make immediate sense, but given that the code is constantly adjusted to accommodate the use of the game, it appears to have more in common with rule than with law. When we apply Baudrillard's understanding of the distinction between Rule and Law to the understanding of MMORPGs, Lessig's Code would be Rule.

From a games perspective Jesper Juul defines rules as both limitations and affordances—rules say what is not permitted, but by creating an arena of limitations they also create an arena of permissions: that which is not denied is allowed (2005, 58). This is the function of code in digital games, and draws a parallel between code and rule. Rules and game code are used by the players to develop strategies, which are their guides for action within the game. As Juul points out, players rarely have complete strategies; they have incomplete strategies, which change when the game changes (2005, 59).

If something has not been permitted by the program, it is not possible. We must however see the distinction between "permitted" and "planned." There are many strategies that have not been planned in the game design process, but are still possible. It is in this area we find the deviance, the alternative strategies used by the players.

Strategy

While rules are universal, strategy is subjective and is the individual's plan for how to reach a goal within the game. Strategies are developed within and in relation to the rules to achieve certain goals.

The strategies I present in this article are different ways players cope with and find pleasure in a thoroughly designed playing field. Unlike physical sports, computer games don't have to submit to the laws of gravity or other physical limitations. In digital worlds the code represents the limit. As T. L. Taylor shows in her article "Does WoW Change Everything?", the code can be, if not changed entirely, then manipulated and circumvented through "mods"—programs created to modify the user interface (UI) of games (Taylor 2006; see also chapter 9 in this book). Without changing the mechanisms of the calculating programs, the mods change the information the players have access to. As the players' strategic choices are based on information, this adjustment of the interface has a large impact on the development of strategies.

But outside this rather technical layer of rules and tools for developing strategies, MMORPGs offer unique chances to develop personal, nontechnological (if we can use this term in a game which is totally dependent on technology) strategies. Some of these strategies were described at the early stages of computer game development. Richard Bartle's player typology splits players into achievers, explorers, socializers, and killers, and shows how these groups can be recognized through their different strategies (1996). These typologies are recognized by Blizzard in the categories for gameworlds. Blizzard has tagged realms to be devoted to some of these major play strategies: PvP, Normal, RP, and PvP-RP, where a quick and dirty use of the Bartle typology indicates that PvP fits the killers and Normal fits the achievers and explorers, while RP fits the socializers.

When they start a character, players have to choose which kind of server they want to play on, something which has a strong strategic impact on the subsequent play. And players continue to make strategic choices, stretching the limits of what the game can accommodate.

Deviance

When behavior bends the rules and norms too much, society considers it deviant, and such behavior is popularly understood as stigmatizing and problematic. The idea of deviance is problematic in current social research. The two main frames for understanding deviance are "objectively given" or "subjectively problematic." According to Rubington and Weinberg (2005, 1–2), the objective understanding of deviance is not valid. In order to understand deviance objectively there needs to be a common set of norms from which to deviate, a social consensus that is not apparent in modern society. Deviance subjectively understood is deviance in an interactionist perspective, where the deviant is defined as deviant both by others and by him/her self, through communicative action, and by the use of symbols—this is deviance understood as an interpretation, not as an absolute standard.

While this appears to be an open and versatile definition of deviance, Blackshaw and Crabbe discuss how deviance is a failed category within sociology. They cite Sumner on a discussion about how deviance is useless as a category as all human behavior simply "is" or "is not." The moral judgment inherent in "deviance" is not acceptable for sociology (Blackshaw and Crabbe 2004, 4). The idea of deviance is, however, still strong both in society and in research, and their own work, *New Perspectives on Sport and Deviance*, shows how the arena of games—in this case sports—can shed light on the relationship between rules, human actions, and irregular practices.

An interesting view on deviance and rules comes from Howard S. Becker (2005, 2). In his discussion the categories of deviance are created by what he calls "the crusading reformer." The crusading reformer considers rules inherently good and obedience to rules a means toward a better life. Most important is the idea of a strict structure to life, a frame defined by a complex network of rules. When the crusader enforces rules it is done independently of the deviant or delinquent act itself: if the rules change, what is considered deviant today is fully acceptable tomorrow. "He is not so much concerned with the content of any particular rule as he is with the fact that it is his job to enforce the rule. When the rules are changed, he punishes what was once acceptable behavior just as he ceases to punish behavior that has been made legitimate by a change in the rules. The enforcer, then, may not be interested in the rule as such, but only in the fact that the existence of the rule provides him with a job, a profession, and a raison d'être" (Becker 2005, 4).

The crusading reformer has a relationship to rules that is definitely gamelike. Rather than being concerned with the common sense or the content of each rule, the crusader thinks rules are inherently good and must be obeyed. Games are sets of rules, and to play games all those who participate must accept them as real, important, and inherently good. They may be discussed, criticized, avoided, broken, and occasionally changed, but nobody questions the need for rules in a gameworld.

This is why it can be relevant to talk about deviance in games though it may be quite problematic in general terms. Games are sets of rules, and have no existence without rules. The act of adhering to these rules is voluntary (Huizinga 2000, 8). There are no sanctions against the deviant other than possible exclusion, but this is used without trial, an automated, rule-determined re-sponse.[2] Games offer much clearer absolutes, and give a clear-cut norm to deviate from. Still, a game like *World of Warcraft* will also display relative, sub-jective deviance. There is for instance no game-based punishment for ninjaing loot, a serious offence among the players. But the players are quite efficient in correcting undesirable behavior. There are strong mechanisms of socializa-tion, the most efficient of these being exclusion. The "ignore" function, the ability to block all messages from other players, is a powerful tool of social sanction. Shunning has been coded into *World of Warcraft*.

Deviance in this Argument

For the sake of this article I define deviance as deviance from the plans of the game designers. There are two types of deviance: counterproductive—that which hinders personal progress—or destructive—that which ruins the prog-ress of others.

If we understand the programmed possibilities as the norm, all behavior that defies or avoids this becomes deviant. Roger Caillois considers breaking rules for the convenience of out-of-game strategies to be a way to corrupt the game. He does however distinguish between cheating, which he considers to still be within the rules of the game universe, and playing the game with a dif-ferent goal than just playing the game, as in professional gaming. Cheats have in-game goals: a way to excel at the game without working as hard; contami-nation has out-of-game goals: a way to move the resources spent in the game out of the game, turn the in-game gain into an out-of-game gain, or the other way around (Caillois 1961, 44–45).

Is in-game deviance the same as corrupting the game? Corruption, unlike cheating, structurally alters the game. Cheating is a re-creation of the game, as it depends on the rules. The players' alternative strategies redevelop the un-expected potential and invite the creation of individual games within games. What, then, is deviance?

Studying Cultural Actions in Games

I have gathered my experience with *World of Warcraft* through play, conver-sations, and interviews with members of a guild I will call "Eternity Fall" (EF), on the Horde side of one of the older European role-play servers. I inter-viewed ten players during a real-life guild gathering in Holland in June 2006.

One player in EF e-mailed me a description of his strategies on bot-spotting and -fighting. One player from a different server was interviewed in Volda, Norway, while another player from another server allowed me to quote from a long conversation we had through MSN, an instant messenger program. My research also relies on Blizzard Web sites and forums, more-or-less-professional information and discussion sites such as Allakhazam[3] and Thott-bot,[4] and player Web sites and forums.

The realm where the majority of the interviewees for this article play is an established RP realm. I have asked most of the sources about their favorite playing strategies and if they have any other particular preferences to their play. I have also asked how *World of Warcraft* rules facilitate their particular strategies, and what they have to do in order to play the game the way they want to. I have had descriptions of photo competitions, world PvP, bot-spotting, battleground encounters, cross-faction role play, gold-buying, grind-ing, instance farming, raids and social pressure, guild leading and guild life—a rich and varied description of humans creating their own space and strategies, adding to the larger picture of the gameworld of Azeroth.

Role Play

A smaller part of the *World of Warcraft* realms are dedicated to role play, RP. In this context RP means acting as a fantasy personality developing a game character. Esther MacCallum-Stewart, Justin Parsler, and Ragnhild Tronstad all discuss this phenomenon in depth in this book (chapters 11 and 12). Per-haps one of the most visible expressions of the servers' role-play nature is seen in the names of the avatars. Naming is discussed by Charlotte Hagström in chapter 13. The distinction between RP, PvP, and Normal realms is discussed as well. I will just note that all of them include certain rules of conduct, more elaborate for RP realms than the others.

If we follow Ragnhild Tronstad's argument about the character's appear-ance, role-playing takes time away from other activities that support role play. Role play is counterproductive in relation to the game progress, and this can harm a character's development.

Players and Role Play

Role play (RP) has a long history online, as is well described in the academic literature, from the digital identity experiments described by Sherry Turkle

(1995), by way of the Holodeck dreams described by Janet Murray (1997) and Richard Bartle's virtual gender-bending (1999), to my own research on role play in MUDs (Mortensen 2003). It's no surprise then that role play is an important focus for many of the players of *World of Warcraft*. The game is, however, not designed to reward RP. All other activities are carefully designed into the game and into the reward systems. PvE is the way to progress through the game, and is the main route to leveling. PvP is an alternative route to mastery of the game. Both play styles are rewarded by equipment, reputation, and increased skills in the process of designing a powerful character.

To role-play slows the avatar's progress toward higher levels, which makes it a counterproductive deviance from the game norm. One such example of RP as counterproductive to the immediate progress was a Warsong Gulch battle with Eternity Fall. This Horde group entered Warsong Gulch as a premade group. Such groups are known to be strong in battlegrounds, as cooperation is a key to victory. Opposing EF at the time was a small group of random Alliance characters. As they were not a full group, the leader of the EF raid decided that a fair game was more desirable than a fast win. The group from Eternity Fall paraded slowly to the midfield to stand in a line across the field, and with gestures indicated that they were waiting for the opposition to find a few more players. The Alliance did a lot more than that: seeing what they faced, by the time the battle started almost all of the characters on the Alliance side had been swapped for others with high PvP rank, meaning they had taken the opportunity to let the less-experienced players leave the field and call the better players to the battle. The Alliance still lost, but the delay and the strategic swapping changed the mood and the meaning of the game.

A fully point-rational behavior would have been to attack as soon as possible, kill as many as possible, and win the game fast. In the time it took the Alliance to get ready for battle, Eternity Fall could have finished the battle and been about to start a new fight, doubling the gain. The fair and "knightly" behavior had two rewards, neither of them given by the game platform: 1) to gain the personal respect of the opponents in the name of fair play, an ideal in sports, games, and competitions everywhere, and 2) to underline the fantasy of the guild members as disciplined heroes, knights of the epic battles of myth and story. But the reward for obeying RP motivation is intangible, qualitative, and highly subjective. It can't be measured and can't be compared, except to the degree it is formed into story and enjoyed by other players. For players whose main goal in the game is to gain measurable advantages—for instance, through raiding—this is quite deviant behavior. Others look for different rewards, and make their own games.

One of the players—let's call the character Daisyhoof—is fascinated by the visual aspect of the game, and her favorite quests are the ones that include stunning visual effects, like curing gazelles in The Barrens only to see the beast leap happily away. She would explore areas normally inaccessible to characters at her level in order to take screenshots or "photos" of the areas: "I announced it on guild forums as an in-character message that my mother had lost all her holiday snaps and she needed duplicates before she found out.... I found nice looking places by chance, I didn't research to see if there were cool looking places, then took pictures of them and then weathered them in Photoshop and then said "these are the damaged photos see who can find new ones and whoever can find the most by Friday wins some gold" (Daisyhoof 2006).

In order to get the original screenshots, Daisyhoof, at the time level 35–40, had to enter areas designed for levels above hers. This means she was frequently attacked and killed; her armor was damaged, which costs game money to repair; and the travel was interrupted and delayed. To get the screenshots Daisyhoof deliberately slowed her progress to higher levels and hurt her ingame economy. Her behavior went against the rules designed into the game, and she suffered for this.

At the same time it was this perversion of counterproductive gameplay that turned her subjective variant into a game: she made the rules for a challenge to her fellow players, one they had to put some effort into meeting. She created a miniature game within the game, and her creativity gained her recognition and status.

As players progress, the game offers new challenges, and at a certain point these challenges are quite time-consuming. This is when the players often have to make a new decision about the gameplay strategy. Are they in the game to role-play or to fight epic battles in raids? Eternity Fall was a guild where the players tried to meet both demands, and in the long run both suffered. Nonani, whose player is a very dedicated role player, describes the conflict between the endgame activity of raiding and the RP. On the question if raiding takes time away from RP, she answered:

To some extent yes, I do find it a little bit frustrating and I was a bit concerned about the guild when we first seemed to be moving heavily into raiding. It's a bit of a Catch-22 really because I know that prior to starting the raiding group we had lost a couple of good players who decided that they wanted to move on to that part of the game, so they left the guild and we haven't really seen or heard much of them since. So I know that if we hadn't got into raiding we would almost certainly have lost more members....

Yeh, I would say it definitely does, but at the same time it keeps us together as a group rather than just having people splinter off to all sorts of different raiding communities. (Nonani 2006)

This was a dilemma created by the way raiding consumed time.[5] When a raid instance took several hours for forty people to go through, and raid groups scheduled six to twelve-hour sessions, often over several days, in order to clear some of the level 60 instances, for EF to take time out of the progress for RP during the raid became meaningless. Even asking for help from another player in a polite manner became a drain on their time. The mages, who produce high-quality "food" and "water" and are often asked to provide for the other players, at one point posted a request that people stop being polite about it, asking guild members to be deliberately rude, as rudeness was quicker.

Under that kind of pressure for time, the niceties of creating a mood through RP or the courtesy of knightly behavior become impossible. For EF it created a tension that the guild, in the end, could not contain. In January 2007 the raid leaders split off into a raiding guild, while EF decided to become a dedicated RP guild. Nonani had in the meantime quit playing her EF characters. The conflict between the behavior they all enjoyed and had sought together to maintain and the behavior the game encouraged and rewarded took its toll.

Guilds

One of the more deviant activities of the game, regardless of server, must be guild-leading. Of all unrewarded tasks in the game, this one must be the most strenuous and least rewarding from a point-hoarding view. Where raid-leading ensures that the raid leader gets into raids with players she enjoys playing with, and hence gains experience, equipment, and raid rewards, the guild leader receives no rewards apart from some respect from their guild mates and a lot of maintenance work. At the same time, all guilds must have a leader. The rules of the game insist on this. The player I interviewed about this was quite relaxed about the efforts of guild-leading:

Torill: So how involved are you in the guild-leading?
Valencia: How involved I am in the guild-leading? I have been an officer for quite some time. I was one of the first two officers. So well, I don't consider the guild being actually led that much but in the things that where we actually do make decisions about I'm involved. Just as involved as the other officers. We discuss issues together and try to find a solution that we all like so in that way I don't know how involved.
Torill: Did you spend much time on it?
Valencia: Not so much, it doesn't require so much time usually. It comes in waves. Sometimes it's more than others. When there's some issue coming up then it requires some time (Valencia 2006).

Valencia took over as a guild leader shortly after this conversation. Only a few months later the same issues which troubled Nonani led Valencia's player to renounce his leadership and then shortly after take his raid character out of the guild and into a pure raid guild. The issues that needed to be solved had grown unsolvable, and the process of leading the players he loved playing with had taken the joy out of the game.

One of the main problems with guild leadership is that the only reward for leading a guild is status and power, while there is no authority outside of the guild leader to bestow these rewards. There are two ways to feel that guild-leading is rewarding: either the leader can desire power and the chance to control the environment for other people, or she can have a masochistic desire to serve, as somebody has to do the job. Both behaviors are considered deviant in and outside of game contexts.

The High Cost of Raiding

Raids are groups of more than five players, and can be as large as forty players. They are needed to solve tasks in some of the more complicated areas in the game, where the objective is to defeat NPCs too powerful for smaller groups and loot them for their good equipment, the "loot" they "drop."

Raids are very well facilitated by the game, as the entire process of quests and instances that a player goes through from level 13 to level 70 is a training process for the raiding, which starts at 60 (and now with *The Burning Crusade* starts again at 70). The easier areas have equipment that makes it possible to enter and fight through the harder areas. There are special raid channels once you are in a raid, and raid leaders are given special permissions.

At the same time raids are extremely player-intensive, and one of the areas where we see the highest emphasis from the players on the use of mods. The prerequisite for most raids is CTraid, a mod for raid administration.

The heavy raid instances are the most intensive and challenging areas in the game, but that is also why they are the most rewarding, and the ones that some players give the most status. Some players see all the other activities as perversions; only raiding is truly the game. A player on a PvE server made the claim that all gamers really wanted to raid, and that only raiders were worthy of research as it was not at level 60 the game started, but at Tier2 ("Stian," in an instant message to the author, 2006).[6] While I disagree strongly with his sentiment about what is worthy of study, his passion was relevant to the opinion of many of the dedicated raiders. In order to keep raiding, you have to believe you do the only thing worthwhile, as raiding excludes most other game activities. In this view anything which slows down the character's progress is meaningless, perverse frivolity and senseless excess. Everything but the raiding becomes deviant. How deviant is such an obsession with one aspect of the game?

It is the raiding which really hooks players and earns *World of Warcraft* its reputation as an "addictive" game, but it's also the raiding that causes burn-out and total withdrawal from the game. One player talked about raiding and the effort of it. He had at the time stopped playing *World of Warcraft* once, because the raiding took up too much of his time. As I did the interview he had just resumed playing. When *The Burning Crusade* was released he refused to buy the update, and so efficiently ended his raiding days. This is a typical story of a dedicated raider: the intensity of the experience and the tightly knit community has a strong hold on the players, to the point that the only way to stop raiding is by making a clean break from the game.

This player, "Raider," had indulged in a deviance that Blizzard punishes with exclusion when they discover it. This is a type of transgression that I would call a destructive deviance, as it harms others by disrupting the balance of the game. Raider had bought gold. He described the process carefully, emphasizing his search for a reliable gold seller. His description and justifications ring with insecurity: "I asked around and made sure I had found a reliable seller. If not, I would never have done it. The process was easy, but I had to make sure the payment went through a reliable card company" (Raider 2006).

This is a player who took great pride in his abilities and his skill. He played for the sake of the social activity, to assist his friends, and for the challenge, not for the quick glory of easy epic loot. What made him take the easy way out? He answered that one himself by explaining it in very simple time versus money terms. What he bought was not gold, but time. The sum he spent on gold bought him hours when he did not have to grind for gold to spend on potions, buffs, and equipment. Raiding is a high-maintenance activity.

When I asked if some new raid instance would not lead to more of the illegal gold trade, the guild talk on Eternity Fall pointed out that not all parts of the game are for everybody. At the same time it is exactly this exclusivity of raiding that makes the raid-connected gold trade flourish: if a player doesn't have the time to invest in grinding for buffs and potions, other resources have to be used, and buying the way to status and advantage is quite common in all walks of life. Perhaps not all parts of the game are for all the players, but the players willing to spend hard cash can still get an advantage over the rest.

Buy Cheap Gold

The contamination of games by mixing resources from different arenas is nothing new to gaming. Caillois describes the problem and calls it corruption: "The principle of play has become corrupted. It is now necessary to take precautions against cheats and professional players, a unique product of the contagion of reality. Basically, it is not a perversion of play, but a sidetracking derived from one of the four primary impulses governing play" (1961, 45).

Part of the magic in the magic circle (Huizinga 2000) depends on how the playing field evens all players. Rich or poor, king or peasant: what happens in the game is only supposed to depend on your skill. This dream of fair play has always been contested. It is no surprise that computer game players try to use their out-of-game advantages in-game, and one way to do that is by buying gold.

Edward Castronova became known to the game research community through his article on the economy of Norrath, the world of *EverQuest* (2001). Here he describes a market that transgresses the game space and brings resources across from one arena to the other. He expands on this in his more recent work *Synthetic Worlds*. "Once a buyer gets to the website, purchasing virtual items and currency is just as quick and easy as buying a book at Amazon.com. Select the items you want, put them in your shopping cart, and head for the checkout" (Castronova 2005, 164).

Shopping for gold, items, or even characters has become as streamlined and commercial as buying a pair of sneakers. And in the same manner as a team can buy the players they need to top the Series, *World of Warcraft* gamers can buy their way into the top levels of the game. This is, however, not an accepted way to achieve status.

Yet for all its successes, IGE and its competitors are not fully accepted within the gaming industry. Game developers in general seem to wish that IGE and the market that feeds it would go away. For the fact is, the developers are trying to build a fantasy existence, and the idea that not only is this alleged fantasy irreparably intermixed with reality, but that some outsider can make millions off of that fact, is troubling. From a neutral standpoint, one can see merit on both sides. IGE merely capitalizes on natural market incentives. On the other hand, the fantasy atmosphere of synthetic worlds is their most precious object, and the crass marketing of goods and currency endangers it quite terribly.[7] (Castronova 2005, 165)

Castronova here points to the problem with the fantasy of the game realms, claiming it is the crass marketing around and in the realms that breaks down the fantasy. This is only partly true. What slows the acceptance is the resistance to contamination of the game. The shame and reluctance players feel about using a gold seller is not because they feel the profits should go to the game company. It has to do with fair play and respecting the arena.

Like all players who can't spend all hours grinding, I have had a peek at the gold-selling pages. The prices are not unreasonable at all, and I understand why people buy. For a slow grinder like me, to make 1000 gold takes at least a month of in-game collecting. I can buy it for $38.99, which is two to three hours in real-life work. The conversion rate of time is very good.

Why don't all players just do it? Interviews with players who do not buy gold explain why. Large groups of players strongly disapprove of gold buying. Social pressure and fear of losing face are important barriers. There is a logic to this disapproval. The real value in multiplayer games is your reputation. Reputation is spread virally through social interaction, but it has few visual or other more explicit expressions. Your reputation—if it is a good one—will, however, often be reflected in your access to groups and raids: your path through the complex areas of the game will be easier and you will have more access to gear. For those who are not in on the social rumor circle, the fancy gear appears to be what garners respect, and they assume that getting similar gear means getting similar respect. Since they don't have access to the same pool of raiding partners, they have to gain what expressions of status they can through the auction house. At the auction house a particular item can run up to several hundreds, if not thousands, of gold. The price of a certain dagger obtained in Molten Core was, in December 2006, 1500 gold (prices vary between servers and factions). For a player with no or limited access to raid groups, this object will either mean months of grinding for gold or a trip to the gold sellers.

But games, as has been repeated to exhaustion, go by their own rules. Mastery is the core of gaming: to get where you want to go not just quickly and efficiently, but beautifully. It's why the Eternity Fall players lined up at the midfield to wait for their opponents to get their group together. It's why *World of Warcraft* players choose enchants with fancy glows over enchants with good weapon effects. It's why players carry spare sets of gear in their characters' bags, filling precious space, and swap between civilian clothing and raid clothing when entering and leaving cities. *How* matters, despite the lack of hard-coded rewards.

Bot-fighting

The resistance to the commercialization of the magic circle has created its own game within the game. Much of the gold farming is done by programs, also known as "bots" (from "robots"). These bots are player avatars, but they are not controlled by a real player at the keyboard, but by a program the player has installed. The bot is designed to perform certain tasks: target, kill, loot, skin, move, target, kill, loot, skin is a very common combination.

Bots can be hard to reveal, as they move in patterns common to players who are farming for something. Farming (the collection of certain items for sale or crafting) is a repetitive activity, and most players settle into comfortable, efficient routines that take little effort—an almost meditative state where multitasking is common. So how do you know if the avatar is a bot or not? For some players, spotting the bots is a game in itself. Margatar claims that most bots are hunters, have pets that keep the default names (Boar, Bird, Cat), and never wear gear from inside instances. He offers this description of his further strategies for botspotting:

And now the most important indicator that the character you're looking at might be a bot: behaviour.

Bots don't notice if a mob gets tagged by someone else after they've sent their pet at it. When I suspect a hunter to be a bot, I hang around and try to see which mob it will attack next. Hunter bots attack by sending in the pet first, so once their pet runs towards a new mob, I tag that mob for myself before the pet reaches it. If the hunter in question is indeed a bot, it will kill that mob anyway, while most players usually will stop attacking since they don't want to do the work for someone else. [...]

Bots don't navigate complex terrain well, especially if there are obstacles between it and the mob it is trying to loot. [...] Some bots can't even go into a proper self-defense mode if they get stuck while trying to reach their loot.

I have seen two different ways of movement that bots use. Some just use their tracking to find a mob to kill. If they run out of mobs, i.e., end up in a place where nothing shows up on their tracking radar, they will stand still. They then slowly turn on the spot, waiting for something to show up. Drag a mob into their tracking range and watch them spring to life again. Slow turning, whether standing or running, is often a sign of bot movement too. (Margatar, e-mail to the author, 2006)

As we see, Margatar has developed a list of checkpoints for recognizing a bot. The procedure includes experiments that cannot be automated. In a way Margatar has developed his own Turing Test for *World of Warcraft* characters. The Turing Test was developed to recognize when artificial intelligence becomes undistinguishable from human intelligence. In a similar manner Margatar is testing for human reason behind routine behavior.

Creating bots to farm for in-game resources is a deviant strategy in many uses of the word, including the derogatory ones. This deviance is treated like cheating: when found out, the account is closed and the character is in effect executed. This is one of the few activities that is treated like a crime against the game. But since the game administrators don't put sufficient resources into this fight against crime, gamers have developed their own strategies. They are thorough, inventive, and in some cases very funny, and the bot vigilante gamers have created their own little perversion of the game as they fight the corruption.

Now how can [you] mess with a bot once you're sure you've found one?

You can tag the mobs they have targeted as described above. They do the work, you get the rewards, and bots who are not getting loot have wasted their time. Report them. It may not have any effect at all, but you never know your luck. If the bot belongs to the hostile faction, you can try to flag them for PvP and kill them. There are several ways to get them flagged for PvP, but none of them is working reliably, from what I hear. You must flag yourself for PvP first, of course.

Spamming them with a /duel macro when they are about to kill a mob works sometimes. Just spam the macro while their current mob is about to die, it might make them attack you, and since they are very bad at PvP, you'll get a pretty easy kill....

And if you have a spare happy fun rock or leather ball, throw it at bots of your own faction. It fills their inventory…one less stack of leather they're bringing home. (Margatar, e-mail to the author, 2006)

This is a great example of how within a multiplayer environment new games are born all the time. If there is a pattern of behavior, somebody is there to play around with it. The trick of making another character turn on PvP unintentionally is common to other activities. One easy strategy with some characters is to turn on PvP and run into range of the Area of Effect abilities. This is basically the same type of strategy as Margatar describes to make the bots go PvP so the player can disable them for a while, but in this case used to annoy and "gank" other players. Ganking is to kill another player character repeatedly, and is mostly used when an overwhelming opposition singles out one target and keeps tracking this one target down. It is a type of griefing, play basically designed to make gaming miserable for other players. Bot-killing is not considered griefing or ganking, but a kind of advanced PvE—the killing of mobs. A bot is controlled by a computer program, and so it's considered a mob by the gaming community and can be killed repeatedly, while the killer still does not become a ganker even if they are killing player characters.

Deviance or Just Another Strategy?

The concept of deviance in human behavior is complex, and while the heavily rule-based arena of gaming makes it easier to pinpoint when an activity deviates from the rules, the activities that are not breaking the rules but simply circumventing them or taking advantage of them, flourish.

Deviance is however still defined by the individual viewpoint. For a raider, all role play is deviant. The only goal of the game from this viewpoint is to reach and master the large raid instances; any other activities are counterproductive. This is a very pietistic view: gaming as a goal-oriented productive activity. Scott Rettberg, in chapter 1, discusses how *World of Warcraft* is a way to train good executives: people who are willing to grind hard for elusive rewards like prestige, status, rank, and reputation. In this view the raiders are the top rank: the ones who are willing to endure more to reach harder goals.

Talking to players it is clear, however, that there are many other reasons to play. One raid group took down the first faction leader on their server. Later they were the first to kill one of the harder bosses in Black Wing Lair, but that is expected behavior for a raid group. To kill a faction leader, however, is not productive for the advancement toward instance mastery. The only thing the raid group achieved by killing that leader was to kill the leader. He didn't even drop any good loot. A whole group of raiders dedicated themselves to several attempts in order to do something that even in game terms was totally unproductive. In the flesh world this would have been considered at best odd, at worst, totally perverse. But this is what makes games something more than a training ground for highly efficient executives: the joy of gaming is as much in playing with the limits of the game as in mastering the rules and solving the riddles.

The main problem with the deviance concept in the flesh world is that it is not a description of an objective position, but of a subjective experience. There are no objective measurements for "normal" or for "deviant." Gameworlds are strongly designed worlds where there is a right and a wrong. Follow the rule = right, break the rule = wrong. But even in this simplified world it turns out to be not that simple. There is a lot of gray space, and humans take delight in using it. Much inventiveness goes into not following the obvious aim of the game. Mastering the game is not submitting to the game: it is to know it so well that the game no longer controls the player.

In this manner games become practice grounds for subversion: a place to learn about rules, how to understand them, how to obey them, how to stretch them, how to break them, and how to avoid them. The deviant is in this case not the one who breaks the rules, but the one who decides not to care about them at all. And so the most likely place to find the deviant use of the game is in the use that is outside of the arena of rules: to use the game to chat, to take pretty pictures, to have cybersex in an inn in Goldshire, to have a group of researchers meeting in a cave in Durotar. Relating to the rules, no matter what type the relationship is, is not deviance. Deviance within a gameworld is to decide not to bother, and stand aside.

At the end here I will try to bring the logic of the game back into the flesh world. If this definition of deviance as not caring about the rules is to work in the mundane world, many of the current popular definitions are not valid. Crime, cheating, sexual explorations: they are all defined by a relationship to the law or to socially accepted norms. The sexual deviant is as titillated by being outside of common norms as by the act; the criminal is aware of the lawlessness of his actions. But not to bother is so common that we accept it as a norm. We rarely consider that lack of understanding, involvement, or participation in the mechanisms of the world around us is one of the greatest problems we have. What gaming can teach us is that it's not the clash of wills and interests, the odd behavior, or the personal, individual strategies that ruin the patterns of our world. Gaming shows us that the real threat to a rewarding, functional system is when the participants don't care.

Acknowledgments

A heartfelt thank you to the players of the guild I have chosen to call Eternity Fall, and the subjects for my interviews. Also thanks to the members of the European researchers' *World of Warcraft* guild, several of whom are contributors here. May we all play again.

Notes

1. My research was done on the original world, but the article was finished just after the advent of *The Burning Crusade*, the 2007 game expansion. This leads to some irregularities in the text, as the research relates to a game which has been altered. While this may be a problem to the description of the game, it also underlines the changeable nature of code.

2. This is like the referee at a football match, who makes the decision then and there. Even if the decision may later be seen to be wrong, the rules say it has to be obeyed while the match continues.

3. Allakhazam is a Web site for information about objects, quests, areas, and other useful information for players. For a fee players gain access to updated information about their favorite game. Information about *World of Warcraft* is available at ⟨http://wow.allakhazam.com/⟩.

4. Thottbot is a Web site for information about objects, quests, areas, and other useful information for players. The information at Thottbot is collected by a program or "bot" which players can install on their machines like an add-on. This reports the information the player accesses within *World of Warcraft* to the Web site ⟨http://thottbot.com/⟩, where players can access the information freely.

5. With *The Burning Crusade* the size of the groups allowed to endgame raid instances has shrunk to twenty-five players, and the instances appear to be shorter.

6. Tier2 refers to equipment. Blizzard has introduced certain equipment sets for the characters, where collecting the whole set would give the characters strong bonuses. This made the sets very desirable, but since they are hard to collect and some parts only drop in raid instances, owning one makes the player easily recognizable as a dedicated raider. There were several tiers before *The Burning Crusade* opened. *The Burning*

Crusade, however, made a lot of the old equipment obsolete, something that caused both anger and sorrow in the players.

7. IGE is Internet Games and Entertainment, a company selling in-game objects to players.

References

Bartle, Richard. 1996. "Hearts, Clubs, Diamonds, Spades: Players Who Suit MUDs," *Journal of MUD Research* 1, no. 1. Available at ⟨http//www.mud.co.uk/richard/hcds.htm⟩.

Bartle, Richard. 1999. "A Wiz by Any Other Name." Available at ⟨http://www.mud.co.uk/richard/abcdec98.htm⟩.

Baudrillard, Jean. 1990. *Seduction*. Hampshire, UK: MacMillan.

Becker, Howard S. 2005. "Moral Entrepeneurs: The Creation and Enforcement of Deviant Categories." In *Social Deviance*, 5th ed., ed. Henry N. Pontell, 2–6. Upper Saddle River, N.J.: Prentice Hall.

Blackshaw, Tony and Tim Crabbe. 2004. *New Perspectives on Sport and "Deviance": Consumption, Performativity, and Social Control*. London: Routledge.

Blizzard. 2004. *World of Warcraft*. Blizzard Entertainment Inc.

Caillois, Roger. 1961. *Man, Play, and Games*. New York: The Free Press of Glencoe.

Castronova, Edward. 2001. "Virtual Worlds: A First-Hand Account of Market and Society on the Cyberian Frontier," *The Gruter Institute Working Papers on Law, Economics, and Evolutionary Biology* 2, no. 1. Available at ⟨http://www.bepress.com/giwp/default/vol2/iss1/art1⟩.

Castronova, Edward. 2005. *Synthetic Worlds: The Business and Culture of Online Games*. Chicago: University of Chicago Press.

Daisyhoof [pseud.]. 2006. Interview with the author.

Huizinga, Johan. 2000. *Homo Ludens: A Study of the Play Element in Culture*. London: Routledge.

Juul, Jesper. 2005. *Half-Real: Video Games between Real Rules and Fictional Worlds*. Cambridge, MA: MIT Press.

Lessig, Lawrence. 1999. *Code: And Other Laws of Cyberspace*. New York: Basic Books.

Mortensen, Torill Elvira. 2003. *Pleasures of the Player: Flow and Control in Online Games*. PhD diss., University of Bergen and Volda University College.

Murray, Janet H. 1997. *Hamlet on the Holodeck: The Future of Narrative in Cyberspace.* New York: Free Press.

Nonani [pseud.]. 2006. Interview with the author.

Raider [pseud.]. 2006. Interview with the author.

Rubington, Earl and Martin S. Weinberg. 2005. *Deviance: The Interactionist Perspective,* 9th edition. Boston: Allyn & Bacon.

Taylor, T. L. 2006. "Does WoW Change Everything? How a PvP Server, Multinational Player Base and Surveillance Mod Scene Cause Me Pause," *Games and Culture* 1, no. 4: 318–337.

Turkle, Sherry. 1995. *Life on the Screen: Identity in the Age of the Internet.* New York: Simon and Schuster.

Valencia [pseud.]. 2006. Interview with the author.

Role-play vs. Gameplay: The Difficulties of Playing a Role in *World of Warcraft*

11

Esther MacCallum-Stewart and Justin Parsler

What is Role-playing?

[R]ole-playing means more than actually playing a role-playing game (FlagRSP 2006).

What does role-playing mean in MMORPGs? This chapter investigates not the game, but the activities within it—the act of role-playing itself. What does it mean? How does it take place? And perhaps most crucially, with so many players and so many different modes of play within *World of Warcraft*, why is it so difficult in a game styling itself as a "massively multiplayer online role-playing game" for players to enact their roles, and how do they overcome this problem?

When discussing role play in *World of Warcraft*, one immediately runs into semantic difficulties: the term "role-playing" has no clear, consistent definition and a computer game that is designated as a "role-playing game" generally does not *require* the player to do any actual role-playing. This confusion can leave players perplexed: some want to role-play, but do not really know what it is, some have no desire to pretend to be someone else when playing, some may see role-playing as esoteric or elitist, and some may simply assume that it must be role-playing because it says so on the box. Similarly, the definitions of a role-playing game have been recently questioned by Joris Dormans, who acknowledges that role-playing games have a "troublesome relation between roleplaying on the one hand and rules, gaming and gameplay on the other" (2007).

A player who is consciously role-playing in *World of Warcraft* is seeking to create a character who transcends the mechanic of the game and takes on a plausible, defined reality of its own. This is not to say that the player lives their character's life (though some do), but rather that they direct that character's actions, not as a player controlling a game avatar, but rather like an author, scripting their protagonist.

The term "role player" has only recently been adapted to suit online gamers, a problematic appropriation. Previously, the term applied to players of tabletop gaming or live action role-playing (LARP). MMORPGs are seen by many as the natural successors to these games; however, they remove some elements, namely the freeform and "acting out" aspects of the game. However, while online gaming in the form of MMORPGs is becoming increasingly popular, most players come not from tabletop or LARP, but from the world of computer games. "Role-playing game" is described in the *Oxford English Dictionary* as "A game in which players take on the roles of imaginary characters, usu. in a setting created by a referee, and thereby vicariously experience the imagined adventures of these characters" (2603). In MMORPGs, the term "role-playing game" describes not the spontaneous acting out of a character, but refers to game mechanics: levels, character classes, and, to some extent, the high-fantasy setting of the game itself. Clearly, the terms are very different ones.

In tabletop and LARP, role-playing involves a willing suspension of disbelief whereby the player seeks to make their role in the gameworld a believable and persistent one, to act out that separate existence, and to have the world respond accordingly in order to substantiate this role. As Sean Patrick Fannon argues, this is chaotic in form, something that MMORPGs simply cannot reproduce: "RPGs...require rules that allow for a wide range of choices by the players. There are no set paths, no specified areas with established rules for what happens when you land on them, and rarely any intended 'endings'" (1999, 35, emphasis his). *World of Warcraft* does not create such a world; in fact, many of the mechanics of the game disenfranchise this randomness. This is due to several factors: player agency is limited within the game, interface causes a separation between player and gameworld (Gee 2003), other players do not respond to role play in consistent ways, and there are invariable differences of culture, linguistics, and age. In spite of this, many players seek to rise above the game environment and create their own reality within the game. Therefore, it is necessary to determine why role play takes place and how it affects play in *World of Warcraft*.

Why Role Play?

I had always assumed that the "RP" in MMORPG was ironic. After all, most MMORPGs have had to deliberately set aside designated role-playing servers, and these have always been in the minority. This suggested that role-playing wasn't something most players wanted to do in an MMORPG. (Yee 2006)

The act of role-playing can seem a curious pastime to the outsider. Unlike the main thrust of the game, it offers no tangible rewards: levels are not gained, better equipment not found. To the vast majority of *World of Warcraft* players a significant part of the game's appeal involves advancing their character, and role-playing does not facilitate this—indeed, as we shall see, it takes up valuable time and actually *slows* progression. The only facet of core gameplay in *World of Warcraft* likely to be affected by role play is the building of interpersonal relationships, which can in turn lead to more productive gameplay. However, these relationships can be built up equally well without the need to role play.

We feel that role players see role-playing in a number of ways: as a testing of personal ideals; as morally challenging, involving issues of teamwork and conflict resolution (or not); as mentally or physically demanding; as opportunities to act out characteristics or beliefs they might not usually express; as granting a sense of agency that encourages feelings of influence, control, and power; as engrossing; and finally, as escapist. To some people, role play increases the quality of the game. Creating a character who shares commonalities with the overall game narrative gives the world meaning for the player. Rather than being simply a game where points are gained and monsters defeated, the "World" of Warcraft—Azeroth (and now The Outlands)—is given a coherent meaning by people who then use it to build their own stories.

Immersion

[T]he player is aware that it is optional to imagine the fictional world of the game. In non-electronic make-believe games, this makes perfect sense since a game of make-believe is not required to be rhetorically persuasive (nobody else needs to be convinced) nor does it need to be logically coherent. We can agree to believe in the fiction, and we can agree not to. (Juul 2005, 141)

One of the central problems with describing role play is the assumption that it automatically involves immersion. Atkins (2003), King and Kryzwinska (2006), and Salen and Zimmerman (2004) have all argued convincingly that immersion is often mistaken for truth; the assumption that a player can become totally immersed in a game is false.[1] King and Kryzwinska argue that games are not realistic, and are not meant to be. No one is about to be sucked physically into the terminal only to find themselves playing a very real game of death, nor can they ever really remove themselves from the fact that playing games requires a secondary interface (keyboard, computer screen, mouse) to interact with their character. In *World of Warcraft*, the player additionally accesses the game through a "picture frame" consisting of health bars, icons, and chat channels.

The block here lies in the flawed understanding that immersion is the only state in which role play occurs: "All players are aware, at some level, that the gamescape is an artificially constructed and limited environment. Players are generally very happy, and willing, to 'suspend disbelief,' however, to allow themselves to be taken in by the illusion that the worlds in which they play are more than just entirely arbitrary constructs" (King and Krzywinska 2006, 119).

Immersion involves a loss of self by the player, who then "becomes" their character. Frequently ignored is the fact that role-playing is very rarely accompanied by immersion, but is instead a creative attempt to get as close to this as possible. Being totally in character is to a role-player something of a Holy Grail, but it is rarely achieved. Indeed, it is more likely to be reconstructed retrospectively through role-played anecdote. However, immersion does not have to be present for role play to occur. For example, if a dwarf who had been following my avatar around politely for weeks suddenly offered her a bunch of flowers, I might roar with laughter, but might instruct my character to behave as if she were mightily offended. The dwarf might weep and run away embarrassed, and the player be genuinely frustrated by the rebuff. However, if the act is convincing, and believed by both, effective role play has still taken place.

Role-play Basics

World of Warcraft has specifically allocated servers for role players to use, and issues them an instruction every time they log in telling them to "respect the additional policies" and giving them a Web address on which to find these. They continue with the assertion that "Creating an immersive world that holds true to the base story line of the World of Warcraft is the driving motivation behind our Role Play Servers. While other servers allow you to play

World of Warcraft, these servers are intended to let you live World of War-craft. Within this environment you will embark on long-lasting adventures, foster enduring comradeships, and wage epic wars" (Blizzard 2007b).

The small number of servers dedicated to role play in Europe (in November 2006 there were only eleven out of ninety-one total), alongside Blizzard's admission that "this level of immersion rests largely upon the shoulders of you, the player" demonstrates that actual role-playing is regarded as secondary to the gameplay itself. This is partly due to Blizzard's perception that role-playing activities are beyond their control, but also indicates that they do not generally consider *World of Warcraft* a role-playing game. Role-playing "rules" are also very summarily sketched, asking players simply to "act and speak as my character should, in the *World of Warcraft* setting" (ibid).

Blizzard's policy for RP realms involves brief instructions about choosing appropriate role-playing names, avoiding antisocial behavior, and tolerating the beliefs of others. Importantly, however, this is a list of "do nots." Blizzard leaves the decision of how role play should be performed entirely down to the player. This causes many problems, since the lack of definition permits the existence of many levels of role-playing, and gives no clear instruction for novices. The next section deals with how role play is created by players and the methods used to effectively portray a character.

Names and Appearance

The fundamental, critical, absolutely core point of virtual worlds such as those found in multi-player online games is the development of the player's identity. (Bartle 2004, 415)

Within *World of Warcraft*, a player can immediately determine two things about another player: what they look like and their name. A player's appearance derives from a selection of avatars dressed and equipped through certain conditions, while names are chosen by players. As players control their name and it is easily perceived by others, it can be paramount in creating a first impression, and thus names aid the construction of social identities. In RP realms, a naming condition prevents "[a]ny Non-Medieval or Non-Fantasy names (i.e., Slipnslide, Robotman, Technotron)" (Blizzard 2007b). Web sites exist to help players choose "consistent" names, and role players often think as carefully about their name as they do when they create their appearance, investing it with strong internal meaning. Naming is discussed more fully by Charlotte Hagström in chapter 13.

Avatar appearance is one of the only ways that a player can lastingly affect their environment, and is an obvious representation of self in the game. The sexual appearance of many of the avatars causes several role-playing issues, and the representation of female avatars in particular has been an issue in game studies for some time.[2] This obvious act of disenfranchising those wishing to play less erotic figures in the game is as important as the fact that in *World of Warcraft*, height and weight cannot be altered—in short, everyone looks broadly the same despite minor changes of hair, facial characteristics, piercings, or skin colors. However, this is partially offset by the ability to choose clothing, which produces both positive and negative effects on role play and therefore sits somewhat on both sides of the fence.

Throughout the game, the ability to choose clothing for an avatar is readily available. However, in order to become as powerful as possible, a small number of items are highly sought after. The low chance that they will drop from bosses and monsters also makes them status symbols. Characters must wear the most statistically powerful clothing should they wish to do well in combat situations and in order to play at very high levels, a uniform appearance is required, with everyone wearing (or needing to wear) the same few items. The ability of a player to customize their clothing in combat situations is therefore limited, and it is common to take part in high-level instances or raids where all the avatars are wearing near-identical sets of armor.

In order to counterbalance this, role players take great care with their appearances. Customizing appearance is however both expensive and time consuming. Clothing may be of a lower level, and therefore can only be worn for show in nondangerous situations. Nevertheless, this act is one that role players take great pleasure in, and is often a requirement: "Leave the Epix in the Bank! We know full well and understand that epic weapons, glowing enchants and shiny phat lewt are all required for raiding. We like to raid ourselves! Remember though—help us make a role-playing community! Get yourself some 'civilian' clothes for whenever you role-play" (SquareRP 2006). In this case, the conscious decision not to wear armor signifies that role-playing activity is taking place and there is a recognition that unless a player has a "deathwish" (ibid.), costumed role play is not always possible.

Blizzard's costuming design sometimes hinders this choice. It is common to find that a piece of clothing that fully covers the male figure is overly revealing on a woman. The most obvious example is the Black Mageweave Leggings and

Vest set. On a male figure this appears as a black shirt and trousers. On a female it is instead stockings and suspenders, with a basque top. Naturally, this differentiation is often seen by female avatars as unjust. Appearing in public wearing underwear is embarrassing, and automatically bestows the avatar with a sexuality that they may not wish. This sexualization of clothing can be frustrating for female avatars, often prompting complaints that, for example, "armor" consisting of a pair of plate-mail knickers is not very realistic or useful in a fight!

However, players can also find the clothing available to them in role-playing contexts useful for establishing a character's identity. Many role players often wear their chosen clothing in cities—frequently emphasizing this by making their avatars walk instead of run to define "normal" movement in busy areas such as the town squares, or they "dress down" especially for guild events.

At the guild meeting shown in figure 11.1, characters were asked to hide their weapons. Most are dressed for the occasion, and many perform actions that define their characters: rogues sit in stealth (bottom left), others have brought pets (bottom right). Someone has also set a fire in the middle of the circle as a rationale for why these people may be sitting together.

Figure 11.1
The Azeroth Elders at a guild meeting.

Language

Speech and emotes are how players express themselves within *World of Warcraft*. Since costuming can only take place in limited situations, conversation and emoted behavior are crucial in establishing how (and if) role play is taking place.

The first and most obvious problem is the differing levels at which people communicate in games. The act of having to type every word a character says places a remove between player and avatar, and the lack of visible or audible inflexion and body language causes a problem for other players—it is very difficult to convey irony through this mode, for example. At the same time, players' linguistic ability is affected by vocabulary, typing speed, and adeptness at the language being typed. Realms are only available in four European languages—English, French, German, and Spanish—so many players communicate through second languages. Even in a role-playing realm, all of these factors act against those who wish to role play.

The three examples below show different types of player speech:

1. Give 20s pls
2. I want mount when I get to 60
3. My horse's name is Twilight. I just bought him.

In the first example, a player is talking in Leet and is not role-playing. In the second, a player is not role-playing but talking out of character, and in the third role play is taking place.

Leet, the shorthand by which so much MMORPG communication takes place, is detrimental to role play. It forces the player to view a conversation in a linguistic form that simplifies speech rather than to regard a conversation as whole. At the same time, this shorthand is more universal than typed English, used crossculturally by many players. Furthermore, in situations where instructions need to be quickly conveyed, "buff pls" or "mage sheep left" are more practical than whole sentences. In instances, raids, or combat situations, Leet and shorthand are logical ways of communication. And without recourse to an excessive use of macros (triggered when a player presses a button), role-playing is not a practical way to communicate during the active parts of the game. Thus it might be safely said that role-playing must almost always take place during downtime—moments when a player is not being expected to react quickly to the game world.

In the second instance, the player refers to their level (60), which is something that their character would not know in direct speech—also known as metagaming. Furthermore, they are also using official game terms: "mount" and not "horse." The last example is one of clear role play. It is in character, it develops identity by talking about something exterior but relevant, and possibly most importantly, it prompts a response—"He's a nice horse." The central problem with language is that it always operates on several levels. At the same time, without this form of expression, there would be no interpersonal role-playing at all within the game. The sophistication with which emotes and speech are used determines role play, but these distinctions often cause accusations of elitism, since it relies heavily on strong communication skills.

In an attempt to manage the vast amount of communication passing through the game, Blizzard supports the familiar MMORPG arrangement of different chat channels, ranging from global to personal. Their diverse nature means that conversation can exist on multiple levels all at once, and also directs chat toward specific groups—parties, raids, or individuals, for example. Chat channels make communication in the game easier, allowing players to select how and where they speak. However, this causes problems for role players. First, the channels act like telepathy, assuming that everyone can hear speech wherever they are. There is no reference to this in the world background, it is simply taken as a very strange given. Second, several channels are global, and role-playing is not regulated across these spaces. No consensus exists on how role-playing should take place (if indeed it should at all) and it is common on role-playing realms to hear players chastising each other for not role-playing properly on these channels. The trade channel (only heard in major cities) epitomizes this conflict:

1. WTS [Imposing Belt of the Whale]
2. Thraye's shirts! From gnome to night-elf, we have a size that's right.
3. Selling silk cloth /w me!

While the first two examples are respectively, out of character and in character, the third demonstrates the difficulties of role-playing through chat channels. The vendor wishes to trade and asks the buyer to whisper her. This initiates a second conversation. It may be in character, but the two communicants might be on different continents. Obviously once again this is an unrealistic action—how could someone hear and then respond from such a distance?

The difficulties of communication in the game highlight how role play remains a difficult act of performance and it is clear that the game has many spaces where role play cannot exist in a practical manner. Multiple types of chat channel are, however, advantageous because they enable speech on many different levels, and place role-playing within certain spaces. As a general consensus, "Say" (/s) is used by players to role-play because having the avatar directly in front of you makes in-character interaction easier.

Breaking Role Play

Blizzard, who we have already shown to have a rather hands-off approach to role play—probably because of the extreme difficulties of making such diverse acting out of character into a series of formal rules—does however warn players that this lack of homogeneity is something they should expect:

- There are no automatic game rewards for role-playing, and no game mechanics are altered (if you give a rose to a felhound it will still try to eat you).
- Not everyone will act as you would like and the experience can sometimes be frustrating, especially on the days you don't feel like "speaking in-character" (Blizzard 2007a).

It is entirely possible to have an individual role-playing experience, in character and away from the main body of people, but the fact that this can never be witnessed makes it impractical to record. Social grouping, therefore, is important to role-playing activity, although not essential. This section outlines ways in which role play is performed by the player, and how this presents obstacles for those wishing to role-play their experiences within the game.

Mackay calls role-playing "[t]he performance that becomes itself through disappearance" (2001, 84). This performance, he argues, is strengthened by those around the participant. In a tabletop game these actions would be enacted through verbal description, in a LARP by physical action. Both require some suspension of disbelief, but in both cases the participants are physically together, collectively sustaining the imaginative process. Within *World of Warcraft*, all the participants are separated from each other by their own bodies, the practicalities of the computer interface, and the "picture frame" of screen and toolbars through which they regard their avatar. Inside Azeroth, items are not made intuitively, but are rendered into signifiers that may bear very little resemblance to what a player is trying to achieve. She cannot sew a dress with her hands, or say "I sew a dress" but must instead gather the requisite icons, select the name of the item, and then click "Accept" to tailor it, defamiliarizing the process. An avatar may be constantly visible to the player, reminding them that their "skin" lies several removes away. Even if two players sit in the same room, they are still not directly in contact with the other characters inside *World of Warcraft*. Thus role-playing in MMORPGs is instantly disadvantaged by the layers of meaning through which it must be interpreted.

Immersion within a game is therefore extremely difficult, as collective behavior becomes even harder to simulate, responses are created and processed at a remove, and answers must be "seen" through the layers of the screen— what Gee calls the projective level of role play (2003, 59–66). King and Krzywinska argue that agency helps to offset this problem, granting a feeling of embodied presence and thus characterization within the game: "[T]he ability to affect its contents in ways at least to some extent approximate to the equivalent in the real world can be a major source of impressions of embodied presence, especially as games are played in the present tense, which gives them a temporal sense of immediacy" (2006, 119). In *World of Warcraft*, this most obviously takes the form of quests (see chapter 8). These tasks give the semblance of player agency, especially since there are many that can be done concurrently, giving the illusion of choice. Superficially then, the player engages with Azeroth through a series of plots. They are not being asked to gain another 3000 experience points (although this is the ultimate outcome), they are collecting the war banners of ten invading orcs. In a very shallow sense a narrative is constructed from which the player gains a sense of purpose. Players may then build stories or enhance their characters, as the feeling of embodiment justifies the existence of the character they have decided to role-play.

However, agency remains minimal. Quests are voluntarily taken, but players must complete them to proceed into the game. More importantly, after the successful completion of a quest, nothing in Azeroth changes permanently:

The game world itself is a protean form in certain respects, with various additions and changes to the game's world included through regular updates, which includes temporary festival related material (quests, items such as fireworks and dresses, and decorations). Some aspects of the game do however lend a sense of stasis (Groundhog Day): you may for example have killed Onyxia, but you will still find her alive in human form in Stormwind Castle and encounter her in dragon form in her lair over and over again. In this sense the game does not have a linear chronology; as with retellings of myths, battles are fought over and over again. (Krzywinska 2006)

This causes problems with role-playing. Since everyone does the same quests repeatedly, free movement is restricted; players are following a set pattern and not acting independently. Once a quest is done, although that player may not (usually) complete it again, other characters will be able to do exactly the same quest, and the monsters that the first player killed will reappear. Trying to change the environment has no effect; if someone holds a role-playing event in a church, she cannot move the resident NPC avatars off the podium in order to give her speech and must stand among them. In short, there is no ability to permanently alter the course of history or the ambient setting. Thus the role player has no lasting effect on the gameworld and might rightly assume that their character has little agency, and no importance in the narrative of the world as a whole.

This lack of free agency can be demonstrated by the way quest chains are followed through for experience points despite not really making sense in terms of role-playing. The Abercrombie quests of Darkshire, which end with the hapless player unleashing a monster on the local town, demonstrate this clearly.

A local quest-giver acknowledges that the town is having problems with "the necromancer to the east," clearly implicating Abercrombie before any actions have been taken (he is, in fact, directly to the east of this NPC). Yet despite this information, the player still continues to gather materials for Abercrombie himself throughout a lengthy series of tasks. Eventually, when the old man is exposed, he cannot be put to a fitting end by the player. It is obvious relatively early in the quest chain that Abercrombie is *not* a harmless old man living in a shack. Even geography fingers him—he lives next door to one of the most dangerous graveyards in the game, seemingly unperturbed! Appropriate role play of this situation might be to take the evidence to the mayor and dispense appropriate justice, or possibly attempting to prevent rather than abet Abercrombie's evil designs before they reach fruition. Yet this option is simply not allowed and at no stage can Abercrombie's chaos be prevented.

Class

Most of the character classes in *World of Warcraft* have long traditions and are recognizable to people who have read fantasy literature or played role-playing games. This is especially true of the warrior, mage, and priest. Rogues derive from the old "thief" classes of early RPGs, while the hunter is essentially a Ranger with the addition of a pet (Castronova 2005).

The use of classes facilitates and stymies role play: facilitates because it gives people an immediate handle on what a character is like, but stymies because they can be stereotyped. The perfect example of this is the druid class. "Druid. n. Member of an order of priests and teachers . . . later reputed to be magicians and soothsayers" (OED, 764).

Druids in *World of Warcraft* roughly resemble these criteria. They possess magic, shapeshifting, and healing abilities. Only tauren and night elves can become druids, and it is no coincidence that it is these two classes that are most closely linked with ecological concerns. Druids are assumed to be relatively ecofriendly, depicted as working in harmony with the land and harnessing its forces. Several druid skills are symbolized by a leaf icon, druidic magic largely concerns control of the elements and the weather, and they can change into animals at will.

It might seem logical, therefore, to suggest that druids were so in touch with the land that they would not wish to harm its flora and fauna. This would be a logical role-playing choice, and in a live or tabletop game could be satisfyingly enacted. A player might decide that they will only kill those corrupted by evil or those who are already dead, and play their character accordingly. The referee would possibly award points for adhering to or breaking this tenet. In an MMORPG however, the decision not to kill any form of creature (including other players) can only be disadvantageous and the capacity to role-play this potentially interesting characterization simply does not exist. Were the druid to try actively seeking out the corrupt and undead, they might find them placed behind animals that would try to attack them. They may find themselves missing huge chunks of quests involving killing animals or humans, or unable to complete many sections of the game. Finally, no points are awarded for making this decision.

Sex, Role Play, and Power Emoting

Many players are dissuaded from role-playing because of its perceived connection with sexual activity and cybersex. Indeed, the highly sexualized nature of many character avatars often prompts sexual behavior. Sex is a contentious issue in MMORPGs, further confused since many successfully role-played acts concern the gradual growth of relationships, culminating in weddings, break-ups, or even virtual "births." Indeed, these events can be some of the most valid and rewarding role-play acts. Furthermore, the graphic descriptions that often form part of cybersex discourage players from experiencing more balanced role-play. "Michael" from MMOG Nation expresses this clearly, distinguishing cybersex from role-playing: "WoW is many things, but roleplaying? Lying 'naked' on a bed, with another guy, cybering via /tells in the Goldshire Inn is not roleplaying" (comment posted to MMOGNation .com January 17, 2007). Cybersex also encourages another aspect that many role-players dislike; power emoting. Power emoting involves a forced act pressed upon another player.

Power Emotes / God Emotes Suck
It is very poor role-play to approach someone and /emote steals your wallet. Power emotes (also known as God emotes,) will often have more sensible people ignore you.
    Instead, try more realistic approaches, e.g. /emote attempts to steal your wallet. Doing this may or may not get you a response, but at least it stands a better chance. (Blizzard 2006)

We define role play as an act demanding personal choice, and this is sup-ported by online guides to role-playing that caution against power emoting (Stratics 2005, Ten Ton Hammer 2005). Power emoting is therefore not role-playing, and players who are exposed to this (which can even be a form of bullying or harassment) often confuse the two.

Recovering Role Play

In order for a collection of individuals to be a subsociety they need to perceive them-selves as such—they must recognise that they have a subculture, and act in accordance with the expectations of their group. (Fine 1983, 36)

We have shown how role-playing is extremely difficult in *World of Warcraft*, but it is not impossible. A series of imaginative, original, and sometimes highly organized actions created by players have helped develop and sustain role-playing in *World of Warcraft*.

    A central question in this paper is why role-playing takes place when it is so very hard to perform in the game. The answer lies in the fact that the world is a sustained one. *World of Warcraft* is always there. The game functions in real time, and Blizzard's servers run in local time. When it is daylight in Europe, it is daylight in *World of Warcraft*. At approximately 7 p.m. it gets dark, and at approximately 6 a.m. it gets light, roughly corresponding to the world outside.

    Locations around the world, including churches, inns, parks, beaches, city squares, and what appears to be an empty lecture hall complete with wooden bleachers and a podium on Fray Island are all readily available and play host to a variety of smaller-scale events. The Darkmoon Faire, which travels be-tween the Horde and the Alliance and appears only one week each month in alternate locations, has become a popular place for people to meet and socialize, perhaps because of its neutral connotations.

There are so many unexplained small details in the game that a player has vast potential to create their own stories. The game is also so large that a player might never encounter some moments of it—moments that other players can explain with their own personalized narratives.

Although no rules on how to role-play exist, players make steps to encourage and sustain role play within realms. These include online guides, the organization of role-playing events, programs that can be added to the game that make role-playing easier and more visible to other players, and community groups that encourage role play as well as set their own criteria for what constitutes role-playing activity.

The most important of these is casual role play. The simple act of actually talking to someone in character prompts reciprocal behavior, teaches other people how to role-play in kind, and encourages role play. It may not be possible to talk in character during raids, but it is possible to write a macro that is automatically generated when an action takes place, or to advertise an item in a colorful and entertaining way rather than using Leet. Peer pressure will always be the most effective method of encouraging role play, simply because it sets standards and encourages group participation. If a mage answers "aloud" the request to make a portal to Darnassus, or a warrior adds an in-character battle cry to one of her macros, the visibility of this act enhances the role-playing experience of everyone around them. A willingness by players to get involved also means that communal areas for role-playing have formed in unofficial capacities on many realms. Smaller-scale events are common, from evening prayers, weddings parties, or staged events such as the one advertised by this proclamation on a guild forum: "Bulwar was my brother and now he's dead. I feel so lost and alone. The Horde are growing in numbers and we need to stop them. I want revenge! Kill the troll that took my loved one, his punishment should be death. Meet me in Darnassus, at 15:00. Shennah, daughter of Aurillia" (Silent Minds 2007).

In role-playing guilds, players use chat channels and forums to their advantage. One of the benefits of guild role-playing is that rules can be clearly determined. Guilds often have extensive forums and Web sites devoted to backstory and in-character conversations. Once again these places function to create role play around events that might be difficult to actually respond to in character—for example, they might provide a guild-generated reason to visit a certain instance. The personal nature of guilds also means that role-playing can be carried out in a less self-conscious manner—only the guild of like-minded players need witness the conversations taking place.

Role-playing events on a large scale are relatively uncommon, due to the difficulties in organizing, advertising, and even participating in such events. The Steamwheedle Faire on the EU Moonglade server (held March 19, 2006) attracted over 240 people from both sides, yet many people found their computers unable to cope with the processing needed to have so many players in one place. Despite these problems, the Mithril Guard held a similar event celebrating one year as a role-playing guild in the city of Ironforge several months later. The lag experienced was no less significant, but once again nearly 150 people attended in a city traditionally known for its slow performance and processing times. One might note not only the perversity of human nature exhibited here, but also a willingness to persevere, and of course, the love of a good party.

Small-scale events, however, are much more frequent, both planned and spontaneous. In the Moonglade EU realm, for example, it is common to find characters gathering in the main square of Stormwind or the tavern "The Pig and Whistle" after the evening raids have taken part to informally chat in-character. Other groups, such as SquareRP, unofficially claim designated areas for role-playing purposes, fictitiously locate their guild headquarters in the surrounding buildings, and work to establish community links for like-minded players. Members of the community register as residents through the Web sites and are expected to adhere to a series of rules, including acting in character while they are in the area. These actions recognize that role-playing may not be possible all the time, but if enough people join during downtime occasions, it is hoped that consensual activity will take place.

Thus a second reason for role play is its potential as a creative activity. While some players may come to the game with experience of tabletop or live role-playing, the vast majority of them have not. *World of Warcraft* provides an opportunity—one which other players are sustaining—for imagination to take hold. And this need not be particularly in-depth or even dramatic to be gratifying. At the workshop that helped this book come about, one participant spoke passionately about how a simple emote like making her avatar bow before others in thanks gave her a greater sense of self within the game. Having never role-played before, this action for her was both rewarding and easy to do (simply by typing "/bow"). Useful role-playing emotes include making silly gestures, telling jokes, and even activating predetermined flirting speeches. It is important that activating these emotes enables a short speech, which enables second-language players to appreciate not only that they are telling a joke that others will understand, but that it is clear what they are doing—the spoken joke (which may be quite long) is accompanied by the typed information "xxx tells a joke to yyy." Players frequently use these quick moments of role play not only to communicate with each other, but through a sense of playfulness. *World of Warcraft* provides not only a vista, therefore, but it also gives players places to play and actions that help them.

Finally, *World of Warcraft* reassures players that role-playing need not be entirely serious. A human joke, ostensibly about *Lord of the Rings*, typifies this—making obvious reference to artifacts outside *World of Warcraft*. Other comic references include NPCs with "real" names—Woo Ping, the weapons trainer in Stormwind, or Clarice Foster of Thunder Bluff (an amalgamation of Jodie Foster and Clarice Starling, the character she plays in *The Silence of the Lambs*). While Tanya Krzywinska argues convincingly that this "thickens" the myth structure of the world (chapter 6), it also calls on the player to both identify with and be reassured by the text, providing a light-hearted view of the world that encourages shared recognition as well as reassuring the player that nothing is entirely serious. Thus there is room for humor in role play, as well as an understanding that it moves between immersive and creative practices that do not always have to be fully sustained.

Add-ons

Blizzard has an open policy regarding add-ons—small programs that allow for more productive gameplay. These include tools to help raiding, the automatic selection of spells and buffs, and programs that choose the most lucrative items in the auction houses. Several exist that have been created to improve role-playing in *World of Warcraft*. These include FlagRSP, Role-playing Helper, and Eloquence.

FlagRSP is perhaps the most visible role-playing tool. It marks players with a small box that gives them a full name and title, with the option to view a longer description of what the person is like.

Since the add-on is relatively inconspicuous unless it is selected, in which case a larger description becomes visible (see figure 11.2), it is a popular tool, and as the name suggests, the Flag is a quick marker for determining

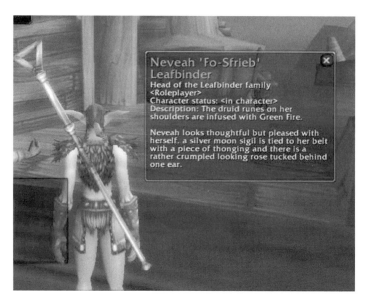

Figure 11.2
FlagRSP (full screen option). This screenshot shows *World of Warcraft* being played with a third party user interface that has been modified by parties other than Blizzard Entertainment.

who is role-playing in a given realm and what they may be like. Unlike Blizzard's role-playing rules, FlagRSP provides a relatively detailed description of basic usage and suggests ways to write a good flag. This inclusion of solid determinants for what makes a clear flag is a good attempt to introduce a more standardized method of role-playing into the game and is perhaps as important as the visual impact of the flag itself.

Roleplaying Helper is a more advanced version of FlagRSP. As well as supporting the flags from the previous program, it enables more in-depth descriptions and contains a generator that broadcasts randomly spoken macros when an action is performed. These are race-specific, so for example, a dwarf who has just been revived might say "Aye! Hit every spot but the vital ones!" Roleplaying Helper not only provides players who are unsure of how to role-play or who do not have English as their first language with clearly written examples, but encourages a coherent worldview by giving clear guidelines on how spoken role play might take place.

Both of these add-ons are visible to other players, but Eloquence is rather different. Billed as "an ambitious addon primarily written for role-players" (Curse Gaming 2005), Eloquence's main function is a personal Leet translator:

ne1 kno wher uc is at → Does anyone know where the Undercity is?
lf1m rouge SCHLO → We want one more Rogue for Scholomance.
CAN SUCK MY A$$ U FUKTARDZ → You can plunge into a gaping chasm for all I care.

Eloquence reinscribes out-of-character speech into full sentences, and changes them into suitably in-character language. In this way it is unique, since it is not only personal to an individual player, but designed to reinterpret nonrole-playing actions in the game. All of these add-ons point to one thing—people want to role-play, yet they find the tools already in place insufficient. They even find other players insufficient, as Eloquence demonstrates, although this add-on also provides a practical solution to the different levels of speech that may be occurring at any one time in chat levels. However, once again these programs demonstrate a genuine willingness to apply imaginative practices to the game, and to expand its potential in meaningful ways.

Conclusion

Role-playing is almost impossible within MMORPGs, even ones with such a developed world background as *World of Warcraft*. The game absolves itself of responsibility, sets no rules, and gives no guidelines on how to role-play within its structure. Role-playing realms are in the minority, with many players choosing not to or being unable to assume a character within the game. There are no gains from role-playing. A priest who holds a role-playing event in a church does not get extra points—in fact, she cannot even move the NPC avatars out of the way while she gives her sermon. These conditions makes the act of role play an act of deviance (Mortensen, chapter 10) within the text of *World of Warcraft*, one which tries to disturb the game's gameplay elements.

In a role-playing game, a player's central aim is the cognitive development of their character. Although statistics, nice weapons, and an interesting look may aid in this, the real engagement from most role players comes through the formation and development of their character as a "real" person. The determination of players to impose role-playing conditions on themselves and to thus inhibit their own gameplay is a clear sign that some people regard role play as equally important to the gameplaying aspect of *World of Warcraft*. Many spend time building reputations and appearances that have no effect on the game dynamic. In some ways this reflects the perversity of human nature—to make things harder by imposing challenges and new ideals on a highly resistant form.

These actions are attempts to find ways of subverting the gameplay into an arena where this agency exists. This aspect of play has its roots in the original game form of role play, and is an attempt to impose the original, full meaning of role-playing into the game. "Live your role" (as FlagRSP instructs players to do when they log in) is an incredibly hard action to perform in MMORPGs, but players are constantly trying to find ways to do this.

The desire to role-play despite these odds is seen in events like The Steamwheedle Faire, or add-ons such as Roleplaying Helper. These events are subversive in that they "break" the game (the lag experienced) or point to its faults (no set rules to role-play). Crucially, all of these actions express the needs that players have to insert themselves into the game more and increase the agency available in MMORPGs. This agency is something that does not yet exist fully in the *World of Warcraft*, but role players' attempts to overcome this show clearly that, in the future, it may well be possible.

Finally, it would be simple to perhaps invent a new definition. Nick Yee, for example, concludes that these games should be referred to as MMOs, excluding the "RPG" because it is not present (2006). But this avoids the fact that these games are marketed with the words "role-playing" as a central part of their brief. What might be more practical, then, is an acceptance that the word "role-playing" is not only misused, but has truly begun to mean the game dynamic that we outlined at the start of this paper: a frame of reference rather than an action undertaken by the player to gain a meaningful, if fantastic, relationship with the game.

Notes

1. Salen and Zimmerman call this "the immersive fallacy" (450–455).

2. See for example, T. L. Taylor (2006), King and Kryswinska's *Tomb Raiders and Space Invaders* (2006), and the Guilded Lilies blog at ⟨http://ninthwavedesigns.typepad.com/guilded_lilies/⟩.

References

Atkins, Barry. 2003. *More than a Game: The Computer Game as Fictional Form*. Manchester: Manchester University Press.

Bartle, Richard. 2004. *Designing Virtual Worlds*. Indianapolis: New Riders.

Blizzard. 2006. "Roleplay Basics." World of Warcraft Forums. ⟨http://Forums-en .WoW-realm-moonglade-en&t-50672&p-1&tmp-1#post50672⟩ (no longer available).

Blizzard. 2007a. "Realm Types." Available at ⟨http:www.WoW-europe.com/en/info/ basics/realmtypes.html⟩.

Blizzard. 2007b. "Roleplaying Policy." Available at ⟨http://www.WoW-europe.com/en/ policy/role-playing.html⟩.

Castronova, Edward. 2005. *Synthetic Worlds: The Business and Culture of Online Games*. Chicago: University of Chicago Press.

Curse Gaming. 2006. "Eloquence." ⟨http:www.curse-gaming.com/en/WoW/ modscreen-2752-8133-1-Array%5Bltitle%5D.html⟩ (no longer available).

Dormans, Joris. 2006. "On the Role of the Die: A Brief Ludologic Study of Pen-and-Paper Roleplaying Games and Their Rules." *Game Studies* 6, no. 1. Available at ⟨http:// gamestudies.org/0601/articles/dormans⟩.

Fannon, Sean Patrick. 1999. *The Fantasy Role-playing Gamer's Bible*, 2nd ed. New York: Prima.

Fine, Gary Alan. 1983. *Shared Fantasy: Role-Playing Games as Social Worlds*. Chicago: University of Chicago Press.

Flag RSP. 2006. "Introduction." Available at ⟨http://www.flokru.org/flagrsp⟩.

Gee, James Paul. 2004. *What Videogames have to Teach us about Learning and Literacy*. London: Palgrave.

Juul, Jesper. 2005. *Half-Real: Video Games between Real Rules and Fictional Worlds*. Cambridge, MA: MIT Press.

King, Geoff and Tanya Krzywinska. 2006. *Tomb Raiders and Space Invaders: Videogame Forms and Contexts*. London: I.B. Tauris.

Krzywinska, Tanya. 2006. "Blood Scythes, Festivals, Quests, and Backstories: World Creation and Rhetorics of Myth in World of Warcraft." *Games and Culture* 1, no. 4: 383–396.

Mackay, Daniel. 2001. *A New Performing Art: The Fantasy Role-Playing Game*. Jefferson, NC: McFarland and Company Inc.

Salen, Katie and Eric Zimmerman. 2004. *Rules of Play: Game Design Fundamentals.* Cambridge, MA: MIT Press.

Silent Minds. 2007. "The Death of Bulwar." Available at ⟨http:www.silentminds.org/forum/viewtopic.php?t-645⟩.

SquareRP. 2006. "Role-playing Charter." Available at ⟨http:www.squarerp.com/charter⟩.

Stratics. 2005. "Roleplay 101." Available at ⟨http:wow.stratics.com/content/features/rpg101⟩.

AnomalousSilence [pseud.]. 2006. "The Do's and Don'ts of Role-Playing," Ten Ton Hammer. Available at ⟨http://vanguard.tentonhammer.com/index.php?module=ContentExpress&func=display&ceid=285⟩.

Yee, Nick. 2006. "Introduction to the Role-Playing Series." *The Daedalus Project.* Available at ⟨http://www.nickyee.com/daedalus/archives/001524.php⟩.

Identity

Ragnhild Tronstad

A Conflict between Capacity and Appearance?

In one of the first issues of the journal *Game Studies,* James Newman presents the interesting argument that, in playing computer games, identification with the character has little to do with the character's appearance. Instead he connects it to the way the character functions and fulfills its tasks in the game: "[T]he level of engagement, immersion or presence experienced by the player—the degree to which the player considers themselves to 'be' the character—is not contingent upon representation. On-Line, 'character' is conceived as capacity—as a set of characteristics" (Newman 2002).

While the argument is convincing, a question remains unanswered: how do we separate capacity from appearance? In this chapter, I will discuss the relationship between character appearance and character capacities and how this relationship affects the possibility of identifying with the character during play. "Capacity" is here understood as the sum of capabilities available for the character, while "appearance" designates its representational qualities.

In *World of Warcraft* (Blizzard 2004), as in most MMORPGs (Massively Multiplayer Online Role-Playing Games), appearance and capacity are closely connected. Players may well choose a character type because of its capacities (a warrior has different capacities than a druid, for instance), and claim that the character's appearance is less important. But inevitably, as we proceed, capacity will become appearance—in other words, a representational quality in the game. Labels signifying the character's class, race, and increasing experience in various areas (level, rank) function as indices of the character's capacities, but they also determine the character's appearance in the game, that is, how it is perceived by both its player and by other players. Before we can discuss how appearance and capacity contribute to the process of identification between player and character, it is necessary to clarify how we understand appearance. In my understanding and use of the term here, "appearance" is closely connected to perception: how we perceive a character is how it appears, and vice versa. Everything that is included in our perception of the character is also included in its appearance, in this sense. Thus, understood as the representational aspects of the character as perceived by an audience (its player and/or other players), "appearance" cannot be reduced to "physical appearance," but must include all kinds of symbolic labels attached to the character, such as name, gender, level, and guild affiliation, to mention a few. Consequently, appearance is not something static but is fundamentally connected to performance, which, in turn, is partly determined by capacity.

There are different ways to play *World of Warcraft*, corresponding to three different types of servers. You may join a Player versus Player server (PvP) and devote most of your playing time to combat with other players; you may prefer a Player versus Environment server (PvE) and be allowed to explore the world without the constant threat of other players attacking you; or you may choose a Role-Playing server (RP), in which the players are supposed to role-play their characters consistently in accordance with the given fictional world of the game. As argued by Esther MacCallum-Stewart and Justin Parsler in chapter 11, dedicated role players will attempt to control their character's ingame appearance to a much greater extent than will PvP or PvE players, in order to project a coherent role. For role players, new capabilities acquired during play will have to be incorporated in a way that is not in conflict with the projected character identity (or alternatively, explained, excused, hidden, or not used.) Conversely, players who care less about role-playing may have their character's projected appearance determined to a greater extent by capacities acquired during play.

As there appears to be a great difference in how the relationship between capacity and appearance occurs in role play compared to when the character is not role-played, I will look at the two types of play separately, arguing that they in fact constitute two very different kinds of game in *World of Warcraft*. In my argument, gaming as a particular aesthetic experience can be identified in the state known as "flow," and my objective in this chapter is to show how the flow experience is obtained and expressed in the two types of game, through different types of emotional engagement with the character. Before I proceed to my discussion of the game, however, the concept of identification needs further clarification.

Identification: "Empathic Identity" or "Sameness Identity"

There are different ways of understanding "identification." On the one hand, identification with one's character may be understood as the player entering a state where he or she has an experience of "being" the character. On the other hand, identification may be understood as experiencing what the character experiences, but without the feeling of being identical to it—that is, with a consciousness of the character as an entity other than ourselves, but with which we can identify. These two types of identification have very different implications in my discussion, and I will therefore separate them using the terms "sameness identity" or "being identical to" for the first type, and "empathy" or "empathic identity" for the second. Additionally, I will use the term "character identity" for that entity other than ourselves with which we may feel empathy. The concept of "empathic identity" is inspired by film scholar Margrethe Bruun Vaage's use of empathy to distinguish between different types of spectator engagement in fiction film (Vaage, forthcoming). She proposes a continuum of empathic experiences ranging from the affective to the cognitive, in which true empathy only occupies the middle position ("embodied empathy" and "narrative empathy") (Vaage 2006, 33), as shown in figure 12.1.

"Emotional contagion" is the affective phenomenon that, for instance, makes us laugh when we witness other people laughing, even if we don't share their reason for laughing and don't know what they are laughing at. The other end of the continuum, "perspective taking," designates the purely cognitive, detached understanding of another person's position, without any emotional experience of how it feels to be in their situation. The reason true empathy is

← emotional contagion — embodied empathy — narrative empathy — perspective taking →

Figure 12.1
Continuum of empathic experiences.

to be found only in the middle of the continuum, thus, is that empathy requires a consciousness of the other with whom one emotionally identifies as different from oneself, and in emotional contagion there is no such consciousness. In perspective taking, however, there is consciousness of the other, but no emotional sharing:

Starting with contagion of other's affective states, emotional contagion is not yet empathy. On the other end of the continuum is pure cognitive understanding of the other's experience. Perspective taking is not yet empathy either. In the middle of these two positions we find empathy. Empathy is thus a dynamic phenomenon. It has both an embodied aspect related to emotional contagion, and a narrative aspect closer to perspective taking. Empathy may start through both perspective taking and emotional contagion, but without some element of narrative empathy, we only experience emotional contagion. Conversely, we only experience perspective taking if we do not have some degree of matching bodily feeling. To some degree both embodied and narrative elements are needed for an experience to be empathy. (Vaage 2006, 32–33)

Narrative empathy, which she also refers to as "imaginative empathy," is the most central term in Vaage's argument, presumably because the narrative fiction film is optimal when it comes to evoking this type of reaction in the spectator. *World of Warcraft*, however, belongs to an entirely different medium and genre where embodied empathy appears to be just as important, as we shall see later in this chapter.

According to Vaage, empathy may cause different types of engagement from the spectator: "fictional engagement," "aesthetic experience," "aesthetic appreciation" and/or "self-reflection." A scene (or, in our case, a scenario) may elicit all these forms of engagement in the spectator/player, but usually not all of them at the same time. Fictional engagement is described as being "successful if the spectator gets a feeling of being transported to the fictional world" (Vaage forthcoming, 10),[1] a state that in game studies is often referred to as immersion, and elsewhere also as transportation.[2] Aesthetic experience is explained as "sensuous feelings of engagement in the fictional world that are no longer strictly narrative or fictional" (ibid. 12), such as gasping at the revelation of a beautiful landscape, or being able to "smell" the flowers growing there. Transferred to the medium of *World of Warcraft*, the concept of aesthetic experience gives an apt description of the moments of intense interaction with the game mechanics, where the player is totally absorbed in whatever action she performs. I will later refer to this as a condition of flow. Aesthetic appreciation is quite a different matter, and concerns the more detached judgment of the aesthetic techniques in use, whereas self-reflection occurs when the player/spectator's focus is turned toward herself and how she would have reacted were she in a similar situation as the one unfolding on the screen.[3]

Fictional engagement may lead to aesthetic experience, which again may lead to aesthetic appreciation and/or self-reflection, all elicited by the empathic engagement in one and the same scene/scenario.[4] In the following discussion on character identification and the relationship between capacity and appearance in regular play, aesthetic experience seems to relate primarily to embodied empathy on the continuum, while fictional engagement (immersion/transportation) appears to be more closely connected to the narrative/imaginative empathy. Nevertheless, as we shall see in the succeeding section on role-playing in *World of Warcraft*, it is possible to have aesthetic experiences elicited by imaginative empathy too, and fictional engagement will often be supported by embodied empathy.

Identification, Capacity, and Appearance in Regular Gameplay

"Appearance" is how we perceive the character, or the projected mental image of it, which may be more or less present during play. "Capacity" encompasses the given possibilities a certain character type has to interact with the game mechanics. This could include race- and class-specific skills, weapon skills, professional skills, and spell-casting skills, but also agility, speed of movement, and the character's armor and weapons. In *World of Warcraft*, such capacities are dynamic and improve during play. And, as I stated in the introduction, improving a character's capacities will also affect its appearance.

In order to illustrate how the character's capacity and its appearance may be considered to be in conflict with each other, and how this conflict may affect gameplay in *World of Warcraft*, I would like to make use of the concept of flow as defined by Mihaly Csikszentmihalyi, a state of "optimal experience" (1990). For flow to be experienced, there must be a perfect balance between the challenges posed and the player's ability to overcome them. The challenges have to be experienced as genuine challenges, not easy to accomplish, but not quite impossible either. In meeting such challenges, the player enters a state of trance-like concentration in which the body seems to perform and react automatically as well as perfectly, without the conscious mind interfering. This state is known as flow. If the player starts to think about what he or she is doing, the state of flow is interrupted and the attempt will most probably fail. When, in *World of Warcraft*, gameplay is experienced as flow, the capacities of the character and those of the player are experienced as being in perfect balance. The player and the character are here perfectly connected, which requires that the player has internalized the controls and game mechanics to such a degree that the medium between himself and the gameworld becomes transparent. The character now becomes an extension of the player while still being perceptible as a separate identity with which the player may identify through either embodied or imaginative empathy (or both), depending, among other things, on the visual, fictional, and ludic context of the gaming situation.

I find that flow is an appropriate concept to describe how gaming can be understood as a specific aesthetic experience. In general, it is difficult to apply traditional theories of aesthetics to games because they differ from other aesthetic objects in that they require (creative) input from the player in order to be realized. This required input most often interferes with any free, disinterested contemplation of the game as aesthetic object, and hinders the player from being momentarily captivated by it, as one can be captivated by a strong or beautiful image, or immersed in it as one may be immersed in an ongoing narrative. Captivation by beautiful images and immersion in narratives may happen in games too, of course, but these are extra-ludic aesthetic experiences, and not of the kind elicited by the gameplay as such. But as Martin Seel writes about aesthetic perception, "[e]ntry into a state of aesthetic perception can come about actively or passively, as an arbitrary change of attitude or as a nonarbitrary occurence. Even if great aesthetic moments—in nature, art, or sport—are usually experienced as something that 'shakes,' 'enraptures,' 'stuns' or 'captivates' us, two driving forces are almost always active in the course of aesthetic perceptions: being spellbound by and concentrating on what is appearing" (2005, 34).

In flow, the player is freed from the burden of interaction, as there is a loss of self-consciousness in which he is delivered from himself. Freedom from oneself, and from self-reflection, is a necessary condition for the aesthetic experience as described by Seel. Flow, then, is my suggested term to describe the aesthetic experience specific to and typical of games. In the state of flow, the character appears to the player in the aesthetic sense of the term, described by Seel as a moment of ephemeral, sensuous presence. Flow experiences in *World of Warcraft* may typically occur in raids or in instances, where the tempo is high, challenges are frequent and sometimes surprising, and one has to cooperate with a group of people in order to reach a common objective. The cooperation factor adds an extra layer of complexity to the game mechanics and makes fluent interaction potentially harder to accomplish, and correspondingly more beautiful to experience when it occurs.

To provide some contrast to this experience of flow, let me give two counterexamples. First, perhaps the most common activity in *World of Warcraft* is the tedious task of repeatedly performing the same kind of action over and over in order to train a skill, solve a quest, collect items to sell, or to enhance one's reputation with a particular faction, as described in the Timbermaw example by Scott Rettberg in chapter 1. Most often this activity consists of killing a particular type of monster, again and again, until the objective is reached (or the player needs a pause). In this kind of activity, the character is often experienced as disappearing, turning transparent—as if magically transformed from a personified character into a depersonalized tool. The character in such cases becomes pure capacity.[5] The other example is to some extent similar to a problem discussed by MacCallum-Stewart and Parsler in chapter 11, when an attempt to role-play fails due to lack of support in the game mechanics. If there are no other role players around to respond so that the action taken results in some kind of effect, this is an example of pure appearance in the game—where appearance is understood in its most radical sense as a superficial play on the surface.

In the introduction to this chapter, I mentioned that the given capacities of a specific class may determine a player's choice of character in the game, regardless of the character's physical appearance. The other variant is of course also common—many players base their choice of character on the given looks of a certain race, regardless of what kinds of class (and class-specific capacities) are available for that race.[6] When a character is chosen because of its initial appearance, with which the player feels she can identify, a problem may arise later in the game when the character is actually played. The function of the character in *World of Warcraft* is double. On the one hand, it represents the player vis à vis other players in the game. On the other hand, it functions as a tool for the player's agency in the game. If the player has chosen a character type with capacities that make it difficult to advance in the game (without the player changing her preferred style of playing), the player may find that identifying with the character's looks is less effective in connecting to the character than being able to identify with its capacities. For example, some character types have capacities that make them popular contributors to a group, but lack the capacities needed to function well in solo play. Another character type may be great to play solo, but less popular as a contributor to group play. Some character types may require a lot of training before they become well-functioning tools for the player's agency in the game, while other character types give the player a feeling of agency and mastery from the start. Discovering during play that the character's available capacities make identification with it difficult, despite its good looks, is most often a newbie problem.[7] Experienced players know the available capacities of the various races and classes, and will make their character choice based on this knowledge. Thus, they will be able to see beyond the initial, superficial appearance of the character to a more realistic, though still not realized, appearance in which potential capacities are already included. This fact alone shows us why it is problematic to assume that capacities and appearance can be clearly distinguished and independently measured in the game.

Identification, Capacity, and Appearance in Role Play

Role-playing is optional in *World of Warcraft*; however, on the special servers reserved for the purpose, role-playing is expected. Nevertheless, even on the role-playing servers many players fail to take the role-playing aspect seriously, to the great frustration of the dedicated role players in the game. As MacCallum-Stewart and Parsler show in chapter 11, despite the special reserved servers, role-playing is not really supported by the game, and the fact that role-playing is in most cases counterproductive in terms of the more agonistically oriented game mechanics may discourage new players from spending time and effort pursuing it. Thus, to role-play *World of Warcraft* is to add to the game an extra set of rules and challenges that is often in conflict with the already existing rules and challenges.[8] However, role-playing also adds a more developed narrative dimension to the gameworld, in which the potential rewards are of a different kind than the usual progress-oriented rewards (such as armor, weapons, gold, or experience points).

Role-playing is to construct and develop a coherent identity for the character, in interaction with other role players, the gameworld, and its mythology. Where identification with the character in the regular game of *World of Warcraft* is often accomplished through embodied empathy, in which the player experiences a kind of physical or bodily connection to the character, role-playing actualizes the narrative/imaginative form of empathy described earlier in this chapter. In role play, the player is more explicitly aware of the character being different from him or herself, having a separate identity with a history, drives, and motivations of its own.

Paul Ricoeur's concept of a "narrative identity" is useful to understand how a character identity is developed in a role-playing game (Ricoeur 1991a, 1991b). According to Ricoeur, what we think of as our identity rests on the (told and untold) stories of our lives more than on the actual experiences we have been through. Actual experiences that are not retrospectively examined and narratively configured in order to fit together with the other stories of our lives have little impact on the image we create of ourselves. In our appropriation of a life story, in which we both construct and discover our identity, certain experiences we have had will count as significant and be included, while others are seen as unimportant and are easily forgotten.

When we create a character in a role-playing game, we invent a set of significant previous experiences for our character in order to provide it with a background story from which we can start constructing its identity. The *World of Warcraft* mythos comprises several stories outlining previous and existing conflicts between the races, as well as their origin and development in the world, and in order to maintain a certain coherence in that world it is important that the previous experiences we invent for our character are somehow compatible with these. However, as with our own identity development, the development of a character identity also involves an element of discovery. It is not unusual that (more or less surprising) aspects of the character's personality will be discovered during play, aspects which were not deliberately constructed from the start. Additionally, since a characteristic of well-performed role play is that it is flexible and open-ended, input from other players with whom we interact will also ideally influence how our character develops.[9] As the actual development of the character identity happens in interaction with other players, the gameworld, and the mythologies of the gameworld, experiences that the character encounters during play will contribute to its narrative identity and its appearance as perceived by its player. But even if one is never in complete control of how the character identity develops during play, it is hardly controversial to assume that a role-played character identity is to a greater extent deliberately constructed and more coherently perceived by its player than are character identities that are not role-played.

As a game genre, role-playing games rely heavily on coherence and realism. Coherent narratives and realistic representations are the formal aesthetic conventions of the genre. These requirements concern form only, and not content, which is often far from "realistic" in the sense that it takes place in a mythical world.

For role players, the demand for coherence functions as a rule in the game, and introduces an extra, role-playing game mechanic on top of the game mechanics already implemented by Blizzard. One consequence of this rule is that the player should respond IC (in character) to approaches directed to the character from other characters in the game; that is, she should respond as if she is the character and only possesses gameworld internal knowledge and reference points, as no references to the real world outside the game can be known by the character. This requires a constant commitment to the game-world that many players find too demanding to adhere to over time. Communicating through the character as if one really is the character, one appears as the character to others. Paradoxically though, there is a greater distance between player and character here than in ordinary gameplay (not role-playing), as role-playing not only requires a consciousness of the character as different from ourselves, but rests on our capability to empathically identify with fictional characters, a capability we are accustomed to through our experience with representational media such as theater, novels, and fiction film. In role-playing, our character is clearly separate from ourselves as a character with which we may empathically identify, whereas in nonrole-played or OOC (out-of-character) communication with other players, the function of our character is merely a tool for representing ourselves.

This difference may lead us to consider whether it is useful to call both types of characters "characters." If not, should the extended, prosthetic, part-of-ourselves type of character be given a different name? "Avatar" is one possibility. Although the avatar concept is often used synonymously with the way I have been using character in this chapter—that is, for both types of player–character relationships—the original meaning of the word clearly distinguishes it from that of character. In Indian mythology, the avatar is a god's representation on Earth; thus it seems reasonable to reserve the term for player–character relationships in which the character functions as a representation of the player in the game—in other words, for relationships where the character (avatar) has no perceptible identity of its own. To describe the player–character relationship of a player who roams the *World of Warcraft* as herself, not role-playing and with no consciousness as to the character (avatar) being separate from herself, "avatar" is definitely a better word.[10] "Persona" can also be used in this respect, and is particularly suitable if the player in question is a "socializer" rather than an "achiever" type of player.

What the term "character" designates, then, is our representation in the game when it takes on an identity separate from our own, in the sense that we can clearly identify the character as separate from ourselves. However, in accordance with Ricoeur's concept of a narrative identity, I believe most player representations in *World of Warcraft* develop into such characters during play, if they are not consciously constructed as separate identities from the start. Even when the character/avatar functions as an extension of ourselves in ordinary gameplay (not role play), the ambience and history of the gameworld that sets the context in which our character appears will contribute to our being able to distinguish our character as an entity separate from ourselves, even if it is never deliberately role-played as such. This separation is also necessary for us to be able to identify empathically with the character and obtain a feeling of experiencing what the character experiences.

In ordinary gameplay, if we obtain a feeling of "being the character," it is most often through embodied empathy with an entity that is partly (an extension of) ourselves, and partly a separate entity that can be identified as a character in *World of Warcraft*. Developing a coherent character identity through role play, which stands out before us as a separate, fictional appearance, makes identification understood as "being the character" less likely. The kind of identification role-playing activates in *World of Warcraft* is the narrative/imaginative empathy, without which we cannot predict how our character would act or respond. To experience flow in role play requires that we have internalized our character's (narrative) identity to the same extent as we have internalized the keyboard controls and game mechanics when experiencing flow in ordinary gameplay. This may be described as a state in which we "know" how the character is going to act and respond without consciously knowing it, as if the character takes over the stage and acts on its own.[11]

As I have stated, role-playing introduces an additional layer of game mechanics to *World of Warcraft*, which may sometimes be in conflict with the given game mechanics. The "world" of *World of Warcraft* does not support this extra layer: its functioning is entirely up to the other players, whose response or lack of response to a fellow role-player's action decides whether the action is valid or void. If an action is not picked up and responded to or further developed by other players, there is no dynamic, and without any dynamic there is very little game. To maintain this dynamic a different set of capacities is required than the ones that come with the character, as previously discussed. In order to master the game of role-playing, it is the player's and not the character's capacities that are important: knowledge of the gameworld, ability to improvise, social skills, and verbal proficiency are among the most relevant skills. As these are the capabilities determining the player's agency in the role-playing game, a player with poorly developed capacities in these areas may have a high-level character in terms of the ordinary game mechanics, and still be nothing but a superficial appearance in the role-playing game. Then again, when role-playing in the context of *World of Warcraft*, character capacities may of course set a limit on the impression one is able to make. It is, for instance, close to impossible to impress anyone role-playing a mighty wizard if one's character is in fact a level 4 Tauren warrior with hardly any spells available. Role-playing in accordance with the character's given capacities is more likely to be accepted by the other players, whose cooperation one needs in order to succeed.

Flow and the Synthesis of Capacity and Appearance

As I have argued, character capacities cannot be treated independently of character appearance in *World of Warcraft*, as capacities improve during the game and determine how our character is perceived by ourselves and other players at every stage. Neither can appearance be separated from capacity, as a certain set of capacities follow each character type and determine how the character functions in play. A character that is not in play is merely a superficial appearance.

Both in role play and in ordinary play, to experience flow requires that the player has internalized the knowledge and controls needed to master the character to such a degree that the character may take over and act without the player's conscious control. In ordinary play what needs to be internalized is primarily the controls and rules defined by the game mechanics, but also to a certain extent knowledge about the gameworld and how it functions. Additionally, in role-playing, extensive knowledge about the gameworld and its mythology, the character's background and situation in this world (its narrative identity), and the social circumstances surrounding the role-play scenario are all required.

Internalizing the controls, game mechanics, and knowledge about the gameworld necessary to experience flow through regular gameplay usually implies identifying with the character through an embodied kind of empathy. This type of flow is embodied and primarily physical, and resembles the type of engagement called aesthetic experience in Vaage's terminology, distinguishable from what she terms fictional engagement in that it may occur independently of any narrative or fictional frame.

Internalizing the knowledge required to obtain flow by role-playing in *World of Warcraft* implies identifying with the character through imaginative/narrative empathy. This type of flow resembles Vaage's fictional engagement, an immersion or transportation into a fictional world. As computer games are not primarily narrative media, this type of flow is much harder to accomplish and almost impossible to sustain should it occur. Nevertheless, if both the other players and the game mechanics confirm one's role-playing by responding appropriately, the flow experience obtained through role play can probably be even more rewarding than the flow experience attainable in the regular, nonrole-played game, as it is a lot more complex and thus harder to accomplish, and additionally involves more of the player's personal capacities and creativity.

Acknowledgments

Thanks to my coauthors and the editors for fruitful discussions and comments during the writing process, and to Margrethe Bruun Vaage for interesting and very valuable comments on an early draft of the chapter.

Notes

1. The article is not yet published, and the page number therefore refers to the manuscript.

2. Transportation theory is described in Green, Brock, and Kaufman (2004).

3. In Sherry Turkle's study on how players use role-playing in Multi-User Dungeons (MUDs) as a means of experimenting with alternative identities, self-reflection is highlighted as the ideal, almost prototypical type of engagement, whereas the other three are largely ignored. Turkle's seminal study thus has limited relevance to studies directed toward the aesthetic and/or fictional forms of engagement these worlds may elicit (Turkle 1995).

4. Identification with the character is at work in fictional engagement, aesthetic experience, and self-reflection, but not in aesthetic appreciation, and I will therefore not

pursue this experience further in the chapter (although preferring a certain character type merely because of its looks could probably be ascribed to aesthetic appreciation).

5. As Tanya Krzywinska argues in chapter 6, narrative and backstory may help make this sort of activity more meaningful. Role players may thus prevent their character from being transformed into a mere tool by evoking some meaningful narrative context to frame the repetitious activity.

6. In the section entitled "Avatar and Identity" in Nick Yee's ongoing study of MMORPGs, *The Daedalus Project*, Yee explains players' different preferences when choosing their avatar type as partly determined by differences in motivation: "Players driven by achievement focus more on the power and effectiveness of their avatar's equipment, while players driven by socialization or immersion are more focused on their avatar's appearances." Available at ⟨http://www.nickyee.com/daedalus/gateway _identity.html⟩.

7. Ducheneaut, Yee, Nickell, and More describe how new players tend to pick their character among the "good" races on the Alliance side, often a pretty night elf, whereas more experienced players, knowing this mechanism, choose the Horde side specifically in order to escape the newbie population accumulating on the Alliance side (2006, 302–304).

8. For a discussion of how role play thus can be seen as a deviant strategy in the game, see Torill Elvira Mortensen's chapter 10.

9. See Nick Yee, 2006, "Faces of Roleplay" and "The Protocols of Roleplaying," *The Daedalus Project*. Available at ⟨http://www.nickyee.com/daedalus/archives/001526 .php?page=4⟩ and ⟨http://www.nickyee.com/daedalus/archives/001527.php?page=3⟩, respectively.

10. An example of this can be found in the comments section of Nick Yee's *The Daedalus Project*, "Through the Looking-Glass": "I play these games not really to become someone different, but to be 'somewhere different.' A place with adventure and excitement, something that you just can't find in the real world. I think it's more fun actually to play who you really are in a RP game. You can experience what it would be like to be in that world as yourself; for the most part that is. I too just like the 'feel' of fantasy games, they bring to the table a whole other world to portray yourself. It's all in good fun =)." Posted by James on April 21, 2004. Available at ⟨http://www.nickyee.com/ daedalus/archives/000755.php?page=3⟩.

11. In Torill Elvira Mortensen's dissertation, *Pleasures of the Player: Flow and Control in Online Games*, one of her informants describes a similar experience to flow in role play, which the informant calls the "role-play high," in the following manner: "[I]t is the point at which you have stopped thinking about; Given this situation, what would my character say? Given this situation, what would my character do?—and start thinking from the point of view of your character and say what you want to say and do what

you want to do. To fully immerse yourself into the character. I find that it's very enthralling" (2003, 164–165).

References

Blizzard. 2004. *World of Warcraft*, Blizzard Entertainment Inc.

Csikszentmihalyi, Mihaly. 1990. *Flow: The Psychology of Optimal Experience*. New York: Harper and Row.

Ducheneaut, Nicolas, Nick Yee, Eric Nickell, and Robert J. Moore. 2006. "Building an MMO With Mass Appeal: A Look at Gameplay in World of Warcraft." *Games and Culture* 1, no. 4: 281–317.

Green, Melanie C., Timothy C. Brock, and Geoff F. Kaufman. 2004. "Understanding Media Enjoyment: The Role of Transportation Into Narrative Worlds." *Communication Theory* 14, no. 4: 311–327.

Mortensen, Torill Elvira. 2003. *Pleasures of the Player: Flow and Control in Online Games*, PhD diss., Volda College and University of Bergen.

Newman, James. 2002. "The Myth of the Ergodic Video Game." *Game Studies* 2, no. 1. Available at ⟨http://www.gamestudies.org/0102/newman⟩.

Ricoeur, Paul. 1991a. "Narrative Identity." In *On Paul Ricoeur: Narrative and Interpretation*, ed. and trans. David Wood. (Orig. pub. 1988.) London: Routledge, 188–199.

Ricoeur, Paul. 1991b. "Life in Quest of Narrative." In *On Paul Ricoeur: Narrative and Interpretation*, ed. and trans. David Wood. London: Routledge, 20–33.

Seel, Martin. 2005. *Aesthetics of Appearing*, Stanford, CA: Stanford University Press.

Turkle, Sherry. 1995. *Life on the Screen: Identity in the Age of Internet*. London: Phoenix.

Vaage, Margrethe Bruun. 2006. "The Empathetic Film Spectator in Analytic Philosophy and Naturalized Phenomenology. *Film and Philosophy* 10: 21–38.

Vaage, Margrethe Bruun. Forthcoming. "Empathy and the Episodic Structure of Engagement in Fiction Film." In *Narration and Spectatorship in Moving Images*, ed. Barbara and Joseph Anderson. Cambridge: Cambridge Scholars Press.

Yee, Nick. 2003–2007. *The Daedalus Project: The Psychology of MMORPGs*. Available at ⟨http://www.nickyee.com/daedalus/⟩.

Playing with Names: Gaming and Naming in *World of Warcraft*

Charlotte Hagström

In Azeroth, no nameless gnomes or orcs are admitted. Every character that crosses the threshold must be assigned a name, which afterward cannot be changed. It will then linger above the character's head for everyone to see, always present and visible. It is through the name the character will be identified by others (as was shown in figure I.1.). Choosing a name is thus an important decision. But *how* and *why* do players choose the names they do? Does a character's name reveal anything about its player? Does it influence the outcome and the experience of the game for the player herself or her fellow players? The purpose of this chapter is to discuss the names of characters and explore the means and motives of players' choices of names.

Naming for Structure

Imagine a society where people did not have names. What would it mean for communication and interaction? How would individuals be recognized and distinguished from each other? Could such a society function at all? A life without names would be very difficult and complicated indeed. In fact, and probably as a result of it being too difficult to muster, there are no such societies. Names are and have always been part of human life. Richard D. Alford states that ethnographic research has not found one single society whose members do not have names (1988, 1). Names are cultural universals, something we have in common whether we live in Amsterdam, Beijing, or Canberra.

But, despite the fact that we all share the experience of having a name, recognizing it as something natural and taking it for granted, there are vast historical and geographical differences as to what is regarded as a possible and suitable name. For example, present-day Spanish and German names are (more or less) exclusively *names*; that is, words used only to identify a person. Chinese names, on the other hand, are also common words.[1] Hoi Ying is a personal name, but it also means "victory" and "wealth."[2] The context determines if the word is referring to a person, a place, or a word (Lu and Millward 1989).

Many names throughout the world have the same origin: Ian, Ivan, Jean, Johan, John, Juan, Hans, and Sean are all variations of the same name. Different languages have different names, or different forms of the same name, and as we grow up we learn to distinguish which name belongs where. We may not know exactly where to geographically place all the names we hear and see, but, in general, we are able to recognize some names as belonging to our own cultural environment and others as different.

Entering the *World of Warcraft* universe entails getting used to totally unfamiliar names. New players encounter and have to adapt to a naming custom that bears little resemblance to the naming practices in the world outside. In Azeroth, it seems, any word, term, or random combination of letters can be a name. Or can they? Gradually players become aware that there are certain naming customs as well as restrictions and limitations in operation. Besides the regulations set up by the game producer, Blizzard, which mimic the name laws executed by nation-states in real life, there is a normative system in place; just as in real life, names can be, and are, questioned, banned, ridiculed, prized, mocked, and admired by fellow players.

Names are present everywhere in Azeroth. Apart from characters run by players, NPCs have names, weapons have names, and monsters have names.[3] Every village and town has a name as do the different zones, lakes, and rivers. When stumbling upon these names for the first time, many of them seem just odd: Sraaz and Agama'gor, Kadrak and Uruson are names without meaning. Even after having met Sraaz and learned that he is a pie vendor in the capital city of the dwarves, Ironforge, or been to Agama'gor and found that it is a place in the grassy zone of the Barrens, they seem to have no obvious connotations. But gradually a pattern becomes visible. An NPC with a name like, for instance, Rebecca Laughlin, is always either human or undead, and surnames like Sparkfizzle or Thistlefuzz belong to gnomes; Kurgul and Gryshka are orc names, while trolls are called Xao'tsu and Zando'zan. Mistina Steelshield is a dwarf as unquestionably as Gishalan Windwalker is a night elf. The names signal a meaning and become tools for the player to use in her exploration and understanding of the world.

Names are, Claude Lévi-Strauss states, essential for creating order and structuring our conception of the world (1996/1962). Through naming people, places, and objects, we make the world understandable. We classify and arrange our environment by separating it into named categories and filling them with named components. For example, a category of beings called "animals" is separated into subcategories such as "dogs" and "cats." Even though not all dogs or all cats look the same, these categories can be distinguished from one another and certain order achieved. Within the dog category, subdivisions may exist such as working dogs, shepherd dogs, and so on. In our language, there are complex systems of main and subcategories; all of them are named and thus distinguishable from each other.

The process of systematization and categorization not only helps us structure our lives and make the world comprehensible, it also regulates our thinking and restricts our perspectives, rendering other possible systems of categorization invisible or even unimaginable. We are so used to our own categories that they seem not only normal but natural. If we are questioned, it is often difficult to explain exactly what makes them so natural—they just *are*. The fact that the members of the different races occupying Azeroth have different types of names thus seems logical and is a system of categorization familiar to all players. People in the outside world also have different types of names depending on where they live or come from; hence it feels perfectly reasonable that this should be the case in Azeroth as well. Once we have identified the pattern, it feels natural to us.

Studying Names

Having decided to investigate the meaning and function of names in *World of Warcraft*, my first step was to let my characters do some fieldwork. On several occasions I placed them around the auction house in the main cities or close to a mailbox, trying to spread my observations throughout the day. I observed both Horde and Alliance names on all available server types, from normal to PvP and role-playing realms, and made a note of their race, class, gender, and level.[4] Altogether I performed 37 observations and gathered 1366 names.[5] My intent was to find roughly the same number for each of the races, but I soon discovered that dwarves and gnomes were less represented than humans and night elves, as is confirmed by the census data at Warcraftrealms.com. On the Horde side the races were more evenly distributed (Ducheneaut, Yee, Nickell, and Moore 2006, 293ff).

Soon I could draw two conclusions. First, neither race nor level seems to matter when it comes to the imagination of the players. The names were as strange, odd, and funny for trolls as for humans, and I found no indications that low-level characters had other kinds of names than high-level ones. One exception was the characters found near beginner areas. Some of these seemed to have been created primarily for testing or dueling, and several were named after real-life objects or expressions. Another exception was the characters with names containing words like "bank" and "cash" in various languages. These were obviously banking alts; that is, characters created to hold items and money for one's main characters, and never meant to reach above level 2 or 3.[6]

Second, I could not verify my hypothesis that there would be a significant difference in names between the role-playing server and the other servers. One explanation is that not everybody on a role-playing server actually role-plays.[7] Another and, I believe, more accurate, explanation is that the name is equally important to someone who does not explicitly role-play as to someone who does.

During my observations I came across numerous fantasy names and names that felt more or less exclusively *World of Warcraft*-ish. But then I also met a cheese in the capital of humans, Stormwind City; a German philosopher in Thunderbluff, the capital city of the tauren race; and a packet of cigarettes in Ironforge. Gods and heroes from Greek, Norse, and Egyptian mythology walked by as did characters from literature and popular culture. Some were slightly disguised with an extra letter or a little twist; others bore their name-sake's full name. Other names were obviously words from other languages than English. Apart from a Swedish Gravedigger, I met a Danish Dwarfwar-rior and a Norwegian Fairhairedgirl. With the help of friends and dictionaries I found I had encountered a Hungarian Whitefang, a Dutch Lampshade, and a Finnish Candyman.[8]

I also noticed several names that included references to war and fighting. Other names signaled that the player wanted to make her nationality known, while yet others used ordinary human names. Names ending with -kid, -boy or -girl were not abundant;[9] neither were names with race- or class-specific elements.[10] These kinds of names are usually brought up in various discussions at the official Web site forum[11] as examples of "bad" names. This may give the impression that there are plenty such names in use, but probably means that the players complaining remember them because they do not approve of them, not because of their actual frequency.

Creating Names

Observing and recording the names of characters was a fascinating experience. However, to learn how and why they had received their names I needed to reach the players. Consequently, I visited various Web sites and forums where names and naming were discussed[12] and wrote a short description of my project on my home page with a notice that I needed informants. I asked friends, colleagues, and students to encourage people who they knew were playing *World of Warcraft* to visit it. Some of them also posted the information on their blogs and Web sites. I soon received answers. Some came through e-mail; others were posted on their blogs. In addition, I carried out three informal interviews with personal acquaintances: one man aged 43, one man aged 23, and three boys in their lower teens.[13]

My informants' stories were interesting and engaging. They revealed inspiration from video games, fantasy novels, sports, mythology, schools, role-playing games, literature, plants, medicines, popular media, music, animals, and family members. Names based on the work of Tolkien were frequent, as were Norse, Celtic, Egyptian, and Greek gods and heroes. It turned out that some used their own name with a different spelling, like Paula, who named her hunter by using the Hawaiian pronunciation of her name, or Juliette, whose character's name is "a corruption of my own name that sounded sufficiently WoWish." Others used Judeo-Christian characters from the Virgin Mary to angels, or Hindu goddesses, or the names of their own pets. Several use a name from a specific book, like *The Four Zoas* by William Blake (1983/1797), *Shardik* by Richard Adams (1974), or *The Book of Imaginary Beings* by Jorge Louis Borges (1970). Some browse the Internet looking for inspiration, while others use words or names that have very private significance; for instance, a nickname given by a brother in childhood, which "also complements my personality," or the name of "the city in Iraq where I grew up."

The search for a suitable name can lead to new knowledge. Curious about whether there were any Irish equivalents to Scottish myths and legends as portrayed in films like *Braveheart* (1995), an informant of Irish heritage "found an entire theology for that culture" and settled for the name of the god of war. "I suppose I'm trying to say that in exploring the name of a simple character, I learned a lot about the rich heritage of my people." Sometimes there is a personal reason behind the choice of a name. After describing how king Creon persecuted his son Haemon's wife Antigone to death and how the king never listened to anybody, especially not his son, until it was too late, an informant explained his choice of Haemon for a tauren warrior: "Needless to say, I felt the same way about my dad who never listens or trusts my opinion until it's too late, hence I choose the name."

Only a few of the informants state that they use name generators.[14] One reason for this may be that those who took the time and effort to explain the stories behind their character names to me, an unknown researcher, had more than an average interest in names. For them, creating names is an essential part of the game and something they want to do themselves, without the help of randomizers. However, sometimes a name generator can be useful even for them. One player described why she used one when she decided to create an orc hunter. She usually plays Alliance characters but "wanted to try 'the other side.' I had no inspiration for her name at all, having no idea of suitable orcish names." With the help of a name generator she settled on Trabyna.

Experienced role players do not necessarily spend more time on creating a name or use different methods or sources of inspiration than others. But, while players in general may or may not find the naming of their characters essential, role players definitely do. One role player explains: "Because I do a lot of LARP, choosing a name is in some ways as important as the visual appearance of a character. After all, in LARP, under all the costume, they are still going to look like me." She also engages in role-playing in *World of Warcraft* and one of her characters shares its name with a LARP character. The best way to make people remember your name is, she says, "to keep it short, within recognizable, simple linguistic patterns, and make sure it is two syllables or less."[15] Several informants comment on long names being difficult or taking too long to type. "I have found that if you are named Alakazzamxerxes or similar you will not be written into as many friends lists," one informant says, and describes how he therefore uses short names with only one syllable.

Others find the names they have created shortened among guild members and friends in-game, much the same way as their names are abbreviated in the world outside.

Names with a History

There is often a pattern or system to the naming done by an individual player. Sometimes the system is obscure and needs to be explained; all characters run by one player may bear modified names of Roman gods, or be inspired by characters found in a certain book. Other times the pattern is more apparent. One player always puts "zar" at the beginning or end of all his names. When he played *Dungeons & Dragons*, for some time he played alongside someone called Zar: "He was the warrior and I was the war-crazy cleric thirsting for blood." They got along well and he was so impressed by Zar, that "when I got WoW, I decided to honour his memory by using the word 'zar' in every one of my names." Another player uses a similar method. His main character is a gnome warlock whose name is a shortened version of a name he used in *A Tale in the Desert*, which in turn was a modified version of another name. All three contain the prefix "Bo," as do all his other character names in *World of Warcraft*. When creating a name he always starts with "Bo" and "uses letters that seem to turn up frequently in game-generated names for the character's race." He also genders the names, ending female names with -a and male ones with -o.

A third player explains the name of one of his characters, a female night elf druid called Boncatti: the first part, "Bon," is his own initials. He has chosen "cat" as the second portion of her name because he is fond of cats, and the elf with her long ears looks a bit like one. His plans also include having her learn how to transform into a panther. The name also needed an ending, and as he wanted it to sound Italian he settled for the postfix -i. Most of his characters, in *World of Warcraft* as well as other games, are female and, in sum, this is how he usually creates their names: "Bon," followed by a part that makes the name more feminine, linked with an ending to place the name geograph-ically, usually in Iceland or central Europe. The name of his main character, however, is not created this way. She is a female human mage whose name is the surname of his favorite guitarist, Ritchie Blackmore, translated into Swed-ish with -ir added at the end to make it look Icelandic: Svartmerir. That he succeeded in this was confirmed when he was contacted in-game by an

Icelander. This player, who uses the Icelandic words for "bald," "beard," and "shadow" as names for his characters, reflecting their looks, thought a character with such a name must be played by a compatriot.

Icelandic and Norse names obviously have something *WoW*-ish about them for many players. Knowledge of the Icelandic language thus makes it easy to come up with an apt name. It also means that a player with a name of such origin can run into a character that is his or her namesake. Einar and Ragnar, who are brothers, have encountered the NPCs Einar Stonegrip in Wetlands and Ragnar Thunderbrew in Dun Morogh. Ragnar also met a player's character with his name. The player, who was from Spain, had found the name in the tabletop game *Warhammer 40000*, where it is the name of a space marine.

Some names have a history that goes beyond the actual character. John, who has been playing role-playing games since the mid-1970s and online ones since the late 1990s, plays a character with the same name as the one he played in *EverQuest*. There he created a druid to whom he wanted to give a name that reminded him of Merlin. However, he felt that "it would be arrogant to name a character Merlin" so he "played around for a couple of hours with a variety of names trying to find the one that worked best for me." Doing so, he came across a Web site with lots of information on Merlin, including spelling variants of the name. One of them was in Welsh. After changing some letters, he had the perfect name and "When WoW came out and the majority of my guild transferred to WoW I went along with the switch and kept the same name." Even though it is not possible to assign more than one name to a character, John's druid has a first name as well as a surname and he uses them both when he talks of him.

Cassandra does the same with her night elf, using a name she originally created when playing *EverQuest*: "I had a very attractive dark elf cleric, and wanted the name to be powerful. *EverQuest* has surnames, whereas WoW does not, so I cannot share my excitement of my creation." When she started playing *World of Warcraft* she was not pleased to find she could not play the character of an evil priest because of her looks. Her character is, she says, "a very beautiful creature and [I] would not want to shame her character since she has been in the company of my imagination for years."

John and Cassandra are forced by the rules of the game to call their characters by first names only. This does not, however, mean they do not *have* surnames.[16] The players think and talk of them using full names, and it is obvious that both their first and last names are significant. Without their names they would not be who they are. The druid and the night elf may not look the same in *World of Warcraft* as they did when they were created, be it in *EverQuest, Dungeons and Dragons*, or somewhere else, but in the eyes of their creators their appearance is only one of many factors that make them what they are. In real life, people change clothes and hairstyles, they lose or gain weight, and they grow older. The altered look of an avatar may thus not be a challenge to its identity. An altered name, however, is something else.

The biography of the self is, as Anthony Giddens phrases it, constantly in transformation and has continually to be rewritten and reformulated, as self-identity is something changing, never to be completed: "A person's identity is not to be found in behaviour. Nor—important though this is—in the reactions of others, but in the capacity *to keep a particular narrative going*" (Giddens 1991, 54, his emphasis). In her biography, an individual must "continually integrate events which occur in the external world, and sort them into the ongoing 'story' about the self" (ibid). In real life people do sometimes change their names. They do not, however, lose their surnames without receiving a new one. The name is intimately linked to personal identity, to who you are. Called by another name you are at risk of *becoming* another person, since, as Giddens states, a person's name is a primary element in her biography. Other players may only see yet another druid and yet another night elf, but John and Cassandra see lives and histories in their characters beyond their images on the screen. In those life histories, names are fundamental.

Losing a Name

Given the essential weight of a character name to many players, the loss of a surname may be annoying and frustrating. Losing a first and only (visible) name can feel like a catastrophe. One informant, who had to change her name, Applesauce, noted that "I guess Blizz didn't like an undead warlock running around with a cute name" and changed it to a name she got out of the novel *The Count of Monte Cristo* (Dumas 1996/1844). Others feel their world collapse. For them, to lose a name is to lose an identity and to be personally questioned. Not only does their character have to be renamed and adjusted to a new identity, their judgment, ability, and talent as name-givers, players, and members of the *World of Warcraft* community are questioned.

In the article "Blizzard Made Me Change My Name," CmdrTaco expresses how he felt when his name, which he had used online for many years and which had followed him "from game to game, both local, networked, and massive," was banned (2005). He does not question the company's right to decide the rules or change gameplay dynamics: "If Blizzard wants to make my mace have 5 less DPS and 3 less stamina because it's unbalanced, well I can accept that." But, he continues, a forced name change is something completely different: "in a massive multiplayer game, your name is different—that isn't about balance, it's about identity." CmdrTaco is not upset out of any pure concern for his character. It is for the *name* as such and for what it represents. For him, the name is not only, or primarily, the name of his character but the name through which other players recognize *him*: "In guild chat, I am a total stranger to people I may have chatted with for months."

Name researcher Leslie Alan Dunkling compares personal names with photographs and remarks that "My name—spoken aloud or written down—is a reflection of me, like my face in a photograph. The name of a friend, or his photograph, serves equally well to bring all my memories of him to my mind" (1977, 11). In a virtual environment like *World of Warcraft*, the name is more than a reflection. The name *is* virtually both the character and the player, as communication usually is carried out via chat between the participants, who are unable to see each other. It is also quite possible to get to know someone fairly well even without seeing her character. Thus CmdrTaco does not exaggerate when he writes that his forced name change means that "My history with other players has been erased."

A similar experience is related by Haya Bechar-Israeli (1995) in connection to using nicknames in Internet Relay Chat. One person called himself ⟨cLoNehEAd⟩ and, curious about the name, Bechar-Israeli sent him an e-mail asking about his choice. In return, she received a long and surprising story told in a humorous tone, beginning like a fairy tale with the words "Once upon a time..." It turned out that the name he had originally used was Bonehead, but one day one of his students had told him that this was what "mislead jerks, miscreants of an unthinkable kind, that spend their time shaving their heads, wearing Nazi-uniforms and burning down the houses of foreigners" called themselves (Bechar-Israeli 1995, 3). His story accounted for how he had found it necessary to change his name but how difficult it was. Then, finally, after thinking he somehow had to clone his name, he suddenly saw the solution: Bonehead would become Clonehead. "He had it. No shadow of a doubt. Not one single voice in his now crystal clear head disagreed. He had found his new identity" (Bechar-Israeli 1995, 4).

Though told in a witty way, the story of how Bonehead found his new name has a serious undertone. Being forced to change a well-established nickname—in Bonehead's case because others might associate it with something not intended—does not only involve having to give up a cherished name. It also causes severe problems, as nobody will immediately recognize Bonehead under another name. On the Internet he *is* his name, and only his name: it is his identity.

Shamanboy meets Lehgolaz

The naming custom of *World of Warcraft* (for example, the naming of NPCs) is set by Blizzard and it thus exists independently of the players, who will get to know it step by step. But the problem for new players is that they have to decide on a name *before* they start playing (Castronova 2005, 32ff). At that time, they are not familiar with the custom and maybe not even aware that there *is* one. This is illustrated by one informant's story about her first character. She gave it the name her son would have been given if he had been a girl. At that time she "was new to WoW and didn't really have any idea about the different cultures in Azeroth, however it doesn't seem too out of place on a night elf." She also has another character, a gnome called Betty, created to help her daughter when she started to play. "I didn't put much thought into her name at the time but it turned out ok as I've decided that Betty can be short of Bettina, which sounds very gnomish." For many players it is important that the name feels culturally appropriate, and there are probably several who have done the same thing as this player did with the name Betty: decide it is short for another name, or a nickname or pseudonym. As the name is not changeable, there are only two solutions if it feels wrong: delete the character or find a way to live with it.

But not all share this view. Another informant says the only names she has "problems with are the ones that are hard to spell. 'Gheritzherten' or nonsense names are just a pain. Humor is always a good one, assuming it's tasteful humor." Her own characters' names come from various sources: characters within *World of Warcraft*, out of anime and fantasy novels, by combining two more or less randomly chosen words, or just out of the blue. One is called Watermelon since "I love naming characters off of fruits," another Airnetc which is "air" combined with "net." As "Airnet" looked funny, she "made it funnier by adding a 'c' at the end." Doubtless there are many players who do not find fruits suitable as names, regarding them as ruining the "feeling" of the game (Krzywinska 2006, 387).

But under which conditions can one player judge other players' taste in names? Several informants stress that with the wrong kind of name, whether it is wrong because it so obviously is based on somebody else's imagination or because it is "stupid," a player has not fully understood what the game is about, and thus cannot appreciate all its parts and aspects. One informant believes that "A person who has the name xxxBadAssxxx is probably a person who doesn't care about the game itself but plays it just because everybody else does." He says it "also feels like the people who have those names are younger players." This is supported by another player who believes that age, at least to some extent, is related to certain types of names. Shamanboy is an example of a name he terms ridiculous, and he thinks "Serious players have more serious names and most of them are not very young." This is however not definite, he says, and there are probably many exceptions as "you can be a serious player even if you are young."

A third informant does not refer to age but says: "I do judge other players by their name in the sense that there are some names that will give me a negative impression of the player rather than the other way around." These are "names that look misspelled or not like names (such as initials), or are too like real life names" as well as the "ones that are obviously dumb." None of the informants states that he or she actually avoids these players, but it seems likely that not many such names are to be found in his or her friend lists.

A frequent statement from informants, as well as in posts on forums, is that names that are too apparently inspired by *The Lord of the Rings* are stupid, tiresome, and show a lack of fantasy and creativity. Primarily, the critique does not so much concern the names as such but rather the players who choose them. Not being able to come up with a better name for a night elf than Lehgolaz is considered obvious proof that you are an uncreative person—a characteristic that is both annoying to other players and disturbs the gaming experience. Creativity is highly valued and as there are limited possibilities for expressing it through the look of the avatar—the combinations of hairstyles, skin color, and facial features are not endless—the name thus becomes a means both to individualize the character and express certain desirable features or qualities.

Blizzard clearly states that some kinds of names are strictly prohibited. On the official Web site the various game policies are listed, of which the naming policy is one. There are several headings with explanations of what the policy entails and which kinds of names fall under each heading. The categories include, for example, Racial/Ethnic, Sexual Orientation, Religions or Religious Figures, Illegal Drugs or Activities, Trademarks, and Popular Culture and Media Figures. The latter contains a clarification that opens it up for interpretation as it states that it includes "references to very well known people, characters, places, or icons from popular culture and media." Most players would probably agree that the phrase "very well known" is applicable to names from *The Lord of the Rings*, especially among players of *World of Warcraft*, but the boundaries between "well known" and "very well known" are vague and imprecise.

Whether the players read the naming rules thoroughly or not, they can easily gain insight into what kind of names they should avoid just by taking a quick glance at them. The policy also declares what will happen if they violate the rules: the player will "be assigned a randomly generated temporary name, to be changed via the online ticket system," "be given a warning," or "be temporarily or permanently suspended from the game." The worst offense is choosing names that fall into the category of pedophilia. If a player is "found to have such a name for their character, guild, or pet, he/she will have his/her access to *World of Warcraft* permanently terminated."

Game Masters are present in the game to assist, but also to monitor players' behavior. A GM will, if notified, contact a player who acts improperly or harasses other players. This is also the case if a GM finds a character to be named in violation of the rules. Furthermore, players can report other players to the GM if they think that they in some way act offensively or sport an inappropriate name. On role-playing servers, the rules are stricter and some players find it extremely annoying when they encounter characters with inapt names. In a discussion on the official *World of Warcraft* forum for Europe, which starts with a post by a person who has created a naming FAQ for the server, interpretations of the rules and suggestions in the FAQ are debated together with individual names. One of the posted topics concerns whether to report offensive and inappropriate names or not, and whether it makes any difference. One person wrote of reporting 200 names but mentioned that none of them had been changed. More interesting than why they were not changed is the fact that this person found it necessary to report them. It is unlikely that all of those 200 names fell into the offensive names category; it is more likely that they were judged inappropriate by the player her/himself.

Discussions like these are sometimes carried out in the general chat channel during play. One informant says this always upsets him. His reaction is usually to say something about it in the chat and then put the name of the person who complains on his ignore list. Just because a person is an experienced role-player, he says, he or she does not have the right to judge other players' names.

Bad Taste

In 1913, the clergyman P. A. Kjöllerström published a book about Swedish naming customs. He argued for stricter regulations and that Swedes should choose only Swedish names for their children. His rationale was that there were too many English names in use, a phenomenon that he saw as a manifestation of bad taste and proof of a lack of patriotism. If Swedes have English names, he reasoned, neither Swedes nor foreigners will recognize their origins (Kjöllerström 1913, 9).

In 2004, almost a hundred years later, arguments submitted in a Swedish chat forum at alltforforaldrar.se dedicated to personal names echoed his belief. Now and again discussions arose about Anglo-Saxon names, and, at times, the debates got heated. On the one side were those who liked British and American names and saw no problems in giving Swedish children names like Brandon, Tiffany, and Ashley. On the other side were those who considered such names out of place, inappropriate, and signs of bad taste. Ultimately the discussions turned to the relation of names and class. The critics declared that English names on Swedish children gave clear indications of a working-class background and referred to them as "Ricki Lake-names." There is nothing wrong with being working class, several others argued, but as a parent you should think of what a name signals. By giving your child such a name you situate it in a fixed category surrounded by certain fixed prejudgments. The advocates, on the other hand, saw these names as new, modern, and exciting; parents who choose them show an open mind and are not, like the critics, trapped in rigid thinking, constantly worrying about what others might think (Hagström 2006).

A recurring argument was that names "belonging" to a certain language or country are not suitable for people who do not have their roots there. American names are thus perfectly fitting for Americans but not for Swedes. Besides running the risk of being regarded as ridiculous or as victims of Americanization, people who choose such names contribute to the confusion and blurring of boundaries. If everybody uses the same names, names lose their function as a means to categorize and distinguish people of diverse backgrounds. As expected, many discussants found this perspective erroneous and questioned the whole idea of categorizing people by and through names.

However, the last argument is also a standpoint embraced by people in powerful positions all over the world: many countries have strict legislation declaring which names are allowed and which are not. A name that is not listed in an officially acknowledged record is not approved. The purpose may be a wish to protect and preserve a language, or a strategy to force minorities to adjust. Whatever the reason and motive, the regulation of people's names has always been an instrument of control for those in power (Konstantinov and Alhaug 1995).

Looking at Kjöllerström's book and the discussions in the personal names forum, nothing seems to have changed in a hundred years. The fact that Kjöllerström felt it necessary to publish a book on proper ways to name Swedish children implies that numerous parents did not share his view. Today many parents still choose names deemed improper. At the same time, many names that once seemed "un-Swedish" and foreign have been incorporated and are no longer considered odd or unusual. The meaning and associations have changed over time and through use, and new and foreign names have become common and apparently native names (Kisbye 1984).

A conclusion to be drawn from this is that all attempts to conserve a certain name style through arguing that it is desirable or necessary are doomed to fail. There have always been and will always be people who do not agree and refuse to follow the rules, be they implicit or explicit. A player can keep on reporting names she does not think are appropriate for a role-playing server, and GMs can continue warning players who use them—but new characters with such names will nevertheless still arise. The same name has multiple meanings and connotations, in real life as in *World of Warcraft*. Different people have different views, tastes, and preferences and a name that one person finds pretty or nice another finds ugly or unattractive. However, as Pierre Bourdieu demonstrates (1984), our taste depends on our social position. What may seem individual choices made out of personal preferences, be it sports or cars, music or food, are essentially socioculturally determined.

Another conclusion is that customs, habits, and traditions change. Culture is not a condition, something constant. It is a process. We may talk about Canadian or Polish culture, as well as the gnomes' or blood elves' cultures of Azeroth and the culture of the *World of Warcraft* community, but must also be aware that they are not rigid and static (O'Dell 1997). Furthermore, people acting within the same culture do not experience and interpret it in the same way. Factors like age, gender, and class, direct our understanding and affect our knowledge, as does our position in our social spaces.

Serious Feelings

But what is the problem with meeting a Lehgolaz in Elwynn Forest or an Orchunterdk outside Crossroads? Why bother worrying about what other players choose to call their characters as long as they do not intentionally set out to interfere, disturb, or obstruct? One player, who has spent much time finding accurate names for his characters, gives an explanation. To him names play an important part in the gaming experience, and "stupid" names are more than just an irritating element: "If you meet someone called Aprikossylt [Apricot jam] it's disturbing. A player who chooses such a name is not sincere and that is what you want it to be: gaming should be taken seriously and be carefully executed." Three boys, all in their early teens, who express their irritation with random-letter names like Fjehwk or Kgnwhnng, share his views. Such names are really bad, they think, and "ruin the game for others as the feeling of the game is lost."

Words like "serious" recur in many informants' narratives and are clearly an appreciated quality in fellow players, as is their understanding of the "feeling" for the game. Such players accept Azeroth as a *world*, separated from the world the players themselves live in.[17] This world has its own history and culture.[18] A player who lacks feeling for the game or who is not serious is thus not necessarily a bad player when it comes to killing monsters or functioning within a group. Rather that player is, in the eyes of the informants, someone who does not act according to what is culturally acceptable in Azeroth, and an absurd name is an indication of such behavior.

In real life, people's responses to different names are often the result of personal acquaintances and associations. But responses are also the result of culturally shared knowledge of where and among whom a name is common: in a certain age group, religion, nationality, class, and so on. Conclusions about an individual drawn through her name can prove correct. However, they can just as well prove incorrect. The culturally shared understanding of what is behind a name can cause much distress and many problems. Numerous immigrants from the Middle East or Africa living in Western Europe experience how their names lead to unjust and discriminatory treatment: job applications are returned, the housing market seems strangely limited. To employers and landlords their names do not represent individuals but members of a specific group: immigrants (Hagström 2006).

In *World of Warcraft* it is the name more than the appearance that distinguishes avatars, and thus players, from each other. If a player finds Legolas-inspired names inappropriate and indicative of a lack of creativity and fantasy, every character with such a name that she encounters will be judged according to this view. The player behind the actual avatar may be both serious and have an intense feeling for the game, and the name may be the result of hours of creative thinking. In the eyes of the player who does not approve of such a name, it is nevertheless a hindrance for further contact (Heisler and Crabill 2006, 14). Erving Goffman's description of how people standing in front of a person they do not know "can glean clues from his conduct and appearance which allow them to apply their previous experience with individuals roughly similar to the one before them" and "apply untested stereotypes to him" (Goffman 1969, 13) is applicable also to their reactions to personal names. Whether in virtual worlds or the real world, names are not neutral. They are an important factor in cultural and social categorization.

The players of *World of Warcraft* consist of a diverse group of people who all bring their own knowledge and experiences into the game. They will gradually learn and become accustomed to both the culture of Azeroth and the culture of the *World of Warcraft* community, and also contribute to them. Culture does not exist without people, and it is the people who shape and change culture—they are thus not only culture-bearers but also culture-builders (Frykman and Löfgren 1987). As T. L. Taylor writes, "embedded within the game world is an emergent culture created and sustained by players" (2006, 126). Whether or not individual players agree with other players' name choices, once a new character and her name have crossed the threshold of Azeroth, the game will never be the same again.

Notes

1. For a discussion of the difference between names and words, see Nicolaisen (2002).

2. Thanks to Fan Chun Yan, Chang Chia Ning, Lee Hsin Ju, Wan Hoi Ying, Li Huiping, and Lin Ching-Wei for interesting discussions of Chinese names and naming customs.

3. I made a bonus discovery when I recorded the names of NPCs, namely the immense domination of male characters. In all cities the female characters are greatly outnumbered, with Darnassus as the only exception. For example, only 28 of 83 NPCs in Thunderbluff and 24 of 94 in Ironforge were female. My purpose was not to record all of them, but to examine their names, and the proportion could differ slightly if all NPCs were taken into account. Nevertheless, the severe discrepancy undoubtedly influences players' impression of Azeroth as clearly male-dominated, a fact that Corneliussen discusses in chapter 3.

4. As I wanted to see not only the names but the characters as well, in case their appearances would reveal anything of the players' ideas behind their names, observation seemed the best method. The characters I observed were the ones that passed me. My material thus consists of a random sample.

5. As the observations were made before *The Burning Crusade* was launched, blood elves and draenei are not included. Neither are the names of pets or guilds.

6. As with the NPCs (note 3), a closer study of the low-level characters revealed an interesting gender aspect: in all races and classes observed, the male characters are in majority, but not here. Thirty-two of fifty-seven level 1, 2, and 3 characters were female. The most common class was warrior: eleven female, nine male.

7. See MacCallum-Stewart and Parsler's chapter 11.

8. There are probably several reasons behind the choice of such a name, such as a wish to subvert the naming rules set up by Blizzard or to make a joke understandable only to players who speak the same language. It can also cement relations in a multinational guild between members of the same nationality as the secret is revealed only to them.

9. Of 1366 names, 15 included the words "boy," "girl," "chick," "man" or "dude." I found 8 at the normal server, 5 at the PVP server and 2 at the RP server. Their levels ranged between 1 (two names) and 60 (three names).

10. Nine names referred to race, like Divinedwarf; nineteen to class, like Funkymage. Two names included references to both race and class. Dwarf was the most common race (four) and mage the most common class (six) in this type of names. Halfgnome, which I counted as a race name, was the name of an orc.

11. forums.wow-europe.com.

12. forums.wow-europe.com, www.worldofwar.net, and www.wowinsider.com.

13. Unless a different source is indicated, all my examples and quotations stem from this material, which consists of stories from 106 players of various ages and nationalities. All quotations are verbatim.

14. See the World of Warcraft Name Generator at Stratics ⟨http://wow.stratics.com/content/features/name/⟩ or Fantasy Name Generator at ⟨http://rinkworks.com/namegen/⟩.

15. Many role players prefer to turn off the name display, as in real life you would not know another person's name before you have been introduced. For a discussion on role play in *World of Warcraft*, see MacCallum-Stewart and Parsler's chapter 11.

16. There are add-ons—for instance, Flag RSP—that can be used for presenting information about the character, adding a surname, a title, and a short description of personalized appearance (see figure 11.2.). This information is, however, only available to players who have the add-ons installed themselves. If John and Cassandra present the surnames of their characters with the help of an add-on, still only a limited number of players will be able to see it.

17. See Espen Aarseth's chapter 5 and others in the "World" section of this book.

18. There are various sources both in and outside the game for gaining knowledge about the world and its inhabitants. Besides the official Web site there are many sites created by players, as well as several books and comics. In the *World of Warcraft Official Strategy Guide* (Lummis and Vanderlip 2005) one chapter is entitled "Learning your place in the world" with subheadings like "The history of Azeroth."

References

Adams, Richard. 1974. *Shardik.* New York: Simon and Schuster.

Alford, Richard D. 1988. *Naming and Identity: A Cross-Cultural Study of Personal Naming Practices.* New Haven: HRAF Press.

Bechar-Israeli, Haya. 1995. "From ⟨Bonehead⟩ to ⟨cLoNehEAd⟩: Nicknames, Play, and Identity on Internet Relay Chat." *Journal of Computer-Mediated Communication* 1, no. 2. Available at ⟨http://jcmc.indiana.edu/vol1/issue2/bechar.html⟩.

Blake, William. 1983. *The Four Zoas: The Torments of Love and Jealousy in the Death and Judgment of Albion, the Ancient Man.* (Orig. pub. 1797.) Chicago: Swallow.

Borges, Jorge Louis. 1970. *The Book of Imaginary Beings.* New York: Dutton.

Bourdieu, Pierre. 1984. *Distinction. A Social Critique of the Judgement of Taste.* London: Routledge & Kegan.

Braveheart, directed by Mel Gibson. (1995, Los Angeles, Paramount Pictures/20th Century Fox).

Castronova, Edward. 2005. *Synthetic Worlds. The Business and Culture of Online Games.* Chicago: The University of Chicago Press.

CmdrTaco. 2005. "Blizzard Made Me Change My Name." *Slashdot.* October 26. Available at ⟨http://games.slashdot.org/games/05/10/26/142243.shtml?tid=166&tid=10⟩.

Ducheneaut, Nicolas, Nick Yee, Eric Nickell, and Robert J. Moore. 2006. "Building an MMO with Mass Appeal: A Look at Gameplay in *World of Warcraft.*" *Games and Culture* 1, no. 4: 281–317.

Dumas, Alexandre. 1996. *The Count of Monte Cristo.* (Orig. pub. 1844.) New York: Modern Library.

Dunkling, Leslie Alan. 1977. *First Names First.* London: J. M. Dent.

Frykman, Jonas and Orvar Löfgren. 1987. *Culture Builders: A Historical Anthropology of Middle-class Life.* New Brunswick: Rutgers University Press.

Giddens, Anthony. 1991. *Modernity and Self-Identity: Self and Society in Late Modern Age.* Cambridge: Polity Press.

Goffman, Erving. 1969. *The Presentation of Self in Everyday Life.* London: Penguin.

Hagström, Charlotte. 2006. *Man är vad man heter: Namn och identitet.* Stockholm: Carlssons.

Heisler, Jennifer M., and Scott L. Crabill. 2006. "Who are 'Stinkybug' and 'Packerfan4'? Email Pseudonyms and Participants' Perceptions of Demography, Productivity, and Personality." *Journal of Computer-Mediated Communication* 12, no. 1. Available at ⟨http://jcmc.indiana.edu/vol12/issue1/heisler.html⟩.

Kisbye, Torben. 1984. "Bonum nomen est bonum omen: On the So-called Idol Names." *Studia Anthroponymica Scandinavica* 2: 55–85.

Kjöllerström, P. A. 1913. *Svenska dopnamn och släktnamn.* Stockholm: Wahlström & Widstrand.

Konstantinov, Yulian and Gulbrand Alhaug. 1995. *Names, Ethnicity and Politics: Islamic Names in Bulgaria 1912–1992.* Oslo: Novus Press.

Krzywinska, Tanya. 2006. "Blood Scythes, Festivals, Quests, and Backstories: World Creation and Rhetorics of Myth in *World of Warcraft.*" *Games and Culture* 1, no. 4: 383–396.

Lévi-Strauss, Claude. 1996. *The Savage Mind.* (Orig. pub. 1962.) Oxford: Oxford University Press.

Lu, Zhongti and Celia Millward. 1989. "Chinese Given Names since the Cultural Revolution." *Names* 37, no. 3: 265–280.

Lummis, Michael and Danielle Vanderlip. 2005. *World of Warcraft Official Strategy Guide*. Indianapolis: Brady Games.

Nicolaisen, W. F. H. 2002. "Narrating Names." *Folklore* 113, no. 2: 1–9.

O'Dell, Tom. 1997. *Culture Unbound: Americanization and Everyday Life in Sweden*. Lund: Nordic Academic Press.

Taylor, T. L. 2006. *Play Between Worlds: Exploring Online Game Culture*. Cambridge, MA: MIT Press.

Contributors

Hilde G. Corneliussen is an associate professor of Humanistic Informatics at the University of Bergen, Norway. She has a PhD in humanistic informatics (2003) with a main focus on computers and gender identity. Her main research interests are gender and technology in various forms: gender and computer education, gender and computer games, gender in computer history, and computer technology and gender identity. She is currently working on a project about Norwegian computer history in a gender perspective. Her blog, "Gender & Computing," is at http://www.genderandcomputing.no/.

Jill Walker Rettberg is an associate professor of Humanistic Informatics at the University of Bergen in Norway, and was the head of the department from 2005 till 2007. Her background is in literature, but her research interests have expanded from her early attraction to hypertext fiction to a broader interest in narrative in new media. In addition to having published numerous articles on narrative in blogs, games, and on the Web, she has blogged her research regularly at "jill/txt" (http://jilltxt.net) since October 2000. Her book *Blogging* is to be published by Polity Press in 2008.

Espen Aarseth is Head of Research at the Center for Computer Games Research at the IT University of Copenhagen, and Professor II at the Department of Media and Communication, University of Oslo. He is currently working on an ontological theory of games in virtual environments. Prior to coming to ITU in 2003, Aarseth was professor at the Department of Humanistic Informatics at the University of Bergen, which he cofounded in 1996. He is also cofounding editor-in-chief of *Game Studies* (Gamestudies.org)—the first academic journal of computer game research, and author of *Cybertext: Perspectives on Ergodic Literature* (Johns Hopkins University Press, 1997), a comparative media theory of games and other aesthetic forms.

Charlotte Hagström has a PhD in ethnology (1999) from the Faculty of Humanities and Theology, Lund University, Sweden. She works as a senior researcher and teacher at the Department of European Ethnology and as an archivist at the Folk Life Archives. Her research interests are mainly in the fields of personal names and identity, and collecting and categorization. Related to the latter are issues concerning archiving and methodology. Her most recent publication is a book on personal names, *Man är vad man heter: Namn och identitet*, 2006 (You are what you're called: Names and identity).

Lisbeth Klastrup is an assistant professor at the IT University of Copenhagen, affiliated with the Innovative Communication Research Group and Center for Computer Games Research. Lisbeth teaches courses in online communication and does research on all forms of emergent forms of communication and interaction online, including MMOG player stories, weblogs, and moblogs. In 2004, together with coeditor Ida Engholm, she published the Danish anthology *Digital Worlds—the Aesthetics and Design of New Media*. She has published articles in Danish and English on online and transmedial worlds, interaction forms in games and Web sites, and the development of weblogs. She initiated the first academic conference on Computer Games in Scandinavia and chaired the 2005 Digital Arts and Cultures Conference on Digital Experience. She is currently coediting an international anthology on internet research, together with an Australian and an American colleague.

Tanya Krzywinska is a professor in the School of Arts at Brunel University. She is the author of *A Skin for Dancing in: Possession, Witchcraft and Voodoo in Film* (Flicks Books, 2000), *Sex and the Cinema* (Wallflower, 2006), coauthor with Geoff King of *Tomb Raiders and Space Invaders: Videogame Forms and Contexts* (IB Tauris, 2006), and coeditor of *ScreenPlay: cinema/videogames/interfaces* (Wallflower, 2002) and *videogame/player/text* (MUP, in press). She is currently working on a monograph titled *Fantasy Worlds*, a crossmedia study of the aesthetic, formal, and interpellative strategies of virtual worlds in popular media, and is the convener of a master's program, "Digital Games: Theory and Design."

Jessica Langer is completing a PhD in science fiction and postcolonialism at Royal Holloway, University of London, and teaches film, literature, and modern Japanese history and culture at Richmond American University in London. Her research interests include postcolonial literature, film, and the   studies in cinema, especially East Asian and science-fiction film; and cultural implica ons/applications of video games and game culture. She has published academic articles in *Asian Cinema* and *AngloFiles*, and her forthcoming publications include book chapters on postcolonial travel writing and on feminism and otherness in the *Alien* films.

Esther MacCallum-Stewart is a postdoctoral research fellow at SMARTlabs, the University of East London. Her work looks at the representation of history in gaming and the potential for educational spaces within games. Recent work has included the exploration of female role-playing, how historical representation can affect player experience, and the ways in which games can create spaces for learning. She runs the weblog "GlodnEpix" at http://www.whatalovelywar.co.uk/glodnepix.

Torill Elvira Mortensen is an associate professor at the media department of Volda College, Norway (since 1991). She has been writing about multiplayer games in text-based universes (MUDs), and from 2005 she has been studying *World of Warcraft* in order to understand massive multiplayer games with graphic representations. Since 2001 Mortensen has been on the editorial board of the international online journal *gamestudies.org*, and she has presented and published articles on games in conferences, journals, and anthologies since 1995. In 2006–2007 Mortensen is the leader of the European game-researcher's guild "The Truants," which works as an academic network and arena for discussions on games and a source for explorations into the *World of Warcraft* universe for the contributors to this anthology.

Justin Parsler writes and runs Live Action Roleplaying (LARP) Campaigns and PBeM games (Play By Email) on a full-time basis, including the groundbreaking "Frail Realities" game system. He is also a postgraduate researcher at the University of Brunel taking part in the inaugural "Digital Games: Theory and Design" MA under Professor Tanya Kryswinska.

Scott Rettberg is an associate professor of Humanistic Informatics at the University of Bergen in Norway. He is a cofounder of the Electronic Literature Organization, and serves on its board of directors. A writer and practitioner as well as critic and scholar of new media, Scott is the coauthor of the hypertext novel *The Unknown*, the e-mail novel *Kind of Blue*, and the sticker novel *Implementation*. His blog is at http://retts.net.

T. L. Taylor is a sociologist and associate professor at the IT University of Copenhagen and the Center for Computer Games Research. She has been working in the field of internet and multiuser studies for over a decade and has published on topics such as values in design, avatars and online embodiment, power-gaming, gender and gaming, pervasive gaming, and intellectual property in MMOGs. Her current book *Play Between Worlds: Exploring Online Game Culture* (MIT Press, 2006) uses her multiyear ethnography of *EverQuest* to explore issues related to play and game culture. For more information see http://www.itu.dk/~tltaylor.

Ragnhild Tronstad is a postdoctoral research fellow and lecturer at the Department of Media and Communication, University of Oslo. Since entering the field of game studies as a doctoral student in 1998, studying questing and character performance in the Multi-User Dungeon Tubmud, she has published numerous papers, journal articles, and book chapters on topics related to computer games, performance, and new media art. Recently she received a three-year research grant from The Research Council of Norway to investigate the concepts of play, performativity, and presence in new media art.

Glossary

Add-on   A user-created program that modifies the user interface of the game. Add-ons are also known as mods. Blizzard does not allow players to change the game code, only to create add-ons that use the existing game code.

Alliance   One of the two playable factions in *World of Warcraft*. Player characters have to belong to one of the factions, and members of one faction can not communicate with members of the other faction, except through a limited set of emotes. The other playable faction is called the Horde.

Alt   An alternative character used by a player in addition to her or his main character.

AOE   Area of effect. Some spells and abilities are not specific to the player's target, but do damage to hostile creatures within a certain area. This includes hostile players.

Azeroth   The planet and site for the gameplay of *World of Warcraft* until the character reaches level 58–60.

Battleground   A designated area of the gameworld in which PvP combat takes place.

Boss   Many dungeons and quest chains are organised so that players first confront a number of moderately difficult mobs, and then are required to fight a "boss" monster, which is far more challenging. See Instance.

Buff   A beneficial spell that players can cast on themselves or on friendly players.

The Burning Crusade   An expansion pack for *World of Warcraft* that was released in 2007.

The Burning Legion   The common enemy of the Alliance and the Horde, threatening Azeroth.

Class   Each character belongs to one of nine available classes: druid, hunter, mage, paladin, priest, rogue, shaman, warlock, and warrior. The class chosen determines the character's skills, abilities, and limitations, and cannot be changed.

Corpse camping   Hostile players sit by the corpse of a character and wait for it to resurrect so that they can kill it again before the character has recovered from the death penalty. See Ganking.

Corpse run   After being killed, the character is resurrected as a ghost at a nearby graveyard, and has to run back to the corpse, which will be where he or she was killed.

Death penalty   Dying is inevitable in a game like *World of Warcraft*, and each time a character dies there is a penalty, among other things reducing the durability of armour and removing friendly buffs.

Emote   A character can express feelings or actions by emoting. Many emotes are pre-programmed, so for example a player can type the command "/dance" to make the character dance on the screen, while "/smile" will announce a message in the chat window saying "⟨Character name⟩ smiles."

Experience points or XP   The reward a character gets for solving quests and killing mobs. After gaining a certain amount of XP the character will level up to the next level. Currently levels range from 1 to 70.

FlagRSP   One of several add-ons that players can install in order to enhance aspects of role-playing.

Ganking   To kill a weaker player opponent many times in short order. See Corpse camping.

Game master or GM   In some role-playing games, the GM coordinates the plot of the game, but in *World of Warcraft*, game masters are employees of Blizzard that players can contact to report harrassment or to resolve issues in gameplay.

Grinding   Repetitive killing of mobs in order to gain experience, reputation, or gold.

Group   A temporary group that can have between two and five players. Group members can communicate over the group chat channel, and group members (normally) share XP and loot.

Guild   Guilds are semipermanent groups of players who like to play together.

Horde   One of the two factions; see Alliance.

In character or IC   Acting and speaking as though one is the character one plays.

Instance   A "dungeon," in which a team of players cooperates to accomplish quests, or to simply complete the challenges inside. Instances usually involve fighting toward one or more boss characters. The group entering the instance will not meet other players, as they are allocated an instance of their own of the particular dungeon they enter.

LARP   Live action roleplaying game. LARPs are role-playing games that are acted out face-to-face, often involving props, costumes, and spending time in isolated locations.

Leet   The shorthand forms of writing used in chat, e-mails and SMS, and MMORPG. Common Leet abbreviations are AFK (away from keyboard), OMG (oh my god), ROFL (rolling on the floor with laughter), or PLZ (please).

LFG   Shorthand form for looking for group, commonly used in chat channels with the aim of gathering players for a task that requires more than one player.

Loot   Mobs carry loot, which can be looted by the player or group that killed it.

MMOG   Massively multiplayer online game.

MMORPG   Massively multiplayer online role-playing game.

Machinima   From machine cinema; videos made by acting out a story or other content in a game instead of using live action or animation techniques.

Mob   A mobile object, common abbreviation for the monsters and NPCs a character fights in a game.

Mod   An alternative word for add-on.

Non-player character, or NPC   An avatar in the game that players can usually interact with at certain points, but that is controlled by the game.

Normal server   A server where players cannot be attacked by other players unless they have chosen to be in a PvP mode or have entered a battleground or other PvP area.

Onyxia   A dragon, and an example of an important boss who can only be killed after completing a long and complicated chain of quests.

Outland   The new planet introduced in *The Burning Crusade*.

Out of character, or OOC   The opposite of In Character. A player is out of character when talking about things from outside of the gameworld.

PvE   Player versus environment. Players do not fight other players, but fight the environment. See Mobs.

PvP   Player versus player. An area or server where players can be attacked by other players. PvP can also refer to the preferred playing style of an individual player.

Quest   A task assigned to the player, usually by an NPC. Players are awarded experience points when they complete quests.

Raid   When more than five players are playing together in one group they have to form a raid, commonly used for combat with strong bosses such as Onyxia, and normally in groups between ten and forty.

Realm   Blizzard's name for individual servers running the game. Each realm has a designated name, for example, Moonglade or Earthen Ring.

Reputation   The character's standing with different factions in the game. High reputation with a given faction means better prices on trades in a certain area and access to better equipment or specialized skills. High reputation with one faction can also lead to decreased reputation and worse deals with other factions.

RP   Short for role play. Can refer to playing style or to servers specially designated for role-playing.

RP-PvP   A server that is designated for role-playing and is also set for PvP play.

Sargeras   The evil leader of The Burning Legion. For other important characters in the game, see *World of Warcraft*'s official Web site.

Soloing   Playing alone rather than in a group.

Tank   The front-line soldier built to tolerate heavy attacks and protect the other members of the group.

User interface, or UI   The representation of the game that the players use to interact with the game.

XP   See Experience points.

Index